Changing Prospects: *The View from Mount Holyoke*

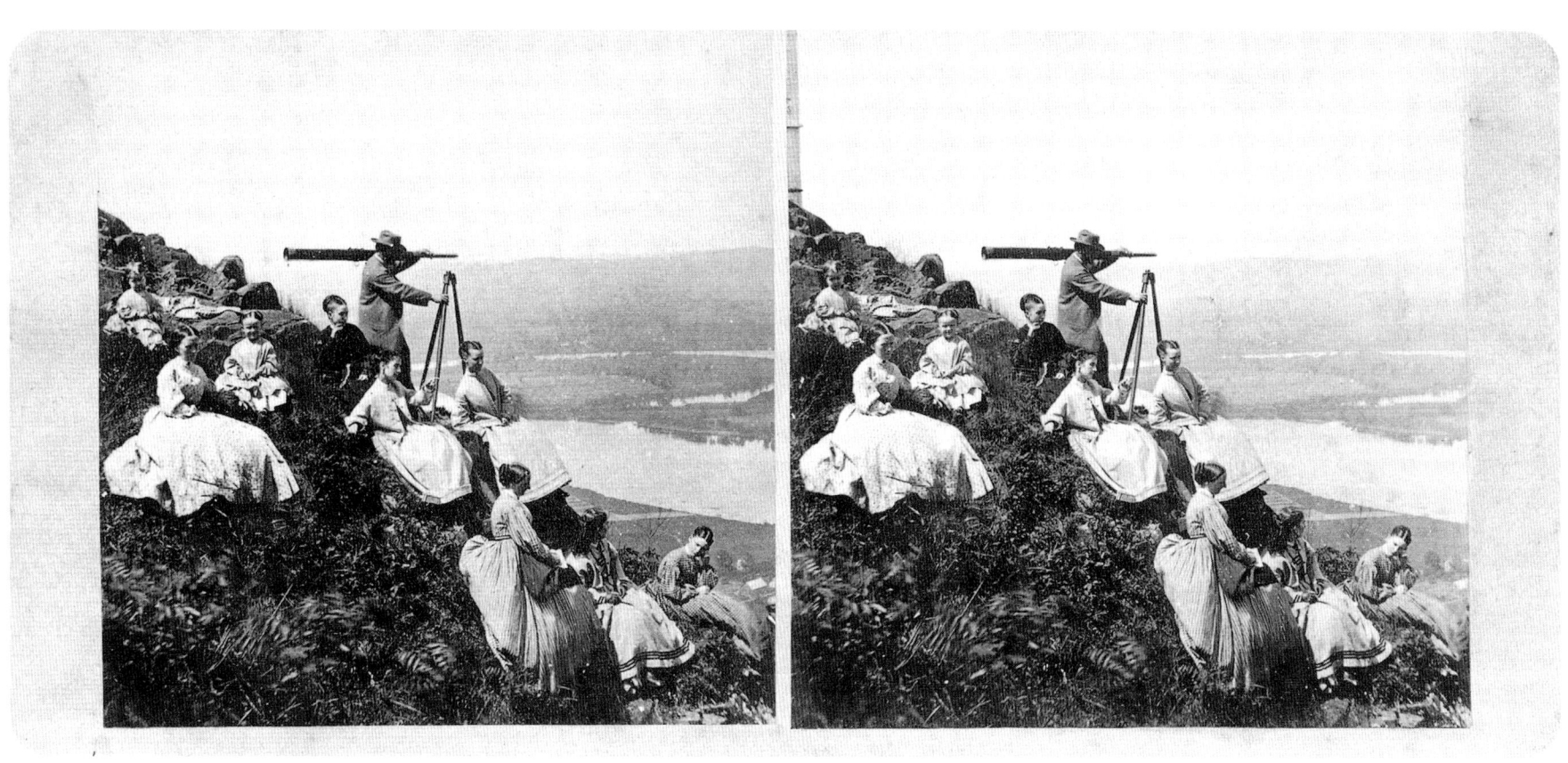

Houghton and Knowlton, *Prospecting on Mt. Holyoke*, ca. 1860s–70s, stereoscopic photograph. Historic Northampton, Northampton, Massachusetts

Changing Prospects
The View from Mount Holyoke

edited by Marianne Doezema

Susan Danly · Martha Hoppin · Ethan Carr
with a foreword by Christopher Benfey

Mount Holyoke College Art Museum

Cornell University Press
Ithaca and London

Published in conjunction with the exhibition *Changing Prospects: The View from Mount Holyoke* organized by the Mount Holyoke College Art Museum, 3 September to 8 December 2002

This book and the accompanying exhibition were made possible in part by generous gifts from Jean J. Beard, the Friends of the Mt. Holyoke Range, FleetBoston Financial, the Lucy P. Eisenhard Fund, the Susan Davenport Page and Margaret D. Page Fund, the Susan B. Weatherbie (class of 1972) Exhibition Development Fund, and a grant from the Massachusetts Foundation for the Humanities, a state program of the National Endowment for the Humanities.

First published in 2002 by Cornell University Press

ISBN 0-8014-4119-6

Librarians: Library of Congress Cataloging-in-Publication Data are available

Designed by Allison Bell
Produced by Arnold Skolnick

Printed in China

Table of Contents

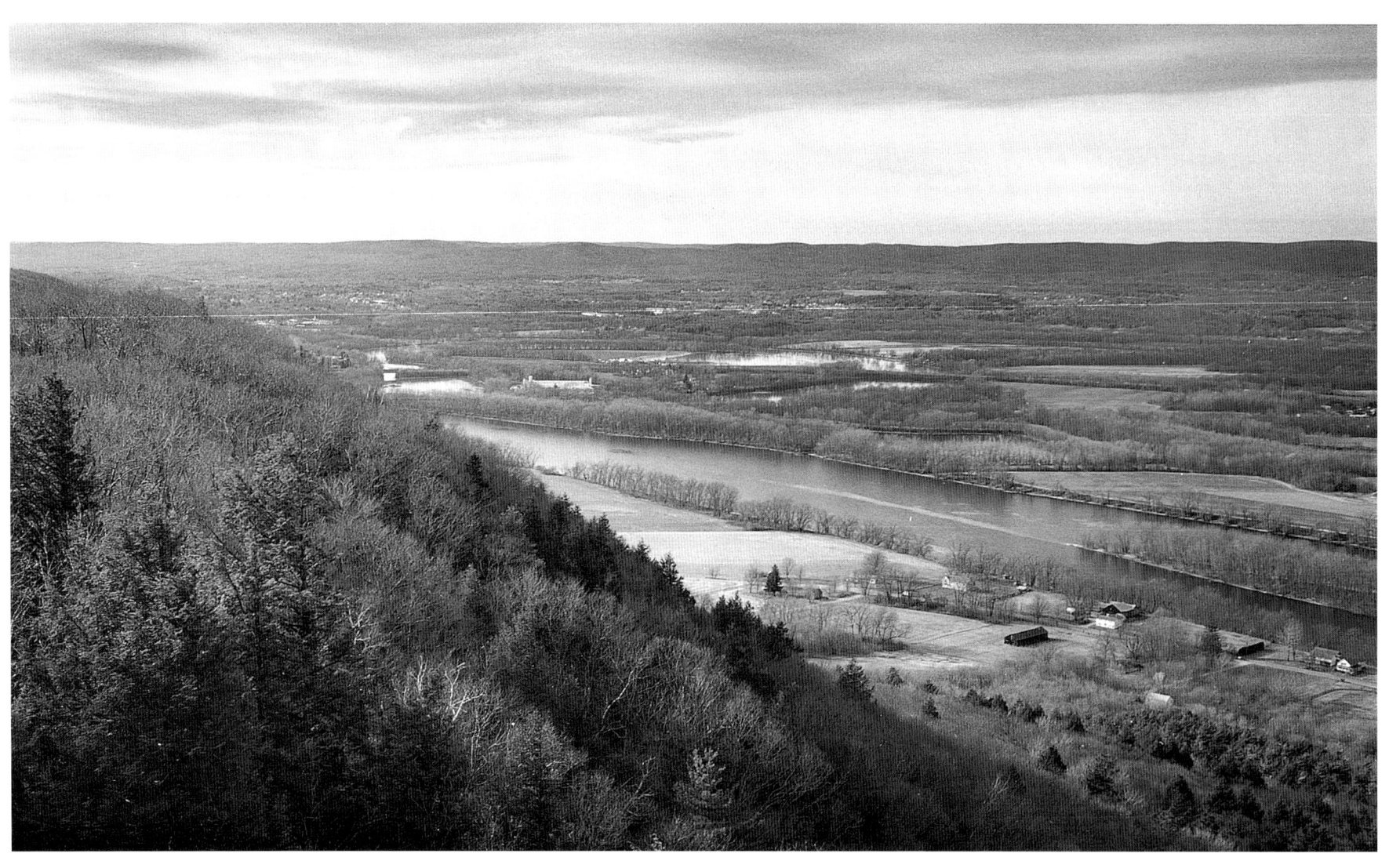

Robert Aller, *Mount Holyoke*, 2001, detail, see figure 39

Preface

Mt. Holyoke, the prominent mountain in western Massachusetts from which this museum's parent institution takes its name, has been a tourist destination as well as an inspiration for artists and writers for almost two centuries. We present this exhibition and the catalogue that accompanies it to convey the story of how this mountain, renowned more for the views from it than of it, became a cultural icon in the nineteenth century and continues to exert influence today.

The story began in 1821 when the first accommodation for tourists was constructed at Mt. Holyoke's summit, a little more than a decade before the opening in 1837 of Mount Holyoke Female Seminary. This new school for women was the realization of a dream for Mary Lyon, a fiercely determined educator who resisted using her own name for the school. She preferred that it bear the title of something more enduring. The exhibition documents and illustrates subsequent connections between the institution that became a college in 1893 and the mountain — traditions such as Seniors' Mountain Day when the class climbed to the mountaintop and slept overnight in muslin nightgowns sewn for the occasion by their sophomore "sisters." Mount Holyoke continues to observe Mountain Day. All students participate (but they don't sleep over).

The exhibition brings together an array of paintings, prints, photographs, and other fascinating objects. One is very likely among the earliest landscape tourism guidebooks produced in the United States. The pocket-size booklet dates from about 1825 and was originally owned by Charles Cramer, who inscribed the back cover, noting that he visited this "Wonder of Nature" on August 28, 1826. To commemorate the event he penned this four-line poem on the page:

> *Oh great Olympus fair Northampton's pride*
> *How hot it is to travel up thy side*
> *Hail mighty mount, grand beacon of our sphere*
> *I wonder how the devil I got here*

Susan Danly's essay elucidates the circumstances of the ascent of Mr. Cramer's contemporaries, why they had a devil of a time scaling the slope and, more importantly, why they made the effort in the first place — why, in fact, Mt. Holyoke was the second most popular tourist attraction in the United States for much of the nineteenth century. Danly also examines the role the mountain played in the history of American landscape painting of the period. Chris Benfey reminds us of the rich literary tradition associated with the site, which loomed much larger in the cultural imagination of the nation then than it does today. Martha Hoppin, on the other hand, demonstrates a resurgence of interest in the site among contemporary painters and photographers who use the mountain regularly as a subject. Ethan Carr discusses ongoing debates about private versus public use of the site and preservation efforts during the second century of the mountain's history as a national landmark.

Organizing an exhibition of this complexity requires the participation of numerous talented individuals. As co-curators Susan Danly and Martha Hoppin developed the conceptual framework of the exhibition and then fleshed out that framework with a selection of paintings and a variety of other artifacts from public and private collections. Their essays in this publication make important contributions to the literature of American art and cultural history.

Mount Holyoke College Art Museum's curator, Wendy Watson, guided us through every aspect of the execution of this exhibition, and Linda Delone Best, the collections manager, handled the intricacies of borrowing objects from across the eastern United States. Sabine Haberland Cray (class of 1972), copyeditor of the catalogue, was critical to its accuracy, clarity and consistency. Marjorie Kaufman lent her sharp proofreading skills during the final stages of this publication, demonstrating the value of another set of discriminating eyes. Designer Allison Bell made the publication an elegant work in itself. Arnold Skolnick produced the book and deserves special mention for the quantity and quality of the color. Debbie Davis handled public relations as well as financial matters with care and precision. Diane Schläppi developed compelling programs for teachers and school groups.

We are extremely grateful for the generous cooperation and assistance provided by many friends and colleagues during the preparations for this exhibition and publication. Paul Staiti, Alan Werner, Patricia McGirr and Robb Strycharz consented to read early drafts of sections of the essays and offered valuable insights. We appreciate their advice and recommendations. Additionally, we would like to thank Lorna Condit at the Society for the Preservation of New England Antiquities; Suzanne Lemakis at Citigroup; Kerry Buckley and Marie Panik at Historic Northampton; Tevis Kimball at The Jones Library, Inc.; Peter Carini and Patricia Albright at the Mount Holyoke College Archives and Special Collections; Sue Rainey at Shrine Mont. We extend thanks to Charles Johnson for sharing information about the history of the mountain house and his grandfather Clifton Johnson. Elaine Kachavos generously provided further information and educational resources about the mountain house. We would also like to express our appreciation to John Arthur, William Baczek, Jill Hodnicki, Peter Johnson, Rich Michelson, Betty Romer, Lawrence Siddall, Peter Tatistcheff, and Eva Zervos, who helped us locate paintings and other objects that are included in the exhibition.

We owe a deep debt of gratitude to the lenders without whose generosity this exhibition would not have been possible. On behalf of the co-curators of the exhibition and the museum staff, I would like to extend heartfelt thanks to Andersen-Boston; Citigroup; the Florence History Project, the Fruitlands Museum; Forbes Library; Jones Library; Historic Northampton; the Episcopal Diocese of Virginia; Vance Jordon Fine Arts, Inc.; the Mead Art Museum, Amherst College; The Metropolitan Museum of Art; the R. Michelson Galleries; the Society for the Preservation of New England Antiquities; Smith College Museum of Art; and the Whitney Museum of American Art, as well as a number of artists and private collectors.

We are extremely pleased to have the opportunity to express our appreciation to Jean J. Beard, FleetBoston Financial, and the Friends of the Mount Holyoke Range for making important contributions that helped make this exhibition a reality. Education programming is made possible by a gift from Victoria McNeil LeVine (class of 1979). The exhibition and catalogue are also supported by the Lucy P. Eisenhart Fund, the Susan Davenport Page and Margaret D. Page Fund, the Susan B. Weatherbie (class of 1972) Exhibition Development Fund, and a grant from the Massachusetts Foundation for the Humanities, a state program of the National Endowment of the Humanities.

Marianne Doezema
Florence Finch Abbott Director
Mount Holyoke College Art Museum

Foreword:
"A Route of Evanescence"

Christopher Benfey

In 1910, Mount Holyoke Professor Mignon Talbot found a dinosaur in a bed of sandstone near the College. It was a savage little predator built for speed, so Professor Talbot called it *Podokesaurus holyokensis*, the "fleet-footed lizard of Holyoke." Talbot had often taken her students to see the ubiquitous dinosaur tracks that crisscross the valley cut by the Connecticut River, between the igneous outcroppings of Mt. Tom and Mt. Holyoke. But to find the fossilized bones of a dinosaur species never before identified — that was something else altogether. She exhibited her discovery in Williston Hall, the science building, where *P. holyokensis* became a sort of prehistoric pet for students. Seven years later, during the Christmas break of 1917, Williston burned to the ground, and not a trace of the fleet-footed dinosaur was found in the rubble. *P. holyokensis* had the peculiar distinction of being the dinosaur that vanished twice, once in the Triassic period, and again a hundred and fifty million years later.

There are two discreet signs along Route 47, where it winds its way between the gentle ascent of Mt. Holyoke and the circular bend, or Oxbow, of the Connecticut River. One points the way to the summit. The other marks the level of the many floods that have inundated the valley over the past two centuries. Driving along this pastoral landscape, with its derelict tobacco barns and low-lying pumpkin fields, it is difficult to recover the furious cultural activity that once surrounded Mt. Holyoke. No sign now of the riverboat landing for sightseers by the hundreds, or the tramway that tugged them up the mountainside, or the poets and painters who came to look once more at the all-too-familiar elms and cornrows — God's plenty laid out for all to see. If we look really hard, we can find their traces. Otherwise, this world can seem almost as far away from us as *P. holyokensis*, the dinosaur that disappeared when the science building disappeared. As Emily Dickinson, Mount Holyoke alumna and connoisseur of lost things, put it, we find ourselves traveling along a "Route of Evanescence."[1]

Ralph Waldo Emerson, fresh out of Harvard in 1823, called Mt. Holyoke a "hill," not once but *twice*, and was happy to encounter no "rattlesnake or viper" on the descent.[2] Sylvia Plath, while teaching at Smith in 1957–58, whittled it down still farther into a "mere truncated hillock." "We have not mountains, but mounts," she wrote in her condescending poem "Above the Oxbow."[3] Hill, hillock, or mount, the allure of Mt. Holyoke was never the view of the summit — think of Mont Blanc, the Matterhorn, or even Monadnock — but rather the view *from* the summit, specifically the dramatic panorama below. It was the carpeted collage of farmland, woodland, river, and road, spreading out into the civilized distance, that drew people by the thousands to the 954-foot peak.

For half a century, from roughly 1830 to 1880, writers vied as much as painters to capture what the early British traveler Basil Hall described in 1827 as "the beauty of the prospect from the summit of this noble hill."[4] The most conspicuous feature of the view — the Connecticut River circling in the Oxbow to the south and winding through the idyllic town of Hadley to the north — inspired some of the most promiscuous metaphors. T. Addison Richards wrote in *Harper's* in 1856 that the river threaded "its silver tide through the tender verdure as capriciously as a vein in the neck of beauty."[5] Two years later, Oliver Wendell Holmes compared the river to a "great lord, swallowing up the small proprietary rivulets very quietly as it goes, until it gets proud and swollen and wantons in huge luxurious oxbows above the fair Northampton meadows, and at last overflows."[6] A nineteenth-century guidebook writer called it, more chastely, "the Nile of New England."[7] No wonder the Hartford poet Wallace Stevens, in the face of such cloying verbosity, settled for "The River of Rivers in Connecticut."

They say familiarity breeds contempt, but under the right circumstances it can also breed contemplation — and further creation. No one looked more fixedly at the proverbially beautiful Holyoke Range than Emily Dickinson. Dickinson climbed Mt. Holyoke on October 9, 1849, with a group of friends, during the period of recuperative roaming that followed her strenuous year at Mount Holyoke Female Seminary. "The Mountains — grow unnoticed — " she began a poem written in 1863, showing off what she had learned by reading and listening to Amherst College president and professor Edward Hitchcock. Hitchcock,

a pioneering collector and explicator of dinosaur traces and tracks, explained how rivers and volcanoes, if given enough time, could make and unmake the most dramatic features of the landscape, such as mountains, whose "Purple figures rise/ Without attempt — Exhaustion —/ Assistance — or Applause."[8]

By 1871, the reputed "drama" of the prospect from Mt. Holyoke was so engrained in the national psyche — it was an obligatory stop on the "Grand Tour" of the eastern United States — that Dickinson wrote another poem in which the mountains got some applause after all. In "The Mountains stood in Haze," she imagined the different components of the familiar Mt. Holyoke panorama — mountain, valley, river, sky, and sun — as characters of a drama on a stage. The poem concludes:

> At leisure was the Sun —
> His interests of Fire
> A little from remark withdrawn —
> The Twilight spoke the Spire.
>
> So soft upon the Scene
> The Act of evening fell
> We felt how neighborly a thing
> Was the Invisible.[9]

This underlying feeling of something mysterious and impalpable in the Mt. Holyoke landscape — as though sublimity is not adequately expressed by Thomas Cole's thunderstorm and blasted tree — recurs in later writings. When Henry James stayed in Northampton during the fall of 1864, looking for a cure for his chronic constipation and the obscure "hurt" that kept him out of the Civil War, there was good reason to believe that this most cosmopolitan of American writers would treat the scenery even more highhandedly than Emerson. Living in Northampton could only be a "misfortune," he wrote in his first novel *Roderick Hudson* (1875).

But when James's fictional counterpart Rowland Mallet, an American art connoisseur visiting from Rome, finds a promising sculptor living in this unpromising town, and the two wander out for a stroll along the Connecticut River, Mallet is surprised and moved by what he sees:

> Rowland watched the shadows on Mount Holyoke, listened to the gurgle of the river, and sniffed the balsam of the pines. A gentle breeze had begun to tickle their summits, and brought the smell of the mown grass across from the elm-dotted river meadows. He sat up beside his companion and looked away at the far-spreading view. It seemed to him beautiful, and suddenly a strange feeling of prospective regret took possession of him. Something seemed to tell him that later, in a foreign land, he would remember it lovingly and penitently.[10]

The elusive and uncanny "something" recurs later that evening, as the two men walk among the "great Northampton elms" in the moonlight:

> There seemed to Rowland something intensely serious in the scene in which he had taken part. . . . And as Rowland looked along the arch of silvered shadow and out into the lucid air of the American night, which seemed so doubly vast, somehow, and strange and nocturnal, he felt like declaring that here was beauty too — beauty sufficient for an artist not to starve upon it."[11]

From the top of Mt. Holyoke, where a few thousand visitors trek annually, one can still experience a hint of the perspectives that led earlier visitors there for creative contemplation. These days, the sign to the summit of Mt. Holyoke points as much back in time as up in space; the layered history of the site is as much a lure as its picturesque perfection. The elms, which Thomas Cole painted so painstakingly and Henry Ward Beecher compared to the columns of the Parthenon, are mostly gone from the river meadows, having joined *Podokesaurus holyokensis* in a scene we can only remember, as Henry James puts it, "lovingly and penitently."[12] For more than a century, many sightseers have journeyed farther up the Connecticut River, to the less peopled landscapes of Vermont and New Hampshire. From the top of Mt. Holyoke you can get a fine view of the highway that takes them there, Interstate 91, which slices through the Oxbow like the line across a bifocal lens.

Even the habits of thought and looking that made Mt. Holyoke such a magnet for artists and writers can seem endangered now. The poet Robert Lowell traveled to Northampton during the early 1960s in a frustrated search for traces of his ancestor, the fire-and-brimstone revivalist Jonathan Edwards. "I found no relic,/ except the round slice of an oak/ you are said to have planted," Lowell wrote in his poem "Jonathan Edwards in Western Massachusetts." Driving up Route 116 a few years later to give a reading in Amherst, Lowell passed a sign near Mt. Holyoke that said: "Nash's Dino Land," with an arrow pointing towards some tracks in the underbrush, not far from where Professor Mignon Talbot found her fleet-footed dinosaur. A few minutes later, Lowell told his audience, "I guess all poets live in dinosaur land."

NOTES

1. "A Route of Evanescence," Poem #1498, *The Poems of Emily Dickinson*, ed. Ralph Franklin (Cambridge: Harvard University Press, 1998).

2. Ralph Waldo Emerson, "Walk to the Connecticut," *The Pioneer Valley Reader: Prose and Poetry from New England's Heartland* (Stockbridge, MA: Berkshire House Publishers, 1995), p. 91.

3. Sylvia Plath, "Above the Oxbow," *The Pioneer Valley Reader*, p. 135.

4. Basil Hall, "The View from Mt. Holyoke in 1827," *The Pioneer Valley Reader*, p. 13.

5. Quoted in Jill A. Hodnicki, "The Connecticut Valley in Literature: A Delightful Excursion," *Arcadian Vales: Views of The Connecticut River Valley*, ed. Martha J. Hoppin (Springfield: George Walter Vincent Smith Art Museum, 1981), p. 21.

6. Ibid.

7. Martha J. Hoppin, "Arcadian Vales: The Connecticut Valley in Art," *Arcadian Vales*, p. 31.

8. "The Mountains — grow unnoticed — ," Poem #68, *The Poems of Emily Dickinson.*

9. "The Mountains stood in Haze," Poem #1225, *The Poems of Emily Dickinson.*

10. Henry James, "An American Landscape," *The Pioneer Valley Reader*, p. 247.

11. Ibid.

12. Henry Ward Beecher, "Village Life in New England," *The Pioneer Valley Reader*, p. 251.

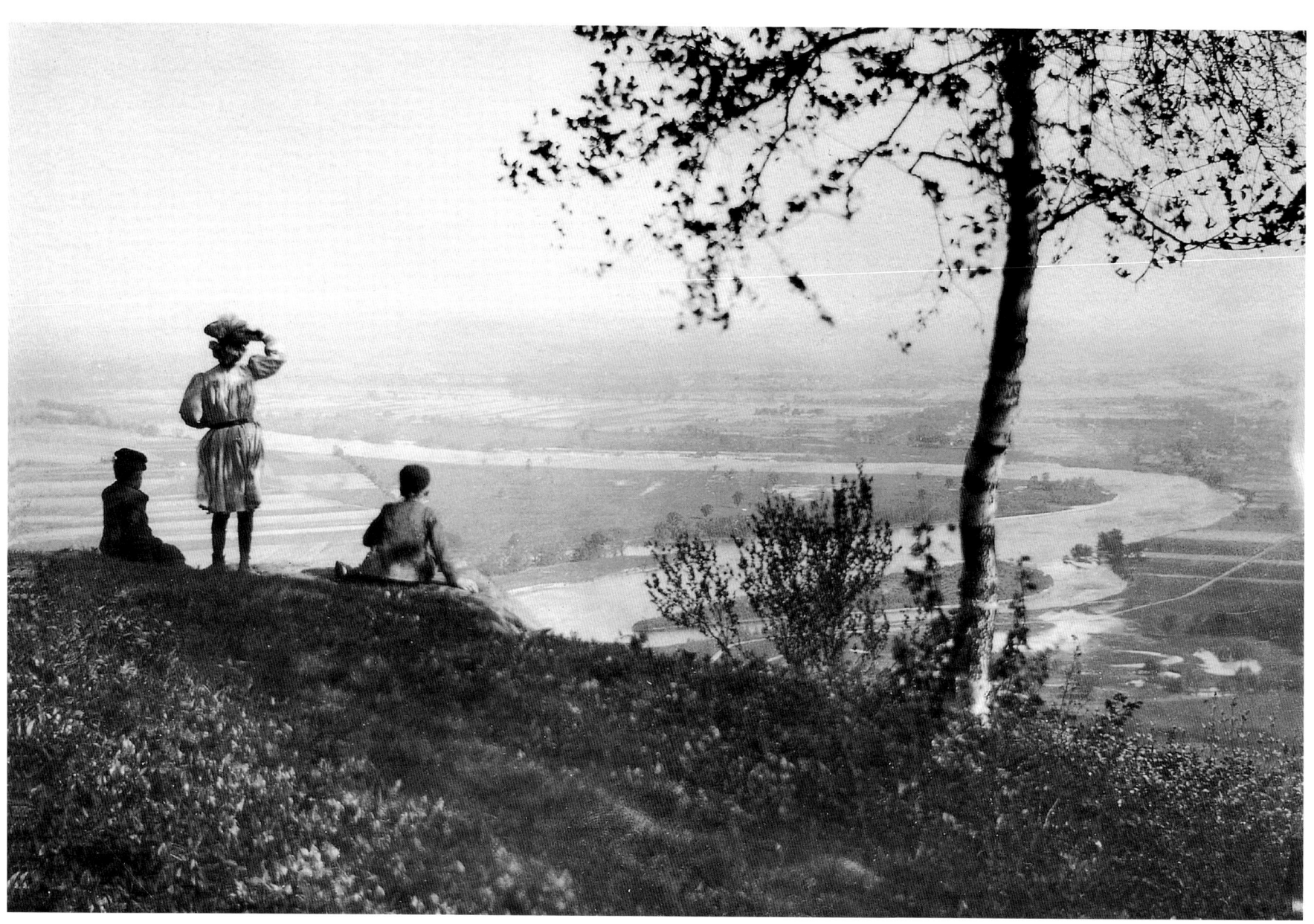

Clifton Johnson, *Hockanum: The Winding Connecticut Viewed from Mt. Holyoke*, ca. 1909, platinum print photograph. The Jones Library, Inc., Amherst, Massachusetts

Mount Holyoke: "The Grandest Cultivated View in the World"

Susan Danly

Mount Holyoke College bears the name of a nearby topographic feature whose rich cultural history far outweighs its rather modest height. Rising to just under a thousand feet, Mt. Holyoke sits prominently at the end of a range of basaltic rock that cuts across the picturesque Connecticut River Valley in western Massachusetts. The mountaintop affords a panoramic view of the valley below and glimpses of other notable New England mountains beyond. On a very clear day visitors can see northward to Mt. Monadnock in New Hampshire, westward to Mt. Greylock, the highest peak in Massachusetts, and southward to East Rock in Connecticut.

Amid the rich farmland and small rural communities surrounding Mt. Holyoke several institutions have helped shape public enjoyment and use of the mountain.[1] But its namesake Mount Holyoke College, founded as a women's seminary in 1837 by Mary Lyon, is most intertwined with the earliest cultural expressions related to this local landmark. In fact, during the mid-nineteenth century the mountain significantly influenced the development of the academic curriculum and social traditions at Lyon's school, which led the way in women's education in the United States. For the general public as well, Mt. Holyoke fig-

ured prominently during this period, not only in the fashionable study of the new science of geology, but also in discussions of religion, literature, and art.

Learning in the Landscape

In the mid-1830s, when Mary Lyon began her search for the site of a new women's seminary, she turned to a group of local ministers and educators, among them her mentor Edward Hitchcock, professor of chemistry and religion at nearby Amherst College.[2] Hitchcock first suggested a learned but unwieldy Greek name for the institution — Pangynaskean Seminary — to suggest a place that would develop a wide range of female powers including physical, intellectual, and moral capabilities.[3] But as soon as the founding committee settled on South Hadley as the site for the school, they appropriated the name of the region's most famous geographic feature for their new institution — Mount Holyoke Female Seminary.[4]

A fundraising circular soon sent to the young women of the Connecticut River Valley advertised the special locale for the proposed school: "located at South Hadley, Massachusetts, on the banks of the Connecticut, at the foot of Mount Holyoke, in the center of New England, easy access from all

quarters, and in the midst of the most delightful scenery."[5] And as Hitchcock further noted, in selecting this specific site, the school offered the advantages of "centrality, retirement, economy, morality, and natural scenery."[6]

The image of a mountain, with its enduring and monumental character, became the emblem of this new educational enterprise (figure 1). The original institutional seal — designed by Orra White Hitchcock, the professor's wife and Lyon's life-long friend — featured a distinctly more biblical mountain peak surrounded by palm trees and

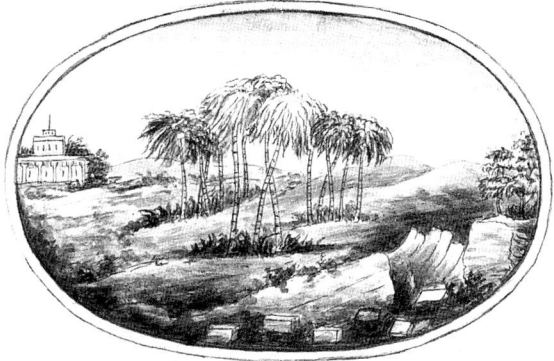

FIGURE 1. Orra White Hitchcock, *Mount Holyoke College Seal*, ca. 1837, pencil on paper. Mount Holyoke College Archives and Special Collections

ancient monuments, suggestive of Mount Zion, the "Holy Hill" of God in Jerusalem. The image makes explicit the combination of nature and religion that lay at the heart of Mary Lyon's educational ideals. Among the principles she wished to impart to her students were an abiding faith in God along with a love of nature. Lyon's attitudes toward God and nature, according to an early biographer, can be traced back to her childhood home nestled in the hills of nearby Buckland: "that wild, romantic, little farm, made more to feast the soul than to feed the body." It was there that she developed a deep spiritual belief in the power of nature as a manifestation of a divine presence. In *Recollections of Mary Lyon*, Fidelia Fiske (class of 1842) draws a lofty analogy between the hilly terrain of Lyon's rural homestead and the biblical story of Moses in the wilderness:

We can hardly feel less interest in Mary Lyon's early home, where Conway, Ashfield, and Buckland made the "Three Corners," than in Moses dwelling in the desert. Her twenty years in that "mountain home" were as surely the Lord's preparation for guiding the thousands of daughters of America, as were Moses' forty years in the wilderness a preparation for leading the thousands of Israel. In that pure mountain air, among those hills and streams and the rocks and the trees, she acquired that physical strength which enabled her to bear the pressure of labor and care in after life that might have carried others to an early grave.[7]

Lyon's abiding love of nature and religious fervor no doubt were reinforced by her earliest contacts with Edward Hitchcock, who in the early 1820s was the Congregational minister in Conway. Lyon first lived with the Hitchcock family when she taught school there during the summer of 1823.[8] From the outset, Hitchcock was impressed with the depth of the young woman's religious convictions and her dedication to women's education. In his biography about her, *The Power of Christian Benevolence*, he noted that from him she learned "principles of natural science and from his wife the arts of drawing and painting."[9] Lyon stayed with the Hitchcocks again in Amherst in the mid-1830s when she was beginning to implement her plans for a women's seminary. At that time she attended his lectures on religion and geology and undoubtedly knew of Orra Hitchcock's vignettes, including views of Mt. Holyoke, for her husband's books on these subjects. In describing Lyon's plans for the curriculum at Mount Holyoke Female Seminary, the College's first historian noted:

Miss Lyon never lost her early enthusiasm for the natural sciences. Believing the God of nature, of providence, and of grace to be the same, she traced his hand alike in history, in science, and on the inspired page. She was never afraid of scientific revelations. "If the Bible," she said, "[would] only take the lead in our schools, I care not how closely the sciences follow."[10]

Not only was Hitchcock one of the first educators to teach geology in the United States, but he also headed the Massachusetts Geological Survey and published its *Final Report on the Geology of Massachusetts* (1841). In *The Religion of Geography and Its Connected Sciences* (1851), he expressed most directly the idiosyncratic nineteenth-century blend of scientific inquiry and religious belief that he shared with Mary Lyon. In this book he discussed a number of geological features that for him were proof of "divine benevolence." Among these were the "disturbed, broken, and overturned condition of the earth's crust" — e.g. mountains like Mt. Holyoke — which exposed valuable ores, minerals, and rocks that were needed by mankind.

For Hitchcock, however, God's benevolence extended beyond the materially useful into the realm of the aesthetic. The creation of beautiful natural scenery was another of God's beneficent acts:

Surely natural scenery does afford to the unsophisticated soul one of the richest and purest sources of enjoyment on earth. If this be doubted by anyone, it must be because he has never been placed in circumstances to call into exercise his natural love of the beautiful and the sublime in creation. Let me persuade such a one, at least in imagination, to break away from the slavish routine of business or pleasure, and in the height of balmy summer to accompany me to a few spots, where his soul will swell with new and strong emotions, if his natural sensibilities to the grand and the beautiful have not become thoroughly dead within him.[11]

Hitchcock believed that Mt. Holyoke was among those few places in New England where the public could easily discern geologic signs of divine intervention: dramatic rock formations, the action of glaciers, volcanoes, and alluvial flood plains. These distinctive landscape features indicated the "numerous changes on the globe which nothing but the power of God could have produced, and which in fact were most striking and stupendous miracles."[12] The most recent and dramatic of these changes noted and illustrated in his *Final Report on the Geology of Massachusetts* was the evolution of what had been a meander bend, an oxbow, in the Connecticut River at the foot of Mt. Holyoke (figure 2).[13] During the spring of 1840, flood waters cut through a narrow neck of land visible in Thomas Cole's painting, *View from Mount Holyoke, Northampton, Massachusetts, after a Thunderstorm (The Oxbow)* of 1836 (figure 8). The river's new course eliminated a three-mile stretch of water and hastened travel. In addition, the abandoned oxbow channel provided visitors to the top of Mt. Holyoke with a new topographic landmark that demonstrated nature's transformative power.

For nineteenth-century educators like Hitchcock and Lyon, Mt. Holyoke provided an outdoor laboratory to study such dramatic geologic and historic change. The establishment of an annual Mountain Day at Mount Holyoke Female Seminary less than a year after the school opened became a means by which its students came to understand the peak's rich natural and cultural significance. In June 1838, Lucy Goodale (class of 1841) wrote of an early morning excursion to the top of the mountain. Some sixty students, as she noted, rose at dawn and piled into a dozen carriages that took them to the end of the road, halfway up the mountainside. "On the way our eyes were feasted with beauteous scenery. The mountains which we were approaching clad in a robe of the most lovely green, the calm blue waters of the Connecticut, the huge rocks, near our path called for the expressions of wonder and admirations." After a strenuous hike to the top of the mountain, they were afforded views not only of nature, but also of the cultural history of the region — from the "churches and institutions of literature and science" in Amherst, to the site of the Indian attacks in colonial Hadley and the "towering spires" of Northampton, "the largest and most beautiful village in our view." The students returned to the seminary by noon "somewhat fatigued by the excessive exercise, but amply compensated with a rich fund of knowledge gained by the observation of the morning."[14]

Just a month later on July 14, Edward Hitchcock led another student excursion to Mt. Holyoke, and he began to lecture at the seminary as well.[15] From the beginning, the tradition of Mountain Day combined physical exercise, aesthetic pleasure, and intellectual enlightenment.

A few years later, inspired by an encounter with a bedraggled visitor from the West Indies, worn out from the steep and rocky ascent, Hitch-

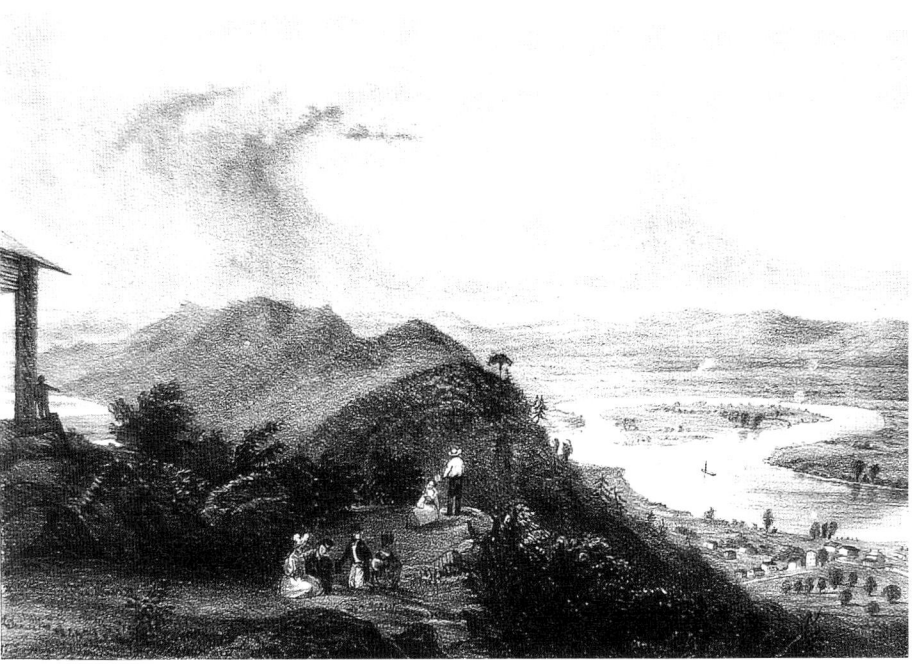

FIGURE 2. After William Henry Bartlett, *View from Mount Holyoke*, lithograph by Thayer's Lith., Boston, in Edward Hitchcock, *Final Report on the Geology of Massachusetts*, 1841. Mount Holyoke College Archives and Special Collections

cock decided to construct a new road up the western slope of Mt. Holyoke. In July 1845, he and Lyon gathered a path-building party made up of his students from Amherst College and provisioned with food prepared by her students at the seminary. Although the local citizenry scoffed at the idea that a path could be built in less than two weeks, the enthusiastic students managed to finish the arduous task in just half a day. When they reached the top, their Herculean efforts were commended in several speeches. Lydia Baldwin (class of 1845) reported in a letter home on the festivities culminating the momentous event. She noted that almost 150 students and most of the faculty of Mount Holyoke Female Seminary had joined Amherst College's junior and senior classes to listen to two hours of lectures delivered by Professors Shepard, Fiske, and Hitchcock. Then the entire group hiked halfway down to a spring to enjoy the refreshments brought by the Mount Holyoke students.[16]

Professor Charles Shepard of Amherst College grandly compared their achievement to Napoleon's conquest of the Alps and went on to talk of the recent "improvement" made by the Connecticut River itself with the formation of the oxbow lake. By eliminating the loop in the river, the new course shortened the downstream journey by an hour; and subsequent deposits of silt provided a bed for the new railroad, making way for more advancements in industry. Shepard also expressed hope that some American sculptor, like Hiram Powers or Horatio Greenough, might provide Mount Holyoke Female Seminary with a marble figure, "the maid of the Connecticut" brandishing a broom, to celebrate the local production of broom corn and to "denote that industry, neatness, and order, are the law of the institution."

Finally, Hitchcock himself addressed the students, giving them a brief geological history of the mountain, and concluded, with some humor, that the latest "geological agency" should be called "Holyoponics" or the "Science of building a road up Mt. Holyoke for ponies." Presciently and somewhat tongue-in-cheek, he also warned that such path-building was a form of erosion (a condition about which environmentalists worry a great deal today): "This is undoubtedly a new force in geologic dynamics, and all visitors to Holyoke will hereafter see that it is a very powerful force. Geologists will undoubtedly introduce it into their future works, as a most important agency in production of *erosions* (in vulgar language called *horse-paths*)."[17]

In 1851 another Mountain Day account, penned by Harriet Lane (class of 1853), observed that once the students had been dropped off at the base of the mountain with the advice to go slow, "each one was responsible for herself." Once on top of Mt. Holyoke, Lane took in the panoramic view as "one continuous scene of loveliness." As she looked down on the fields and villages below, the young woman's thoughts turned to the clash between nature and industrial progress — echoing two major concerns of nineteenth-century American culture, especially to transcendentalists like Henry David Thoreau:

I thought of what Paradise must have been, before Sin came to scathe and desolate this, our beautiful Earth, and of days far back of those, ere man was created; I looked at the woods, and the waters, but saw not the bridge and the rail-car. Suddenly a shrill whistle broke the spell, and most provokingly put an end to all my poetizing. I woke to find myself in this 19th century of Steam and progress, when Art seems so vainly striving to outdo Nature in beauty as well as utility.[18]

By the 1870s a special Mountain Day at the seminary was established for members of the senior class who would spend a day and night at the summit just before graduation. Clad in prized white muslin nightgowns sewn by their underclassmates, the seniors held a banquet, put on "stunts," and stayed overnight in the Prospect House hotel, which had been built on top of Mt. Holyoke in 1851 (figure 3).

The Class Book of 1912 provides a typical schedule of that year's event which included a late afternoon hike up the mountain, dinner, numerous toasts until midnight, an "authorized décolleté with cap and gown" at 1:00 a.m., and a sunrise observation "before a small, select audience" at 4:22 a.m. The next morning featured breakfast, "a sing, a stroll, many snap-shots," and the delivery of "Mountain Mail," numerous handwritten note cards sent by their fellow students to commemorate the occasion.

In 1895, Mount Holyoke College president Elizabeth Storrs Mead established a fall Mountain Day as an official holiday for the entire institution. Faculty accompanied students and provided mountaintop lectures. By 1929 Senior Mountain Day had become a one-day affair; at the beginning of World War II it was discontinued altogether.[19] Although the style of hiking clothes has changed dramatically over the course of the twentieth century (figure 4), horse-drawn carriages still delivered students to the foot of the mountain as late as the 1940s, maintaining ties to the nineteenth-century tradition. These days, in early October at the peak of fall foliage, Mount Holyoke College's administration declares an unannounced Mountain Day celebration and cancels classes with an early

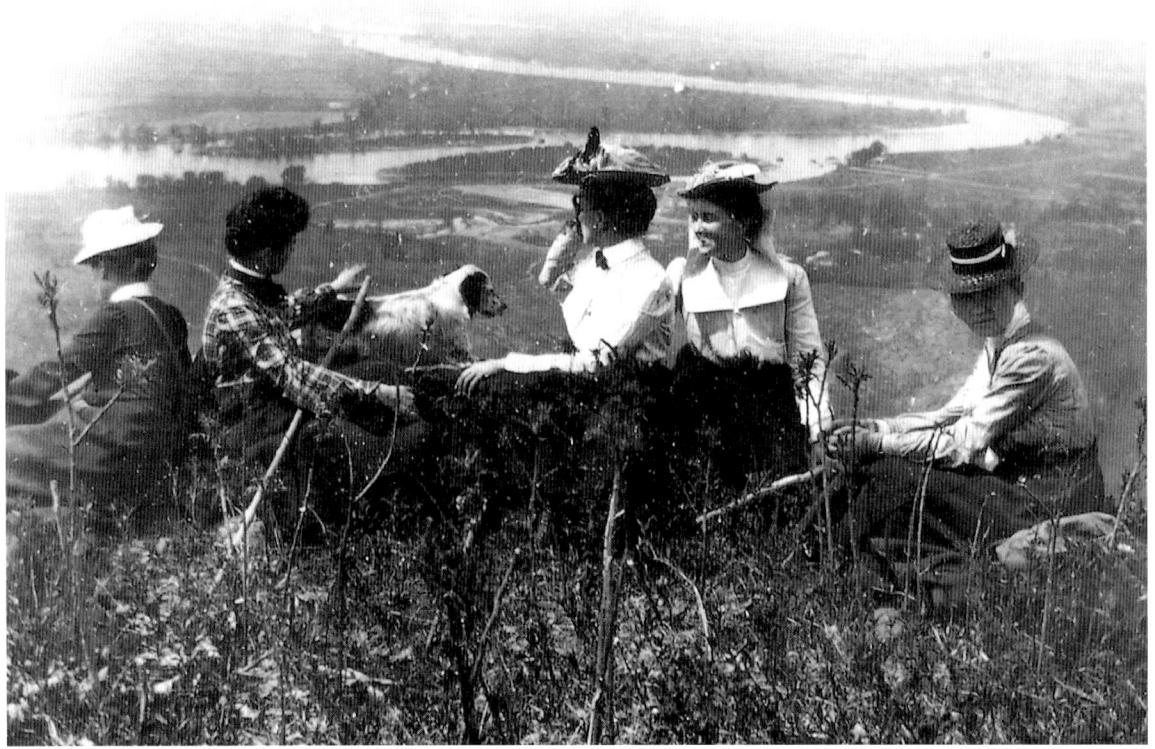

FIGURE 3. Unknown photographer, *Mountain Day Seniors*, 1912, gelatin silver print photograph. Mount Holyoke College Archives and Special Collections

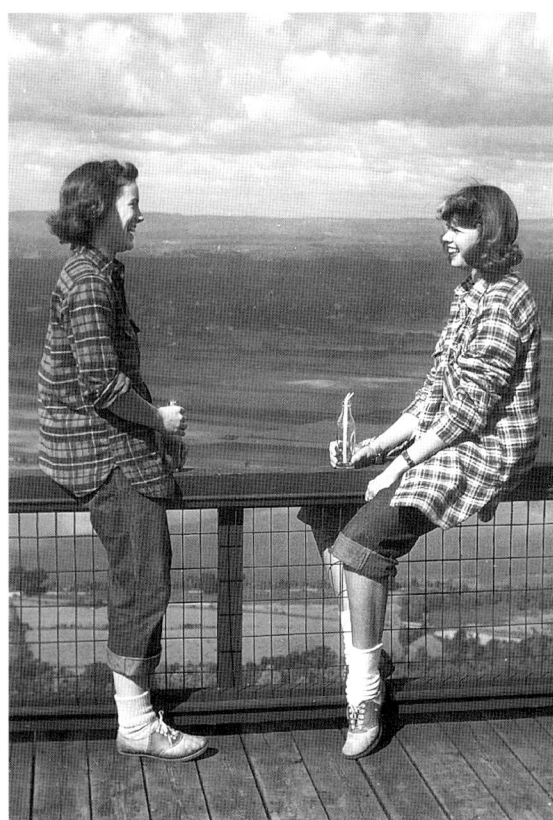

FIGURE 4. Unknown photographer, *View from Mount Holyoke*, 1940s, gelatin silver print photograph. Mount Holyoke College Archives and Special Collections

morning tolling of the school bells. Unencumbered by faculty chaperones and scripted social events, students still hike up Mt. Holyoke to take in the view.

The mountain has always figured into Mount Holyoke's curriculum as well as its social life. Geology and natural history appeared in its first course catalogues and Hitchcock's books were listed as required reading.[20] Today's students do field studies on Mt. Holyoke for introductory courses in physical and environmental geology and advanced courses in surface processes and structural geology.[21] The mountain is an especially revealing site for the study of stratigraphy, glacial striations

and gouges, and columnar joints of basalt. And it figures prominently in the programming and website of the college's Center for Environmental Literacy.

The Tourist Experience During the mid-nineteenth century, local students and faculty were by no means the only people who hiked up the slopes of Mt. Holyoke seeking edification and enjoyment. As tourist facilities on the summit expanded, so did the number and range of the visitors.[22] Although the land was privately owned, the first public amenities on top of the mountain resulted from the efforts of a group of nature-loving citizens from neighboring Northampton. Construction of the first mountain house began patriotically on June 17, 1821, the anniversary of the Battle of Bunker Hill and a local holiday in parts of the Commonwealth of Massachusetts. With festive fanfare, Northampton's church bells rang out at 6:00 a.m. and by noon upwards of fifty volunteers from the town had gathered on top of Mt. Holyoke to build an eighteen- by twenty-four-foot, log-framed structure with a porch that would serve as a vantage point overlooking the valley below (figure 5, center). This rustic structure was leased to Zadock Lyman, a tavern-keeper in Hockanum, the village at the foot of the mountain. But almost immediately Willis Pease of Hadley, who originally had hoped to lease the first building, erected a rival structure. By May of 1823, Pease advertised in local newspapers a range of refreshments offered on top of the mountain. For nine cents a glass (twice the price charged in town), visitors had a choice of "Jamaican spirits, St. Croix rum, Cognac brandy, Holland gin, Cherry Rum, Wines." Water could be had for three cents. He also sold "Spanish segars."[23]

By 1825 a number of wealthy Northampton residents began to pool their financial resources and established the Mt. Holyoke Association that purchased the original mountain house and moved

it next to the shack that Pease had built. Over the next twenty years subscribers to the association bought more land and improved the roads, though carriages could travel only two-thirds of the way to the summit. From that point visitors had to hike the remainder of the way up a steep path laid with man-made stone steps. Nevertheless it was quite an improvement over the original horse trail that led to the summit from the south side of the mountain and the 1845 path constructed by

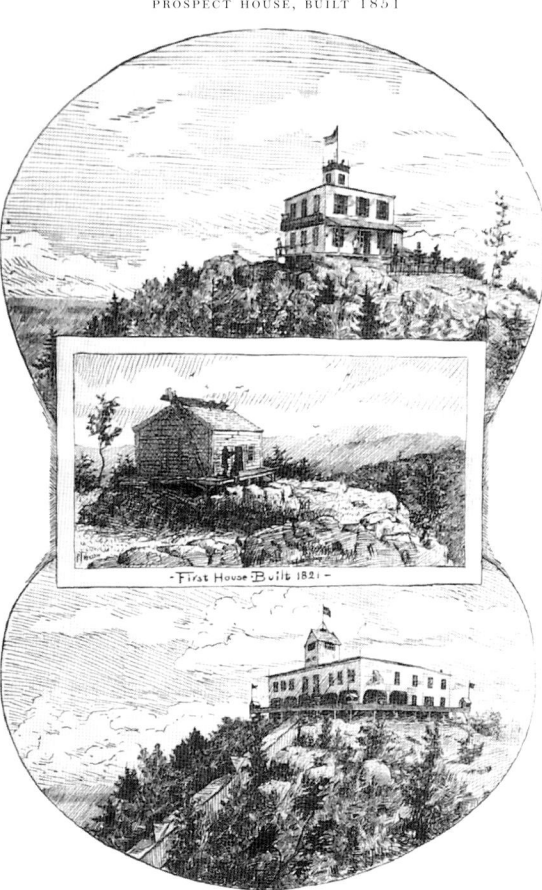

PROSPECT HOUSE, BUILT 1851

First House Built 1821

PROSPECT HOUSE, BUILT 1861

FIGURE 5. Clifton Johnson, *[Three Views of the Mountain House]*, photomechanically reproduced etching from *Mount Holyoke*, brochure, 1887. Mount Holyoke College Archives and Special Collections

FIGURE 6. Knowlton Brothers, *Prospect House, Mt. Holyoke, from foot of railway,* ca. 1870s, stereoscopic photograph. Historic Northampton, Northampton, Massachusetts

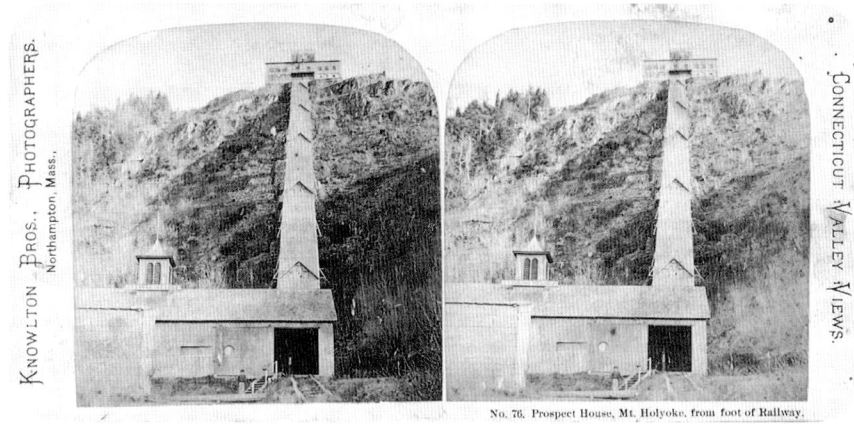

FIGURE 6. Knowlton Brothers, *Prospect House, Mt. Holyoke, from foot of railway,* ca. 1870s, stereoscopic photograph. Historic Northampton, Northampton, Massachusetts

FIGURE 7. Unidentified photographer, *Thatched Roof Summer House,* ca. 1900, platinum print photograph. Historic Northampton, Northampton, Massachusetts

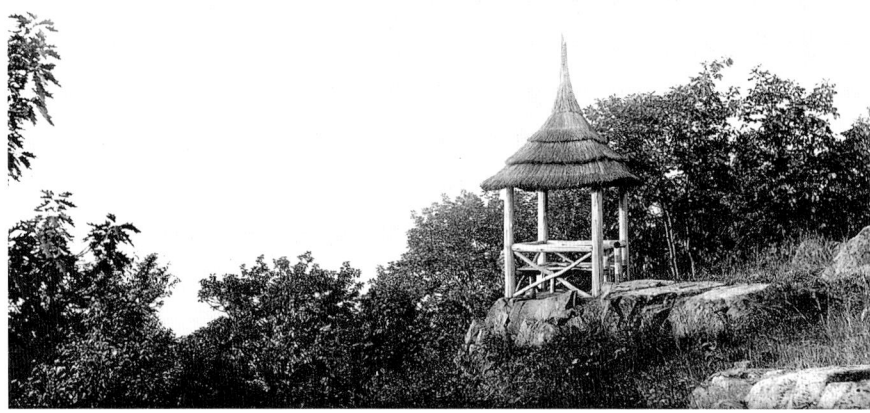

French began construction of Prospect House (figure 5, top). The twenty-five- by thirty-two-foot building featured two stories. The first floor provided a dining room, office, and sitting room, and the second floor had six guest rooms. A twelve-foot-square cupola housing a telescope topped the building.

Perhaps French's most dramatic innovation on the mountain was the addition of a horse-powered inclined railway in 1854. Running on wooden rails, the two "sleigh" cars were pulled by a horse-drawn rope up the steep mountainside from the "half-way house" — a distance of 600 feet with a rise of 365 feet. French added a steam engine in 1856, and in 1867 he laid a second track for the funicular. The entire railway was encased in a wooden shed with dormers to admit light and provide a view (figure 6).

To accommodate the increasing number of visitors, French expanded the hotel in 1861 and after the Civil War provided a steamship to bring guests across the river from the Mt. Tom railway station. Once they reached the summit, guests could enhance the dramatic views by using a variety of telescopes mounted in the "Lookout Room" or outdoors in the rustic gazebo (figure 7). In addition to enjoying mountain hikes, visitors participated in other resort-style amusements such as musicales, dancing, tennis, bowling, and croquet.

In 1871, John Dwight, a South Hadley native and prosperous manufacturer of bicarbonate of soda, bought Prospect House. The renamed Mt. Holyoke Hotel continued to be managed by John French and his wife, Frances (Fanny). In due time Dwight installed the newly invented telephone and improved rail connections to the riverboat landing. In 1894, he significantly expanded the hotel with a sizeable addition that could accommodate forty overnight guests and seat 200 visitors in the dining room. With Dwight's death in 1903 and increasing competition from other local mountaintop hotels, the Mt. Holyoke Hotel faced difficult times.[25]

Amherst College students that went to the top from the old carriage road on the west side.

Although management of the mountain house changed hands frequently during these years, the relatively remote site attracted notable visitors from up and down the eastern seaboard and Europe. In the summer of 1847, the eminent Massachusetts Senator Charles Sumner lavished effusive praise on the site claiming: "I have been all over England, have traveled through all the Highlands of Scotland; I have passed up and down the Rhine, have ascended Mount Blanc, and stood

on the Campagna at Rome, but have never seen anything so surpassingly lovely as this."[24]

It was not until 1849, however, that plans for a proper hotel at the summit were realized. That year John French, a bookbinder from Northampton, purchased the property and petitioned the county commissioners to build a new public road from Hockanum at the base of the mountain to within a short hiking distance of the top. With the subsequent construction of a road from the "half-way house," visitors could soon reach the summit by pony cart. In 1851, with a business partner,

Once again a group of local businessmen, spearheaded by Christopher Clarke, a successful Northampton merchant and music promoter, formed a private organization aimed at preserving the mountaintop for public use. The Mt. Holyoke Company, headed by Joseph Skinner, an affluent silk manufacturer in Holyoke, added the first automobile road on the mountain in 1908 and made improvements to the pier at the Hockanum Ferry that enabled more passengers to transfer from the railroad station across the river. Despite these efforts, the tourist business on the mountain continued to decline. In 1915, after a failed attempt by Clarke and the Mt. Holyoke Company to transfer ownership of the hotel and other buildings on the grounds along with 256 acres to the Massachusetts State Forestry Association, Joseph Skinner offered to buy the property.

As a private owner, Skinner quickly advanced forest management of the site, added electricity, and converted the inclined railway from steam to electric power. Even in the face of the severe economic downturn of the Great Depression, Skinner further modernized the hotel by adding private baths and purchased additional acreage for the grounds. The devastating blow to the summit hotel, however, came not from financial problems but from a destructive hurricane in September 1938.

The 1894 addition fared the worst and even the wealthy Skinner could not afford repairs. A bill before the state legislature proposing to purchase the hotel and grounds stipulated that the Commonwealth of Massachusetts would have to tear down the damaged section of the building. Because of the financial burden it posed, the legislature was reluctant to act. Faced with the twin forces of nature and government, Skinner decided in 1939 to give the entire property to the Commonwealth with the condition that the state park would bear his name.

Although in a state of decline by the 1930s, Mt. Holyoke had been one of the most popular tourist destinations in New England for almost a century. It received notable visitors such as the writer Ralph Waldo Emerson, the famed Swedish opera star Jenny Lind, who called the region "The Paradise of America," and the poet Henry W. Longfellow. During the same period a local visitor, Mary Allen of Amherst, described the experience of the ordinary tourist:

> *A span of horses, in themselves an excitement, drew us and our guests to the Half Way House. From there we had our choice of walking up the road encircling the mountain to the summit, or of being pulled up the incline of the wooden funicular, or even of climbing the 522 steps of the long stairway that paralleled the track. The floor of the old Prospect House, at the top, was smooth for dancing, and between dances we might have the rare privilege of taking the Claude Lorraine glass from its locked security and looking into it to see the meadow's patchwork of colors, below, like a pattern in a real kaleidoscope — evenly cut fields of wheat, rye, and barley, and peaceful farmhouses, and the river winding to the Ox-bow.[26]*

Advertising broadsides for Prospect House in the 1870s illustrated improvements made to the mountain house over the years and emphasized special qualities of the view: "Many other peaks have a higher altitude and offer wilder and more unmixed natural scenery — but no other blends in its wide prospect so much that is rich in soil and cultivation, or presents so much agricultural wealth of beauty, mingled with so much that is wildly majestic, grand and inspiring." As a tourist destination Mt. Holyoke provided a combination of the pleasures of leisure culture and an idealized vision of agrarian labor. Visitors could survey a pastoral landscape, rich in both natural scenery and agricultural accomplishments. In the late nineteenth century, as the nation and the Connecticut River Valley were becoming industrialized, maintaining views of American farmland became increasingly difficult. Private pastoral vistas became more and more the purview of the rich who could afford to build grand country houses. But public places like Prospect House, which catered to the middle class, served an important niche in the growing demand for rural experiences.[27]

As late as the 1920s, when automobiles could reach the top of Mt. Holyoke, the hotel still advertised its vantage point as "the grandest cultivated view in the world," echoing Edward Hitchcock's claim from the previous century. Importantly, the privately owned hotel also touted the ease of public access to the summit that was made possible by the local citizenry: "Mt. Holyoke has been purchased, and the costly road built by public-spirited citizens, to save a beautiful spot from disfigurement. It is not held as an investment, but for the benefit and enjoyment of all the people."[28] These two aspects of the mountain's history — "the cultivated view" and "the public-spirited citizens" who promoted it — lie at the heart of its significance as a cultural icon today.

Nineteenth-Century Aesthetics

During the nineteenth century Mt. Holyoke attracted not only keen academic and tourist interest, but the attention of numerous artists as well.[29] The images they created underscore the value of rural landscape in our understanding of regional and national identity and the ongoing urge to preserve such areas for posterity. Mt. Holyoke, like all elevated vantage points, offers the possibility of taking in the large picture, of thinking about aspects of nature on a grand scale, of contemplating the role of humankind in the natural world.

Nineteenth-century artists (and the general public) further enhanced their vision of the land with the aid of viewing devices such as the camera lucida, telescope, Claude glass, and stereoscopic

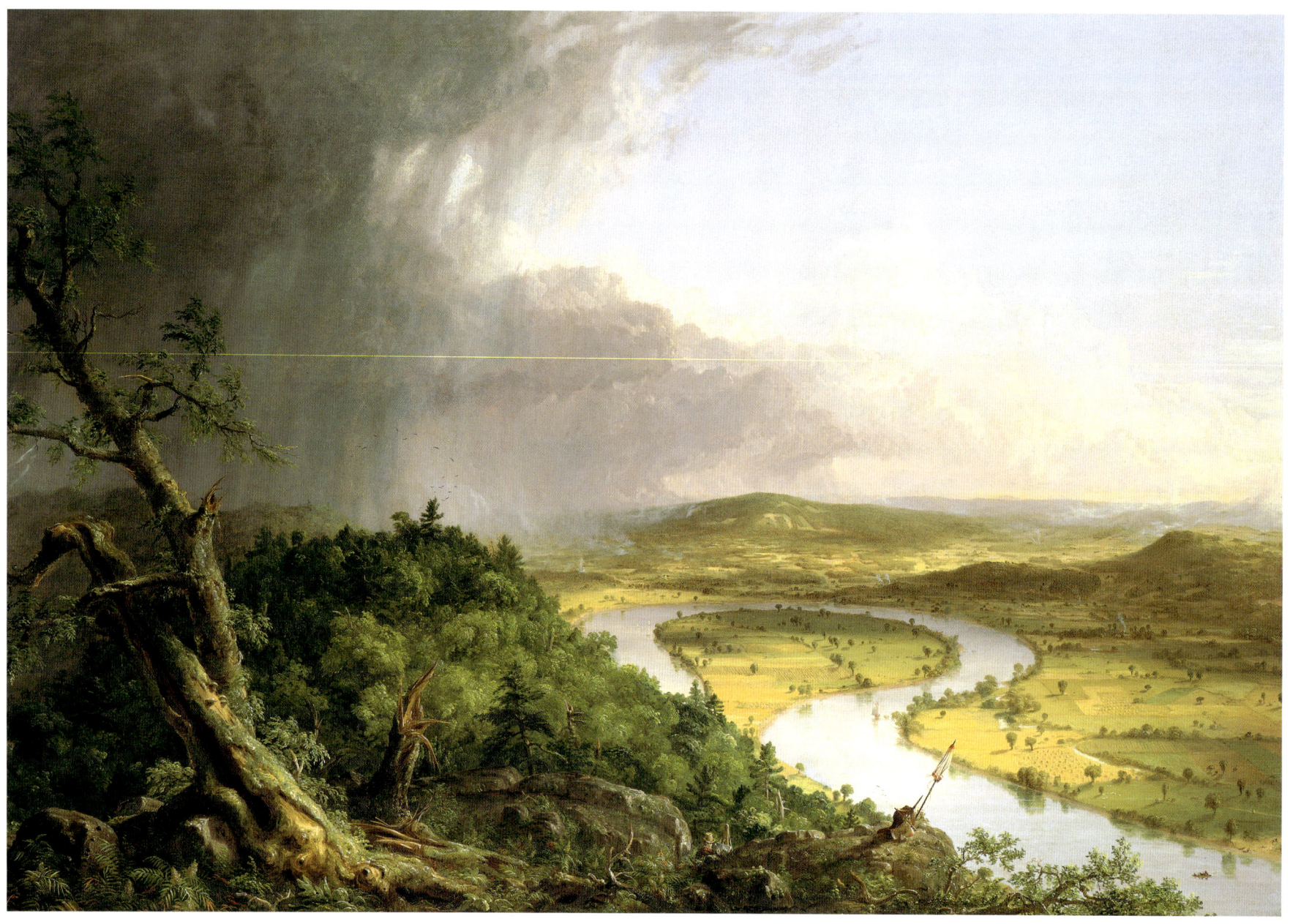

FIGURE 8. Thomas Cole, *View from Mount Holyoke,
Northampton, Massachusetts, after a Thunderstorm (The Oxbow)*,
1836, oil on canvas. The Metropolitan Museum of Art,
New York City, Gift of Mrs. Russell Sage (08.228)
Photograph ©1995 The Metropolitan Museum of Art

photograph. By fixing the sweeping panorama, capturing details in the far distance, and bringing out the three-dimensionality of the landscape, technological innovations made viewing the prospect a more emotionally moving experience.

Thomas Cole (1801–1848) was the first American artist to understand that landscape painting could convey elevated ideas and emotional feelings to the public. His *View from Mount Holyoke (The Oxbow)* of 1836 (figure 8) is one of the most romantic statements of his belief in nature's evocative power. It is a painting about time and place, about wilderness and cultivation, and about art and divine creation. As scholars have noted, *The Oxbow* appeared just after the publication of Cole's important *Essay on American Scenery*, in which he stated that by viewing the wilderness Americans could not only envision "freedom's offspring — peace, security and happiness dwell there, the spirits of the scene" but also contemplate their future — the "mighty deeds [that] shall be done in the now pathless wilderness."[30]

The scene that Cole depicted here is the view from the top of Mt. Holyoke toward the southwest, and the most obvious feature seen below is the dramatic curve in the Connecticut River, known in geological terms as an oxbow. Cole centered his work on the small neck of land that once connected the peninsula formed by the bend to the easterly riverbank. This distinctive bend is dramatically cut off by an elevated mass of trees and a rocky outcrop on the left side of the picture — the wilderness side of the composition. Flanked by a blasted tree trunk and storm clouds on the left, the more pastoral right side of the painting is filled with sunlit fields and clear skies. Often unnoticed at first glance, an artist sits nestled among the rocks in the center foreground with his sketching equipment marked by the umbrella silhouetted against the placid river.

As Cole's contemporary Edward Hitchcock had noted, the Oxbow itself was visual evidence of the river's power and great age as it slowly mean-

dered toward the sea.[31] The fragile neck of land connecting one side of Cole's picture to the other, linking wilderness and civilization, was forever altered by the powerful flood waters of the Connecticut River in 1840 just a few years after the painting was completed. The crescent-shaped oxbow lake, formed in the place of the river bend, appears in images of the same site by contemporary artists (see accompanying essay by Martha Hoppin) and serves as a further reminder of Cole's interest in dramatic alterations to the landscape. His view of the Oxbow is about change and creativity: both slow and rapid geologic erosion, dramatic shifts in the weather, and natural and man-made alterations to the topography. And in the midst of all this sits an artist, making a record of these changes.

Cole believed in the nineteenth-century notion of progress, although he often lamented the scourge of the axe as it cleared away the wilderness. In *View from Mount Holyoke* he bathed the cultivated landscape in sunlight, and his artist's furled umbrella pointedly directs the viewer's attention to the beneficence of American agriculture.[32] Almost every literary portrayal of the panoramic view from Mt. Holyoke in the nineteenth century likewise stresses its cultivated

beauty. Writers Ralph Waldo Emerson, Nathaniel Hawthorne, and James Fenimore Cooper all described the bucolic view from the mountaintop.[33] And popular literature of the day echoed their admiration of the surrounding farm fields and meadows. An 1855 newspaper article, extolling the virtues of the vista, noted:

> *The peninsula rich, fertile and covered with fields of grain, the Northampton meadows, the river at our feet, the numerous village spires, seen in every direction, level fields, orchards, gardens almost without number, and the whole view bounded by mountainous ridges, all going to make up a scene which is called the most beautiful on the river.*[34]

The first recorded visual image of these rich fields appeared in Basil Hall's *Forty Etchings, From Sketches Made with the Camera Lucida, in North America, in 1827 and 1828* (figure 9).[35] Captain Hall, a retired officer of the Royal Navy, was a noted author of popular British travel guides. Thomas Cole most likely encountered this book on the scenic wonders of the United States while visiting London in 1829. He traced Hall's etching and, later in 1833 when he visited Mt. Holyoke,

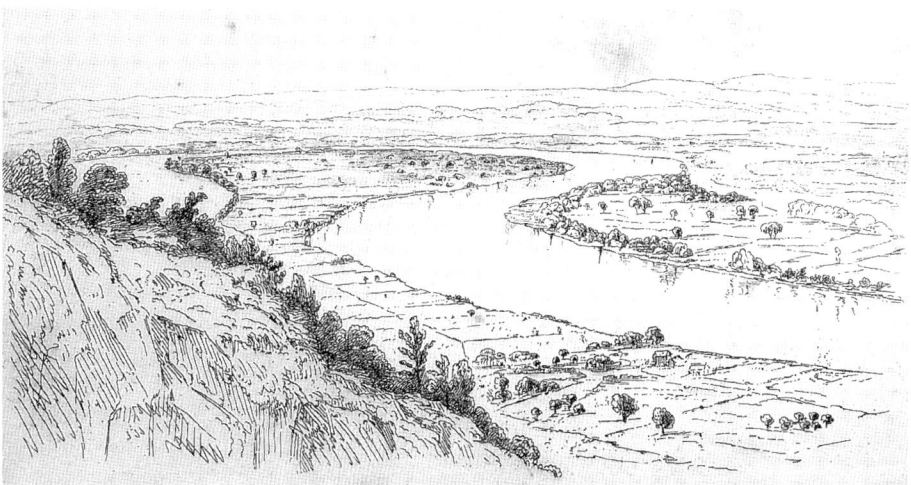

FIGURE 9. Basil Hall, *View from Mount Holyoke*, etching, from *Forty Etchings, from Sketches Made with the Camera Lucida, in North America, in 1827 and 1828*, 1829. Mount Holyoke College Archives and Special Collections

FIGURE 10. Houghton and
Knowlton, *Prospecting on
Mt. Holyoke*, ca. 1860s–70s,
stereoscopic photograph.
Historic Northampton,
Northampton, Massachusetts

FIGURE 11. L.H. Kingsley,
Half-way Barn, ca. 1880s,
albumen print photograph.
Historic Northampton,
Northampton, Massachusetts

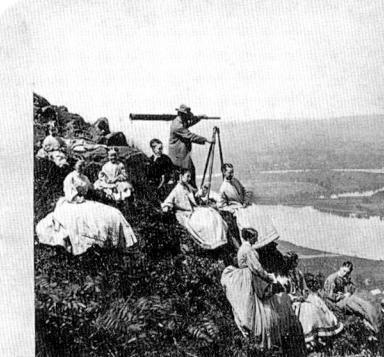
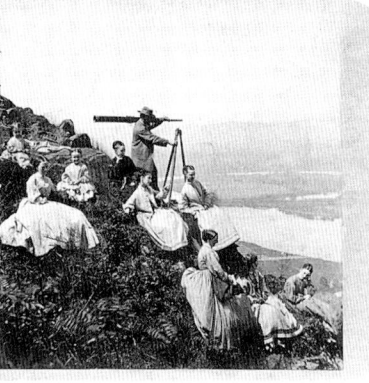

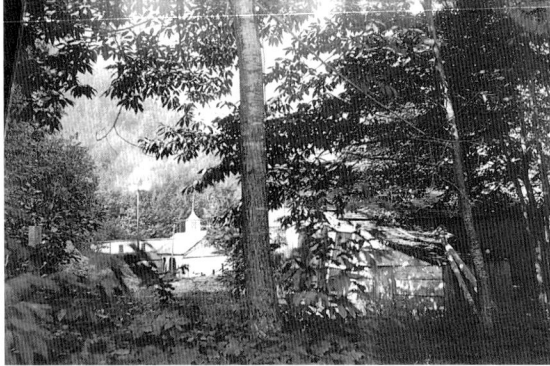

made a freehand sketch of the same view.[36]

The original source of Hall's etching was an image produced by a camera lucida, an optical viewing device invented in England in 1806 to aid landscape artists. The device consists of a prism on a long arm that can be attached to a sketchbook. The scene in the prism is reflected on the paper below, allowing the artist to trace an outline of the view. In the early nineteenth century the camera lucida provided artists with a means to render accurate topographic views that complemented and verified the text of travel guides. Hall declared the view from Mt. Holyoke "one of the most beautiful in America," and he described the river's course as "highly characteristic of the manner in which American streams wind through alluvial grounds."[37]

While the camera lucida projected an accurate, panoramic view, it was difficult to use and never became a popular device. With the advent of photography, however, the public demand for panoramic images increased dramatically. During the mid-nineteenth century, Knowlton Brothers of Northampton produced a popular series of stereo views from the mountain and scenes of the hotel and grounds (figure 10). These photographic images concentrated on technological innovations at Prospect House: the funicular railway, the telescopes, and the steamship. In contrast, L. H. Kingsley, a photographer from nearby Hatfield, sold more picturesque views, hiding these modern amenities behind the leaves and rocky outcroppings of the site (figure 11).

The Prospect House hotel proudly advertised its own modern viewing devices — numerous telescopes and an imported viewing device called a "Claude Glass." Named after Claude Lorraine, a seventeenth-century French landscape artist, the glass enabled a layperson to frame sections of the landscape, isolating aesthetically pleasing views. An 1887 illustrated guide to Prospect House described the popular gadget:

> *A dark, heavy, convex glass, known as the
> "Claude Lorraine," (it being invented by that
> painter) set in a solid frame of wood with
> leather handles at the ends, is much used by*
> *visitors to mirror the landscape, and the rich
> effects obtained delight every one.*[38]

When held up over the shoulder, the dark glass mirrored the vista seen behind the viewer. By framing and sharpening scenic vignettes, anyone could simulate the aesthetic practice of locating the most desirable vantage points.

The author and illustrator of this 1887 guide to the Mt. Holyoke vicinity was Clifton Johnson (1865–1940), a local photographer and publisher noted for his views of the Connecticut River Valley. An inveterate promoter of rural New England life, he was born in the village of Hockanum at the foot of Mt. Holyoke, and as a young man worked in a Northampton bookstore. Drawn to illustrated books, he decided to become an artist and went to New York to study. In 1890, he took up the camera as a means of providing studies for his illustrations. Johnson was best known for nostalgic genre scenes of rural activities: plowing with oxen, maple sugaring, and gardening. In depicting such scenes he adopted the pictorialist mode of photography, well suited to his narrative subjects. *The New England Magazine* noted, "Not things as they are, but things as they look, is his motto: in other words, he is a photographic impressionist." The article goes on to describe his penchant for cloudy days, his practice of photographing into the sun, and his retouching of negatives to add clouds or mask unwanted details.[39]

Typical of Johnson's artful approach is the platinum print photograph with three of his children posing on top of Mt. Holyoke (figure 12). With their backs to the camera, the children look northward over a panoramic view of the Connecticut River as it makes its dramatic curve around the town of Hadley. Johnson reproduced this image in *Historic Hadley*, his commemorative book about the town's history, in the midst of a discussion about Native American life in the region.[40] In this context his children (and by extension the

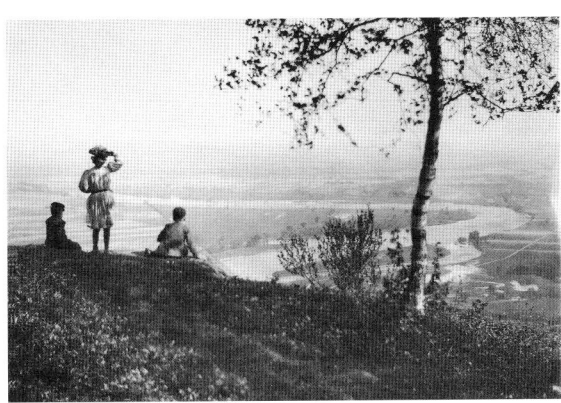

FIGURE 12. Clifton Johnson, *Hockanum: The Winding Connecticut Viewed from Mt. Holyoke*, ca. 1909, platinum print photograph. The Jones Library, Inc., Amherst, Massachusetts

photograph's viewer) survey not only the landscape but also the history of the Connecticut River Valley.

Several nineteenth-century guides to Mt. Holyoke similarly evoke romanticized tales of Indian life in the colonial era, among them the *Mt. Holyoke Pathfinder*, the newspaper published at Prospect House. An edition from the 1870s, for example, included a story about the Nonotuck chief, "Wawhillowa, A Legend of Quonnecticut," by D.M. Elwood. Because the hotel's steamship that plied the Connecticut River was called the Wawhillowa, the romantic origin of its name would have likely offered special interest to mountain visitors. Similarly, Johnson linked his photographs of the Mt. Holyoke area with local Indian tales in *Picturesque Hampshire*.[41] Accompanying his photographs was a long narrative poem about the Connecticut River that lamented the Indians' demise and marked the passage of time along the river's edge.

Elbridge Kingsley (1842–1918), another local artist whose photographs and writing appeared in Johnson's *Historic Hadley*, reminded readers that Mt. Holyoke had always been of strategic importance to the Indians and to the white settlers who displaced them. In his memoirs Kingsley recount-

ed a winter outing to Mt. Holyoke when he first made the connection between the landscape and the Native Americans who had long before inhabited the space:

> And here for the first time I had a realizing sense of the vastness of nature viewed from a height, the lower levels all in white, the glistening frozen river losing itself in the blue haze of the distant hills, all combined to make the perfect picture shadowed in dreams. Here was the fair land of Indian tradition, and this is what the leaders saw from their hill forts, and called on their "Manitou" for help to drive back the invading hosts of the pale faces, with their thunders and lightenings [sic].[42]

Traveling about the countryside in a horse-drawn caravan outfitted with his painting supplies, Kingsley often camped on Mt. Holyoke. In addition to his "sketching car," the artist had a rowboat with which he located artistic vantage points

of the mountain from the river or from the oxbow lake. Hotel managers John and Fanny French would supply him with food so that he could make plein-air sketches and prints all day. During summertime, he and sometimes his brother, photographer L.H. Kingsley, would often spend weeks camping out in the sketching car (figure 13):

> I could look out of my car window and see the whole of Hadley in the loop of the river, and Hatfield beyond. And Mts. Sugarloaf and Toby rising in the background. It was a novel situation to be able to stay in my bunk and see all this under different conditions of cloud and sunshine.[43]

Trained by Deerfield painter James Wells Champney, and in New York, Kingsley had traveled to France in the late 1880s and became an exponent of the fashionable Barbizon style of landscape painting. The suffused light, loose brushwork, and soft color palette in his 1889 *Springtime — Meadow and Mount Holyoke* (figure 14) are typical of

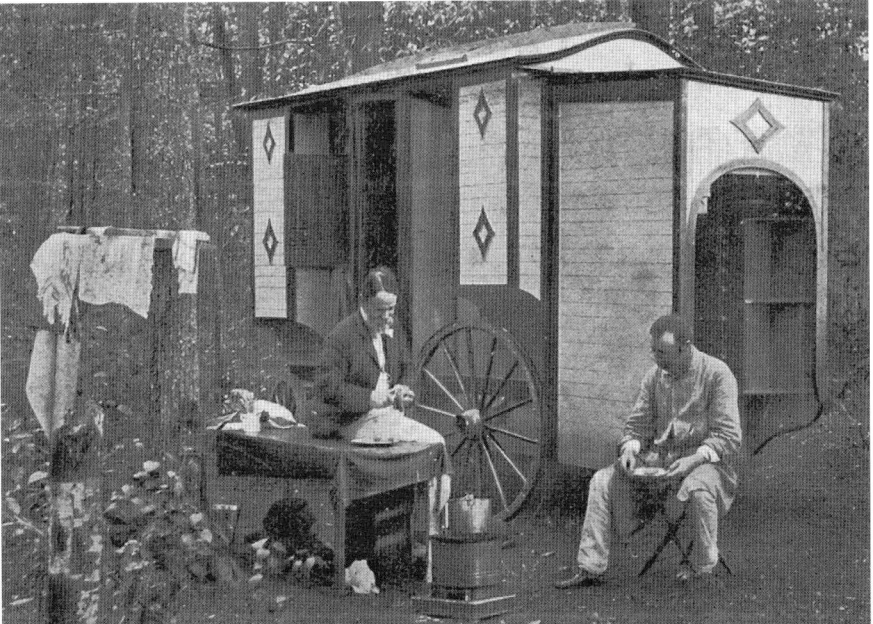

FIGURE 13. Elbridge Kingsley, *Sketching Car on Mount Holyoke*, ca. 1880, photograph, reproduced in *Historic Hadley*, ed. Clifton Johnson, 1909. The Mount Holyoke College Library (not in exhibition)

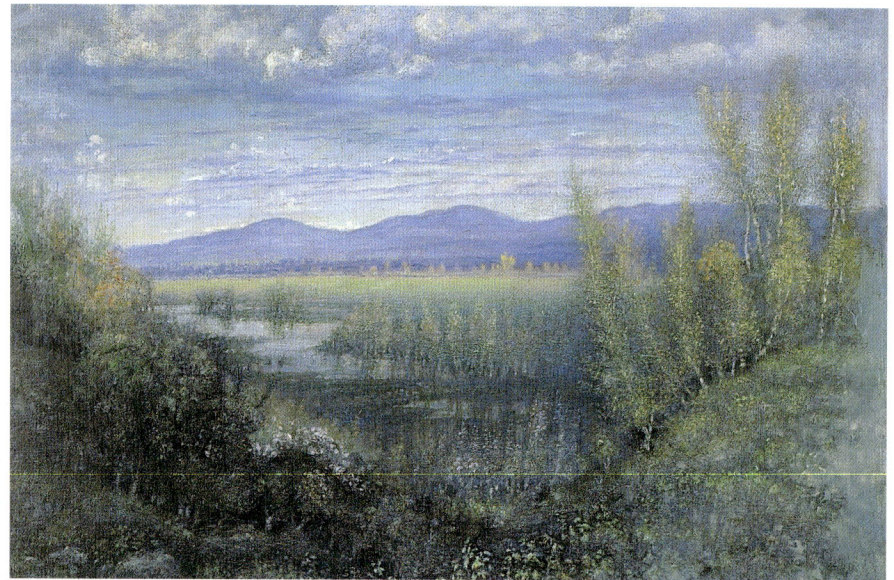

Barbizon paintings that concentrate on effects of atmosphere rather than on closely observed details of nature that characterize earlier nineteenth-century American painting. Also active as a printmaker, Kingsley made wood engravings that, like his paintings, were often based on his photographs of the local landscape.

Another artist working in the Connecticut Valley, David John Gue (1836–1917), painted two important landscapes related to Mt. Holyoke (figures 15 and 16). According to Kingsley's autobiography, John Dwight, the owner of the Prospect House Hotel, commissioned Gue to execute these landscapes, as well as his portrait.[44] Gue's 1903 *View from Mount Holyoke* (figure 15) was painted from the same wooded grove where Kingsley had frequently parked his sketching car.

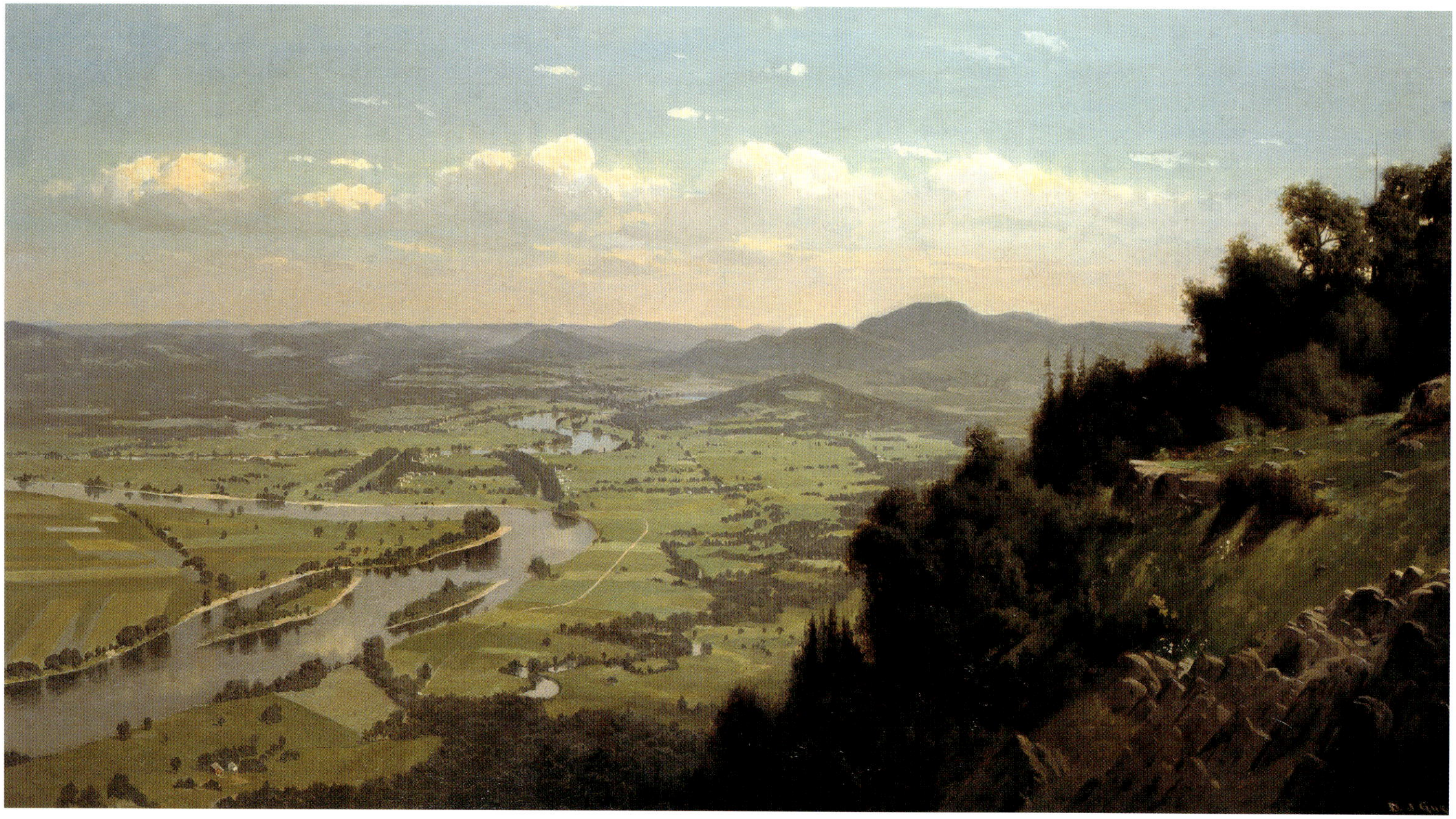

FIGURE 14. Elbridge Kingsley, *Springtime — Meadow and Mount Holyoke*, 1899, oil on canvas. Forbes Library, Northampton

FIGURE 15. David John Gue, *View from Mount Holyoke*, 1903, oil on canvas. Mount Holyoke College Art Museum, Gift of John Dwight

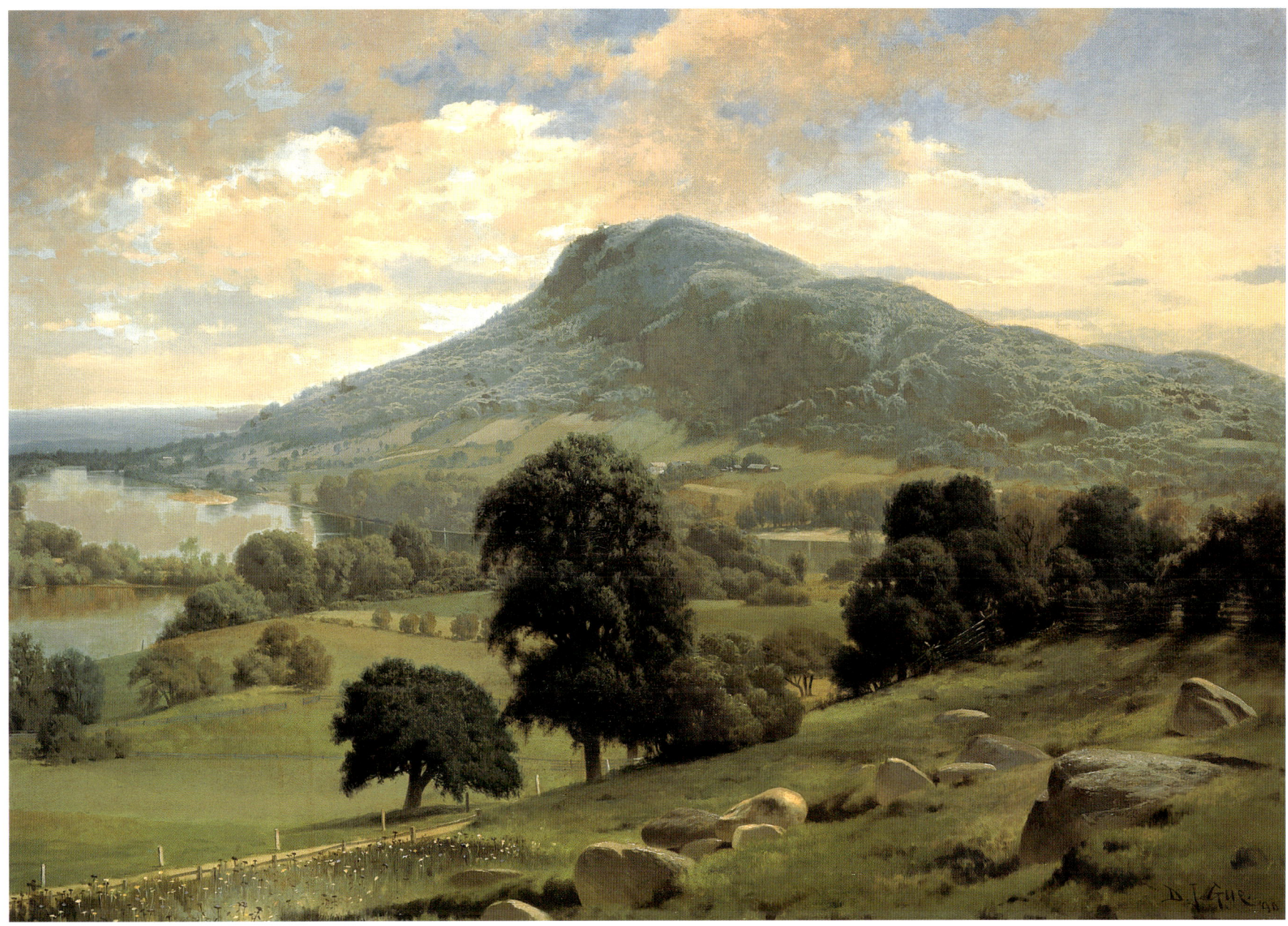

FIGURE 16. David John Gue, *View of Mount Holyoke*,
1890, oil on canvas. Mount Holyoke College Art
Museum, Gift of John Dwight

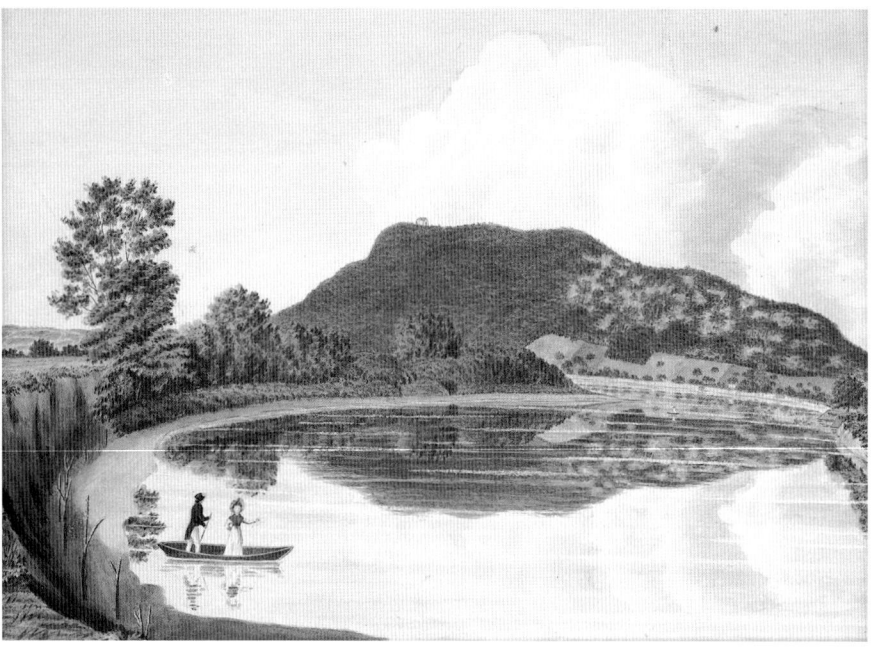

FIGURE 17. Eliza
Goodridge, *View of
Mount Holyoke,
Massachusetts, and the
Connecticut River*,
1830s, watercolor on
paper. Mount Holyoke
College Art Museum,
Purchase with the
Elizabeth Pierce Allyn
Art Acquisition Fund
and Art Acquisition
Fund

Although the two artists may have worked from the same vantage point, their painting styles were quite dissimilar. While Kingsley espoused the looser, atmospheric effects of contemporary French painting, Gue adopted a style reminiscent of the older, American, Hudson River School. According to Kingsley, Gue was a "careful and painstaking artist" who worked in a manner attuned to the realist taste of his patron, Dwight. The details of Gue's landscapes are more tightly rendered and the lighting is brighter — full of sharp contrasts of light and shade, especially in the foreground details. This is particularly evident in *View from Mount Holyoke* where the massing of dark green trees and the sharp lines of basalt outcroppings at the right of the composition are balanced by the more expansive, but softly rendered details of the distant view on the left. The scene Gue painted, looking northward along the dramatic bend in the Connecticut River at Hadley, is significantly devoid of people.

Earlier nineteenth-century artists, such as William Bartlett, Thomas Chambers, and Victor de Grailly, created views from the mountaintop that showed visitors in the foreground admiring the panoramic vista. Other painters, who focused on more distant views of the mountain, also added the human element. One of the earliest depictions of Mt. Holyoke, a landscape by Eliza Goodridge (1798–1882) probably from the 1830s, was painted from the Oxbow and shows a gentleman ferrying a woman across the river (figure 17).[45] The English Pre-Raphaelite painter Thomas Charles Farrer (1839–1891) not only depicted a rowboat with figures in his view of Mt. Holyoke from the Oxbow, but also included a train (figure 18). The railroad, constructed in 1845, ran across the spit of land that had formed at the mouth of the Oxbow after the river changed its course five years earlier. By 1865, when Farrer visited Northampton and made two other detailed views of the area, visitors to Mt. Holyoke frequently arrived by train at the Mt. Tom station and were ferried across the river by steamboat.[46] Farrer directly linked boat, train, and mountain house hotel in the center of his composition.

David Gue, however, assiduously limited such references to human activity in his 1890 *View of Mount Holyoke* (figure 16). He selected a slightly more elevated and southerly vantage point from across the river on the lower slopes of Mt. Tom that blocked out the railroad. He focused instead on the few small farmhouses and fields visible in the far distance. His painting does provide a glimpse of the Mt. Holyoke Hotel just to the left of the mountain's apex as it gently rises above the surrounding landscape. The overall quietude of Gue's clouds, the muted blue-green tonality of the vegetation, and the sense of tranquil harmony in this painting set his work apart from the more grandiose, dramatic statements of Cole and his followers. In place of the railroad tracks, Gue draws the viewer's attention to the old-fashioned split-rail fence that climbs the hillside in the foreground.

By the late nineteenth-century, landscape artists like Kingsley and Gue had abandoned the dramatic romanticism of Cole and the Hudson River School generations and instead chose to emphasize more ephemeral effects of color and tone that evoked quieter, poetic moments in the landscape. Drawn to the verdant meadows at the base of the mountain, rather than its more overwhelming heights, they appreciated the nocturnal glow of the moon as much as the dazzling sunsets viewed from the hotel:

In the evening we would gather in the conservatory on the southeast side of the house, and watch the full moon come up over Mount Holyoke College. The slopes of the mountain on that side were mostly wooded, and the deep ravines darkly shadowed, while here and there the bright pools of water reflected the light. Groves of trees outlined against silver flashes. Perhaps the sky would be filled with light fleecy clouds flitting across the face of the moon, receiving a faint tinge of rose as they approached the light.[47]

Late nineteenth-century artists depicted the intimate and fleeting changes in nature, not the grandiose and permanent. Their "changing prospects" had more to do with varying the viewpoints of Mt. Holyoke itself rather than capturing the sweeping panorama from the summit. More nostalgic than didactic, their bucolic landscapes are filled with poetic longings for a quieter, slower pace of life. Their images carefully avoid any reference to the railroads, steamships, and factories that surrounded the mountain and were clearly visible from the mountaintop. In their reverie of rural life, these late landscapes of Mt. Holyoke are part of the growing Colonial Revival movement in American art — an aesthetic trend that was particularly strong in the Connecticut River Valley, from the furniture making and photographic efforts of Wallace Nutting in Hartford to the architectural preservation and Arts and Crafts society in Deerfield.[48]

For generations, Mt. Holyoke, rising above the valley, has represented a solid and permanent fixture in a changing landscape. It was one of those increasingly rare places in the American landscape that not only has afforded physical exercise but also visual stimulation to nourish the soul and intellectual stimulation for the mind. Today, however, its place in American culture is not so assured. Recently listed as one of the ten most endangered scenic vistas in the United States, Mt. Holyoke stands amid struggles to protect the undeveloped lands that still skirt its slopes and to restore the historic structure that once graced its peak (see the accompanying essay by Ethan Carr).[49] But with the support of nonprofit environmental groups, state forest management, and the general public who continue to hike its trails and enjoy the view, the prospect for positive change looks more promising.

NOTES

1. Besides Mount Holyoke College, Amherst College, the University of Massachusetts at Amherst, Smith College, and Hampshire College lie within sight of the mountain.

2. Edward Hitchcock (1793–1864) was a founding trustee of Mount Holyoke Female Seminary in 1836; see Sarah D. Stowe, *History of Mount Holyoke Seminary During Its First Half Century, 1837–1887* (South Hadley: Mount Holyoke Seminary, 1887), p. 49. He also taught at Amherst College from 1825 to 1845, serving as president there from 1845 to 1854.

3. Stowe, *History of Mount Holyoke Seminary*, p. 49.

4. The school changed its name to Mount Holyoke College in 1893.

5. Quoted in Stowe, *History of Mount Holyoke Seminary*, p. 54.

6. Edward Hitchcock, *The Power of Christian Benevolence, Illustrated in the Life and Labors of Mary Lyon* (Northampton: Bridgman and Childs, 1860), p. 212.

7. Fidelia Fiske, *Recollections of Mary Lyon, with Selections from Her Instructions to the Pupils of Mt. Holyoke Female Seminary* (Boston: American Tract Society, 1866), pp. 22–23. (Note: The author's name is incorrectly spelled Fisk in this edition.)

8. For a discussion of the long relationship between Mary Lyon and the Hitchcocks, see Elizabeth Alden Green, *Mary Lyon and Mount Holyoke, Opening the Gates* (Hanover and London: University Press of New England, 1979), especially pp. 36 and 130–34; and Beth Bradford Gilchrist, *The Life of Mary Lyon* (Boston and New York: Houghton Mifflin Company, 1910), pp. 190–92.

9. Hitchcock, *The Power of Christian Benevolence*, p. 12.

10. Stowe, *History of Mount Holyoke Seminary*, p.147.

11. Edward Hitchcock, *The Religion of Geology and Its Connected Sciences* (Boston: Phillips, Sampson, and Co., 1852), p. 183.

12. Ibid., p. 481.

13. Hitchcock amended a special footnote on the formation of the Oxbow and included an altered version of a print by William Henry Bartlett to show the new course of the river in *The Final Report on the Geology of Massachusetts* (Northampton: J.H. Butler, 1841), p. 242. The Bartlett print is discussed in Martha Hoppin's

essay, pp. 34–35.

14. Lucy T. Goodale, Notebook entry for June 23, 1838, Mount Holyoke College Archives and Special Collections.

15. Green, *Mary Lyon and Mount Holyoke*, p. 188, and for a further description of early Mountain Day activities, see pp. 289–91. For a discussion of Hitchcock's lectures at Mount Holyoke Female Seminary, see Gilchrist, *Life of Mary Lyon*, pp. 298–301, and Frances Lester Warner, *On a New England Campus* (Boston: Houghton Mifflin Company, 1937), pp. 234–46.

16. Lydia R. Baldwin, Letter dated July 2,1845, Mount Holyoke College Archives and Special Collections. Hitchcock's later published account dates this event to July 4, no doubt wishing to associate this local triumph with the national holiday.

17. Edward Hitchcock, *Reminiscences of Amherst College, Historical, Scientific, Biographical, and Autobiographical* (Northampton: Bridgman and Childs, 1863), pp. 220–26.

18. Harriet Lane, Letter dated June 9, 1851, Mount Holyoke College Archives and Special Collections. For a fuller analysis of the railroad in the visual arts, see Susan Danly and Leo Marx, eds. *The Railroad in American Art* (Cambridge: MIT Press, 1988). On Thoreau, see Leo Marx, *The Machine in the Garden, Technology and the Pastoral Ideal in America* (London: Oxford University Press, 1964), pp. 248–55.

19. Janet L. Dimase, "On Top of Mount Holyoke," *Mount Holyoke Alumnae Quarterly* (fall, 1977), pp. 30–31. For further descriptions of Mountain Day celebrations, see Warner, *On a New England Campus*, pp. 234–46.

20. Gilchrist, *Life of Mary Lyon*, pp. 437–40.

21. I would like to thank Alan Werner, associate professor of geology, Department of Earth and Environment, Mount Holyoke College, for sharing information on current curricular practices and the geology of the Mt. Holyoke Range.

22. For a detailed discussion of the development of the site see David Graci, *Mt. Holyoke: An Enduring Prospect* (Holyoke: Calem Publishing Co., 1985).

23. Newspaper clipping, dated May 7, 1823, from photocopy in Lois Bliss scrapbook, Mount Holyoke College Archives and Special Collections.

24. See Mt. Holyoke register book, August 12,1847, Historic Northampton; and quoted on undated Mt. Holyoke broadside, ca. 1860s, Mount Holyoke College

Archives and Special Collections.

25. The first local rival was Eyrie House on neighboring Mt. Nonotuck in 1861. Another mountain house appeared up river at Mt. Sugarloaf in 1864. But the most competition came from the hotel on Mt. Tom, opened in 1895, just across the Connecticut River, which had easier access to railroad and streetcar connections on the west bank. In 1908 yet another mountain house opened on Fisher's Hill in Westhampton.

26. Mary Adèle Allen, *Around a Village Green, Sketches of Life in Amherst* (Northampton: The Kraushar Press, ca. 1930), p. 70.

27. For a history of the growth of rural tourism in New England, see John Sears, *Sacred Places: American Tourist Attractions in the Nineteenth Century* (Amherst: University of Massachusetts Press, 1989), pp. 49–56, and Dona Brown, *Inventing New England: Regional Tourism in the Nineteenth Century* (Washington, DC: Smithsonian Institution Press, 1995). Her discussion of Mt. Holyoke centers on its earliest phase of development in the 1820s and 1830s, pp. 33–34.

28. Advertising brochure for Mt. Holyoke, Mount Holyoke College Archives and Special Collections.

29. For a more complete history of artists painting in the Connecticut River Valley, see Martha Hoppin, "Arcadian Vales: The Connecticut Valley in Art," *Arcadian Vales, Views of the Connecticut River Valley*, ed. Martha Hoppin (Springfield, MA: George Walter Vincent Smith Art Museum, 1982), pp. 31–51.

30. The essay was first delivered as a lecture to the New York Lyceum in May, 1835, and printed in a pamphlet that same year. See the reprint in John McCoubrey, *American Art: Sources and Documents* (Englewood Cliffs: Prentice-Hall, 1965), pp. 98–110. For a discussion of the genesis of the Cole painting, see Matthew Baigell and Allen Kaufman, "Thomas Cole's 'Oxbow': A Critique of American Civilization," *Arts Magazine* 55 (January 1981), pp. 136–39. See also, Hoppin, "Arcadian Vales," pp. 31–51; Oswaldo Rodriquez Roque, *The Oxbow* by Thomas Cole: Iconography of an American Landscape Painting," *Metropolitan Museum Journal* 17 (1984), pp. 63–73; William Cronon, "Telling Tales on Canvas: Landscapes of Frontier Change," *Discovered Lands, Invented Pasts*, (New Haven: Yale University Press, 1992), pp. 40–44; and Alan Wallach, "Making a Picture of the View from Mount Holyoke," *American Iconology*,

ed. David C. Miller (New Haven: Yale University Press, 1993), pp. 34–44.

31. For Hitchcock's discussion of the Oxbow's formation and the importance of the view from Mt. Holyoke, see *The Final Report on the Geology of Massachusetts*, pp. 242–43. For a more detailed discussion of Cole's interest in geology, see Rebecca Bedell's chapter "Thomas Cole and the Fashionable Science," *The Anatomy of Nature, Geology and American Landscape Painting, 1825–1875* (Princeton: Princeton University Press, 2001), pp. 17–45.

32. A similar interpretation of the painting appears in Alan Wallach's "Thomas Cole: Landscape and the Course of America," *Thomas Cole: Landscape into History* (New Haven and Washington, DC: Yale University Press and the National Museum of American Art, 1994), p. 74.

33. Jill Hodnicki, "The Connecticut Valley in Literature," *Arcadian Vales*, pp. 11–29.

34. Unidentified clipping titled "Local Intelligence," July, 1854, in Bliss scrapbook, Mount Holyoke College Archives and Special Collections.

35. Basil Hall, *Forty Etchings, From Sketches Made with the Camera Lucida, in North America, in 1827 and 1828* (Edinburgh: Cadell and Co.; London: Simpkin, Marshall, and Mann, Boys & Graves, 1829), see plate no. XI; and Hoppin, "Arcadian Vales," p. 35.

36. Both of these drawings are in the collection of the Detroit Institute of Arts. For a detailed discussion of their genesis and meaning, see Allan Wallach, "Making a Picture of the View," pp. 80–91.

37. Hall, *Forty Etchings*, p. 94.

38. Clifton Johnson, *Mount Holyoke and Vicinity Illustrated* (Northampton: Gazette Publishing Company, 1887), p. 18. The landscape paintings of the French artist, Claude Lorraine (1600–82), were much admired by Thomas Cole and other American art collectors in the nineteenth century.

39. Mary Bronson Hartt, "Clifton Johnson and His Pictures of New England Life," *New England Magazine* (n.s. 24, August 1901), p. 667. Typical of Johnson's numerous photographically illustrated books is *Highways and Byways of New England* (New York: Macmillan Company, 1915).

40. Clifton Johnson, *Historic Hadley* (Northampton: Souvenir Publishing Company, 1909), p. 29.

41. Clifton Johnson, *Picturesque Hampshire: A Supplement to the Quarter-centennial Edition of the Hampshire County Journal* (Northampton, 1890), pp. 80–81.

42. Elbridge Kingsley, "Life and Works of Elbridge Kingsley, Painter-Engraver" (typescript manuscript, Forbes Library, Northampton, ca. 1915), pp.18–19.

43. Ibid., p. 114.

44. Ibid., pp. 134 and 263–264. John Dwight donated the two Gue landscapes and his portrait to the Mount Holyoke College Art Museum in 1903.

45. Eliza (Elizabeth) Goodrich from Templeton, Massachusetts, was primarily a painter of miniature portraits. According to Nina Fletcher Little, the frame for this rare landscape painting was made by Anson Clark of West Stockbridge, Massachusetts, in the 1830s. See curatorial file, Mount Holyoke College Art Museum. Given the style of clothes worn by the figures and the view from the Oxbow, made before the 1840 rerouting of the river, it seems likely that this work dates from the late 1830s.

46. For more information on Farrer's Northampton landscapes, see Linda S. Ferber and William H. Gerdts, *The New Path, Ruskin and The American Pre-Raphaelites* (Brooklyn: Brooklyn Museum, 1985), entry nos. 11–12 by May Brawley Hill; Linda Muehlig, ed., *Masterworks of American Painting and Sculpture from the Smith College Museum of Art* (New York: Hudson Hills Press, 1999), pp. 74–77, entry no. 21 by Betsy B. Jones; and Gina Greer and Andrea Smith, *American Paintings, 1860–1940* (New York: Vance Jordan Fine Art, 2000), p. 46.

47. Kingsley, *Life and Works*, p. 265.

48. For a general discussion of the Colonial Revival and Arts and Crafts movement in Massachusetts, see *Inspiring Reform: Boston's Arts and Crafts Movement* (Wellesley: Davis Museum and Cultural Center, 1997).

49. Mt. Holyoke is listed by Scenic America, a nonprofit land preservation organization, on their annual ten most endangered sites for 2000. See their website at *www.scenic.org*.

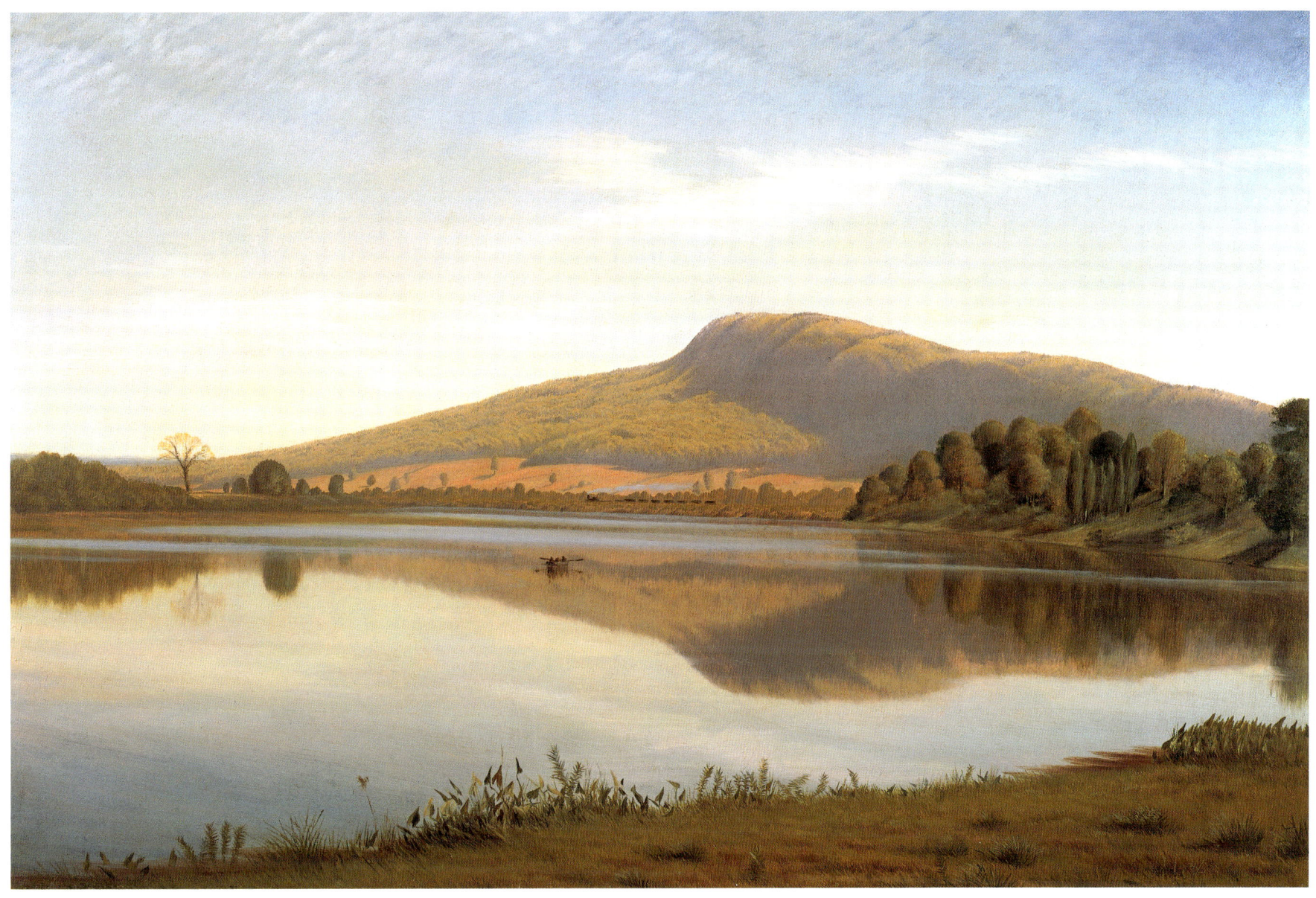

FIGURE 18. Thomas Charles Farrer, *Mount Holyoke*, 1865,
oil on canvas. Vance Jordan Fine Art, New York City

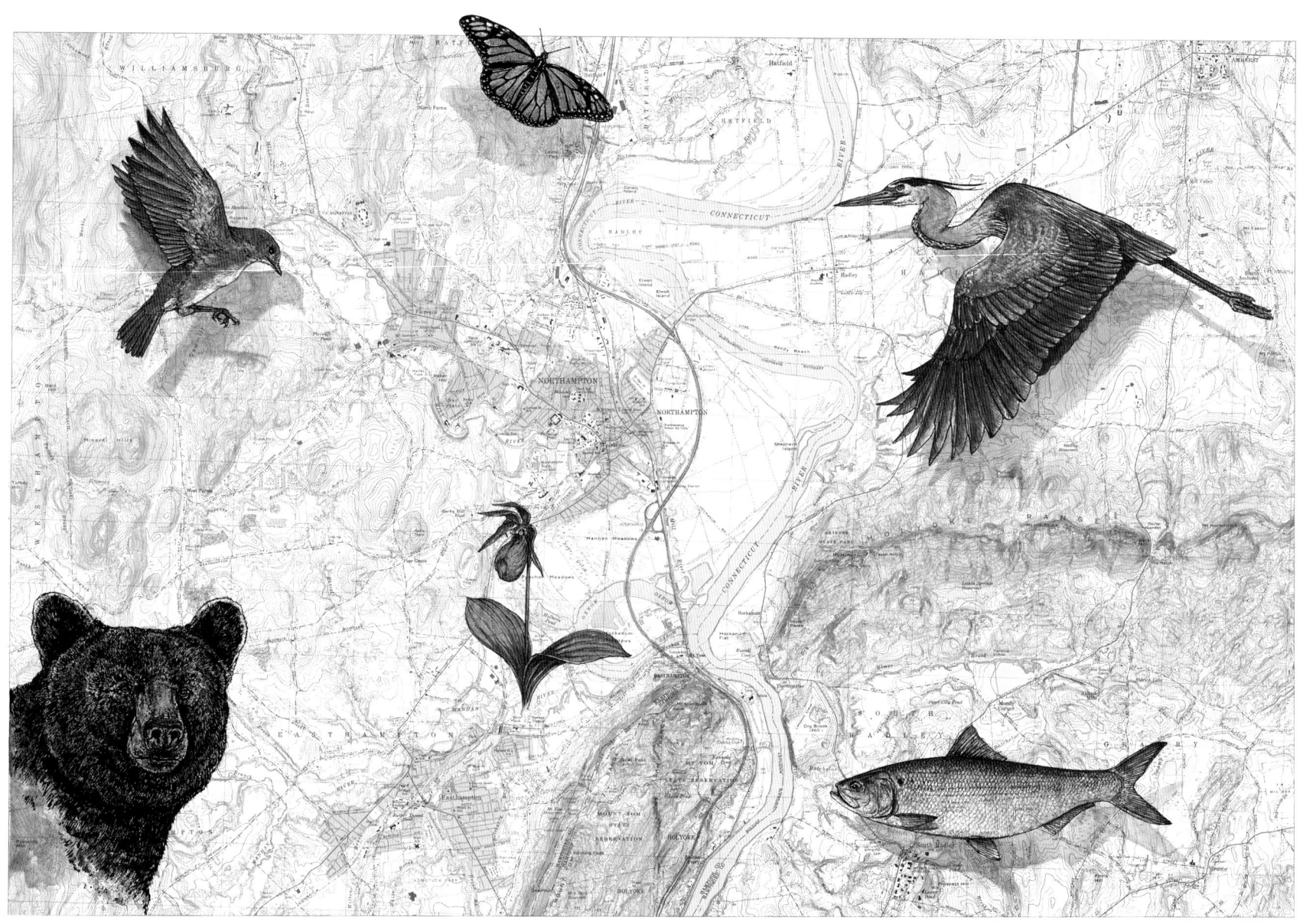

FIGURE 19. Alan Robinson, *The Oxbow*, 2001, watercolor and gouache on topographical map. R. Michelson Galleries, Northampton

Depicting Mount Holyoke: A Dialogue with the Past

Martha Hoppin

Inescapable. That is what Erwin Panofsky called art so authoritative that it conditions the vision of any artist who attempts the same subject.[1] Thomas Cole's *View from Mount Holyoke, Northampton, Massachusetts, after a Thunderstorm (The Oxbow)*, painted in 1836, is one of these works (figure 8). It led Cole's Hudson River School colleagues to adopt his panoramic composition but probably to avoid copying or reinterpreting his subject. In contrast, today's artists regularly paint the view of the Oxbow from Mt. Holyoke and openly acknowledge their debt to Cole.

Contemporary artists have also been influenced by nineteenth-century American landscape painting as a whole. In depicting Mt. Holyoke, most use a realist style similar to the close description of nature found in nineteenth-century examples, especially those of the Hudson River School. The views of Mt. Holyoke that have become standard — one from the top of the mountain looking north to Hadley, a second from the top looking southwest to the Oxbow of the Connecticut River, and a third of the mountain's profile rising behind a foreground of rich farmland — were developed and codified in the nineteenth century. These earlier scenes present an idyllic harmony between man and nature that has strong appeal in today's world of encroaching development and environmental threats. Moved by personal ties to the landscape, contemporary artists mostly choose to convey the pastoral beauty that still characterizes the Connecticut Valley. By suppressing signs of modern life, they return to, or insist on, this vision of Arcadia. They warn against destruction in the present by alluding to art of the past, and current environmental movements provide a climate favorable to the creation and reception of their works.

Nineteenth-Century Views from Mt. Holyoke

In mid-summer 1833 Cole climbed to the top of Mt. Holyoke as part of a general tour he was making from Catskill, New York, to Boston. Today, as then, a visitor to the Summit House (more often referred to as Prospect House or Mt. Holyoke Hotel in the 1800s) sees a panoramic sweep of the Connecticut Valley laid out neatly along the river directly below. Because the mountain rises suddenly out of the flat, alluvial meadowlands, it offers a spectacular vista of many miles (see map used as ground in Alan Robinson's watercolor, figure 19). Straight across the river to the west is Northampton; to the north lies the town of Hadley, and to the southwest is the almost circular configuration of the river known as the Oxbow. Across the river, south of the Oxbow, lies the Mt. Tom Range, partially visible from the Summit House. Further south the river winds past South Hadley and Holyoke. Cole chose to draw the view looking southwest towards the Oxbow. In the center of two facing pages of his sketchbook (Detroit Institute of Arts), he arranged the peak of Mt. Holyoke, elaborating on the mountain's right slope with the Oxbow behind it. He noted in the margin that he could see elm trees and rows of corn below.[2]

Three years later Cole decided to produce a painting of the Oxbow from Mt. Holyoke because he thought it would sell. Although he preferred to create elaborate series of paintings mixing landscape with history or religion, the public wanted to buy pure landscapes. In March 1836 he wrote to his patron Luman Reed, "Fancy pictures seldom sell, and they generally take more time than views, so I have determined to paint one of the latter — I have already commenced a view from Mount Holyoke; it is about the finest scene I have in my sketchbook and is well known — it will be novel and I think effective."[3] The work's impact derives

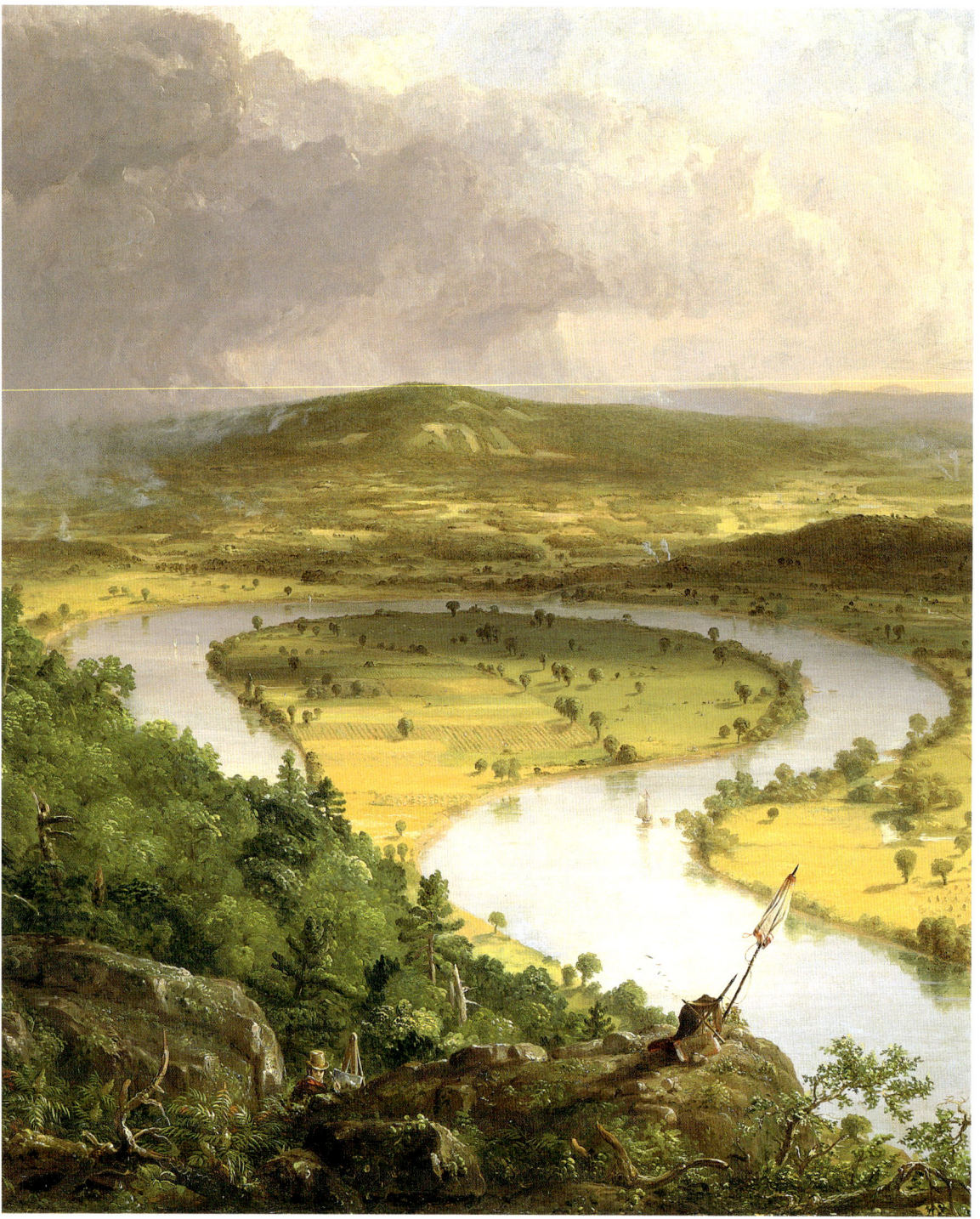

partly from its monumental scale, influenced by the grand size of his *Course of Empire* series underway at that time. Cole commented to Reed that he had only the one large canvas available in his studio.

By calling the site "well known," Cole meant that Mt. Holyoke was becoming an important tourist destination. As early as 1821 local business-men had cut a trail to near the top of the mountain and built a simple shelter there to accommodate the growing number of visitors. In Cole's day the climb involved first riding and then walking via a primitive "staircase formed by nature and art," according to one tourist.[4]

Early guidebooks publicized Mt. Holyoke's attractions. Timothy Dwight, in his *Travels in New-England and New-York* of 1823, described the view from Mt. Holyoke as "the richest prospect in New-England, and not improbably in the United States," and observed that the fertile fields below resembled gardens.[5] Echoing his uncle's remarks, Theodore Dwight in *The Northern Traveller* of 1826 wrote that the "ascent of this mountain has lately become very fashionable," and noted the unfenced farmland and natural meadows.[6] At about the same time, the British Mrs. Basil Hall, who was accompanying her husband, found the countryside visible from the mountaintop to be more settled in appearance than parts of New York State owing to the absence of "rough wooden fences," stumps, and girdled trees (girdling, cutting away a ring of bark, was a typical method of clear-ing land).[7] It was particularly the lack of fencing that distinguished the landscape and inspired com-parisons to a garden.

When Cole eventually painted the view, he added elements symbolic of nature's power — storm clouds and blasted tree — on the wilderness half of his composition but remained close to ob-served reality, as recorded in his on-site drawing, for the Oxbow half. In the distance rounded trees dot the fields, recalling Timothy Dwight's observa-tion that "everywhere forest trees standing singly, of great height and graceful figures, diversify the

FIGURE 20. Thomas Cole, *The Oxbow*, detail, see figure 8

landscape."[8] Dwight also remarked on the scene's distinctive mix of cultivated and uncultivated lands, a feature Cole preserved in both drawing and painting with his division of the Oxbow peninsula into half fields and half pasture.

Other details are rendered with considerable accuracy: the Hockanum ferry crosses the river, the Mill River winds through fields along the Connecticut's banks to empty into the Oxbow, and on the Oxbow's far side, an opening leads to Hulbert's Pond, a remnant of an earlier abandoned oxbow cut off by the present one (figure 20).[9] For this particularly meaningful feature, barely (if at all) visible from the mountain, Cole may have hiked into the area, looked through a telescope, or consulted a map, such as the one published in 1831 (figure 21). Departing from topography, on the other hand, he greatly enlarged some low hills in the distance, limiting the vastness of space. He also added the small figure of an artist at work on the mountain's slope and signed his name on the artist's portfolio.

Cole accentuated the Oxbow's form, rendering it as a nearly perfect circle and tipping up the landscape to make it more visible. At the same time he eliminated the near bank of the river. The resulting abrupt juxtaposition of mountain and river not only reinforces the contrast of wild and settled landscape, but also creates two large shapes, a wedge and a circle, which have a dramatic visual impact. Cole made the riveting form of the Oxbow the focal point of his painting. This geological feature that evolves over time had special meaning for him as a symbol of the cycles of human history and natural history.

Cole was obsessed with what he saw as the inevitable rise and fall of civilization, which he equated with the birth-death-decay cycle of nature. In his view from Mt. Holyoke, the thunderstorm passes off the mountain after nourishing the land below. The sun again shines on the Oxbow's fertile fields, predicting a promising future for the nation. For Cole, the Oxbow's existence implied

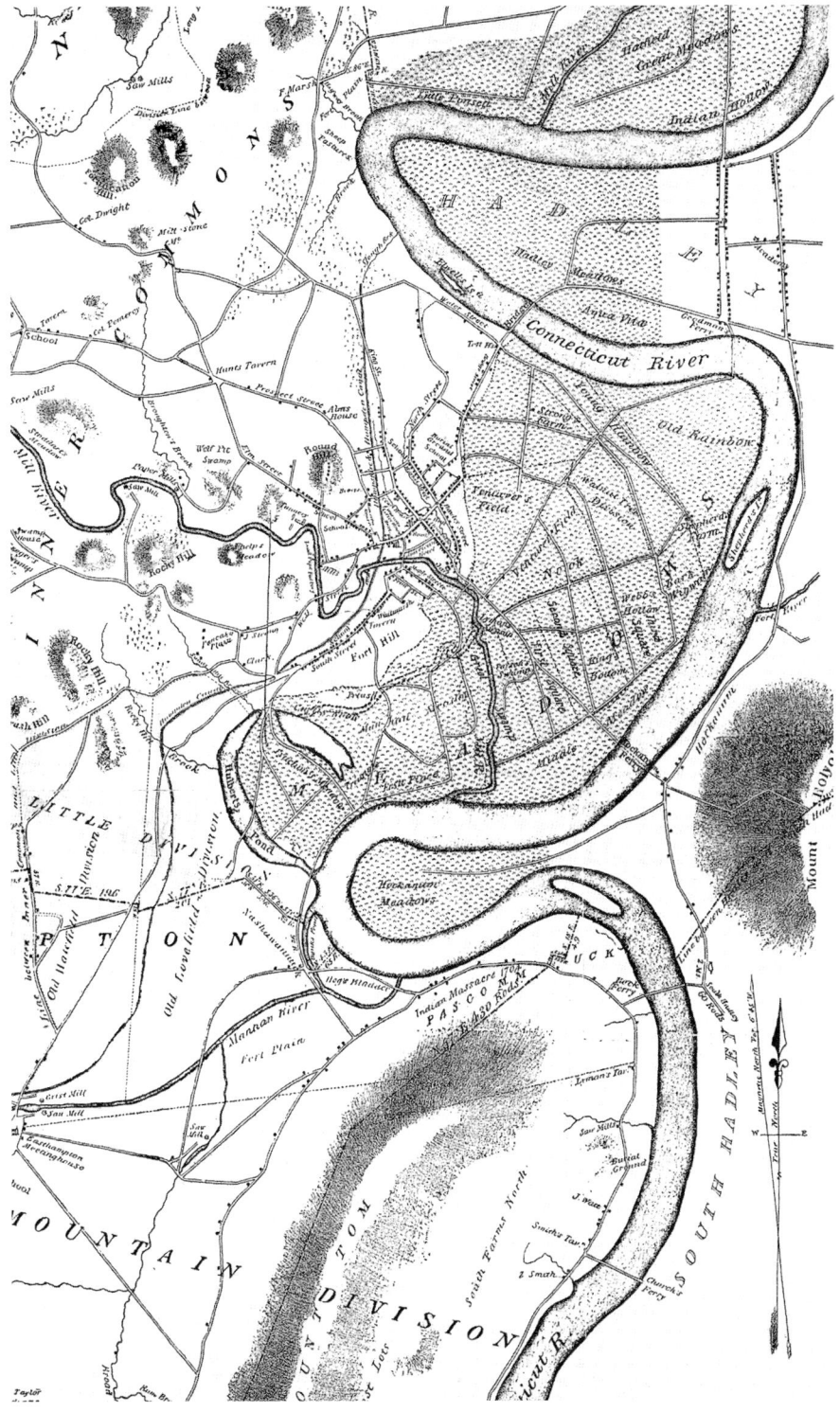

FIGURE 21. *Plan of the Town of Northampton*, detail, see figure 63

FIGURE 22. William Henry Bartlett, *View from Mount Holyoke,* ca. 1838, steel engraving. Collection of Jill A. Hodnicki

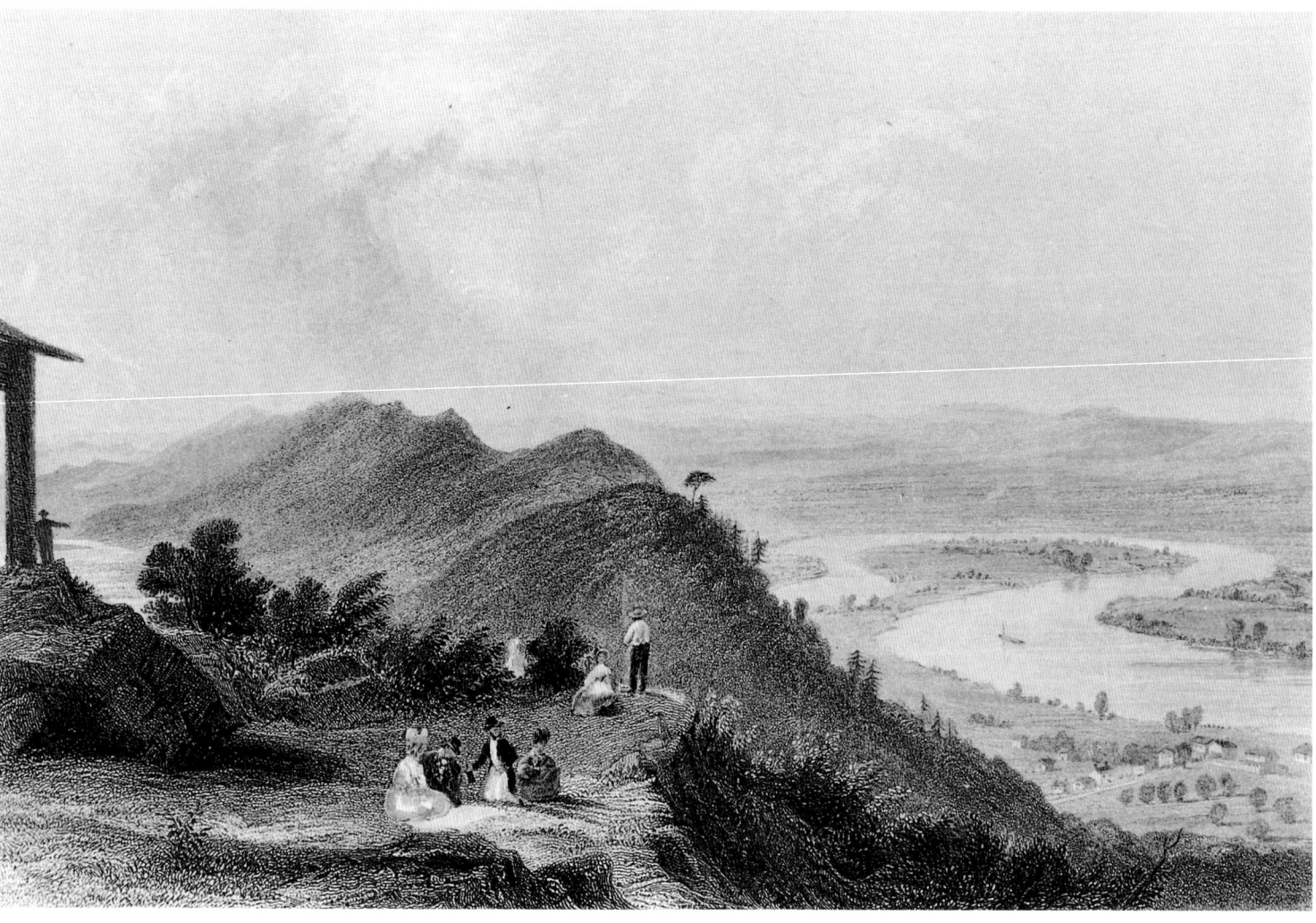

the hand — and the blessing — of God, but it also contained a warning. Cole surely knew that the Connecticut River meandered through a prehistoric lakebed, forming and reforming loops and bends and oxbows over thousands of years, and that repeated flooding nourished the rich soil he immortalized. He must also have realized that the natural process that created the Oxbow also predicted its eventual destruction. Four years after Cole painted it, in fact, the Oxbow loop dramatically changed. After a particularly high flood, in March of 1840, the river cut through the narrow

neck of land and the Oxbow's shape became a completed circle (see figure 2).[10]

While Cole may have conferred special status on the view from Mt. Holyoke, most later nineteenth-century artists who depicted the Oxbow based their images on neither Cole's monumental canvas nor the actual site. Instead they used a small black and white print by English topographical artist William Henry Bartlett. Just months after Cole completed his painting, Bartlett arrived in America to tour the northeast for a London publisher. In covering western Massachusetts,

Bartlett selected four views to illustrate: two from the top of Mt. Holyoke — one southward and one northward (figs. 22 and 23), one from the river looking up at Mt. Tom, and one of downtown Northampton. Bartlett's drawings, over one hundred in all, were engraved and issued first in portfolio form beginning in 1837, and then as a group in 1840 in the book *American Scenery.*[11]

It would be hard to overestimate the importance of this landmark publication. *American Scenery* provided the most widely accessible images of views from Mt. Holyoke. Cole's painting

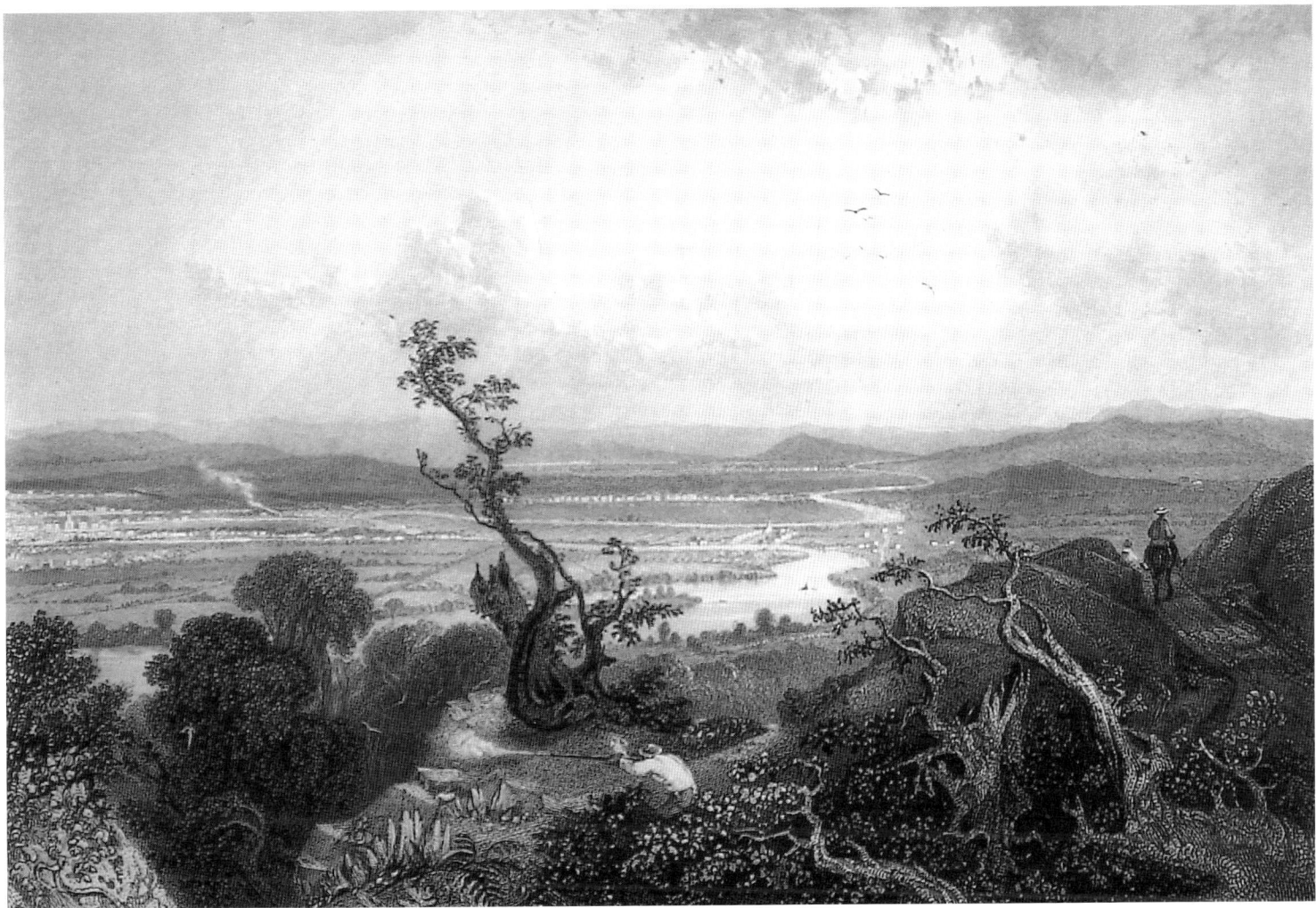

FIGURE 23. William Henry Bartlett, *Valley of the Connecticut (from Mount Holyoke)*, ca. 1838, steel engraving. Collection of Jill A. Hodnicki

of the Oxbow was shown at the annual exhibition of the National Academy of Design in the spring of 1836, when New Yorker Charles Talbot bought it for $500. It was exhibited in New York City only three more times in the nineteenth century: in 1838 at the Stuyvesant Institute; in 1848, just after Cole's death, at the American Art Union; and in 1862 at the Artists' Fund Society.[12] Unlike some of Cole's historical and religious subjects, it was never reproduced as an engraving. By contrast, Bartlett's prints were republished numerous times, lending them an unprecedented authority

and providing a ready model for the many trained and untrained artists who produced images of both the Oxbow and Hadley during the nineteenth century. As a result of *American Scenery*, the Hadley view became almost as important as the one of the Oxbow.

Highly competent but impersonal, Bartlett's depiction of the Oxbow, *View from Mount Holyoke* (figure 22), stresses the scene's civilizing aspects: a calm day; partially cleared and unobtrusive vegetation in the foreground; and, to tame the wilderness even further, a corner of the mountain house

with a party of picnickers. He included a section of the near shoreline, complete with small buildings, but his angle of vision excludes some of the distant farmland so prominent in Cole's painting. Bartlett neither stressed the geometry of the Oxbow's shape and nor tilted its plane forward.

Numerous later paintings, such as *The Oxbow of the Connecticut River* by an anonymous American artist (figure 24), show their debt to Bartlett in retaining his composition, picnickers, and landscape details. Because his engravings were so straightforward and descriptive, they allowed

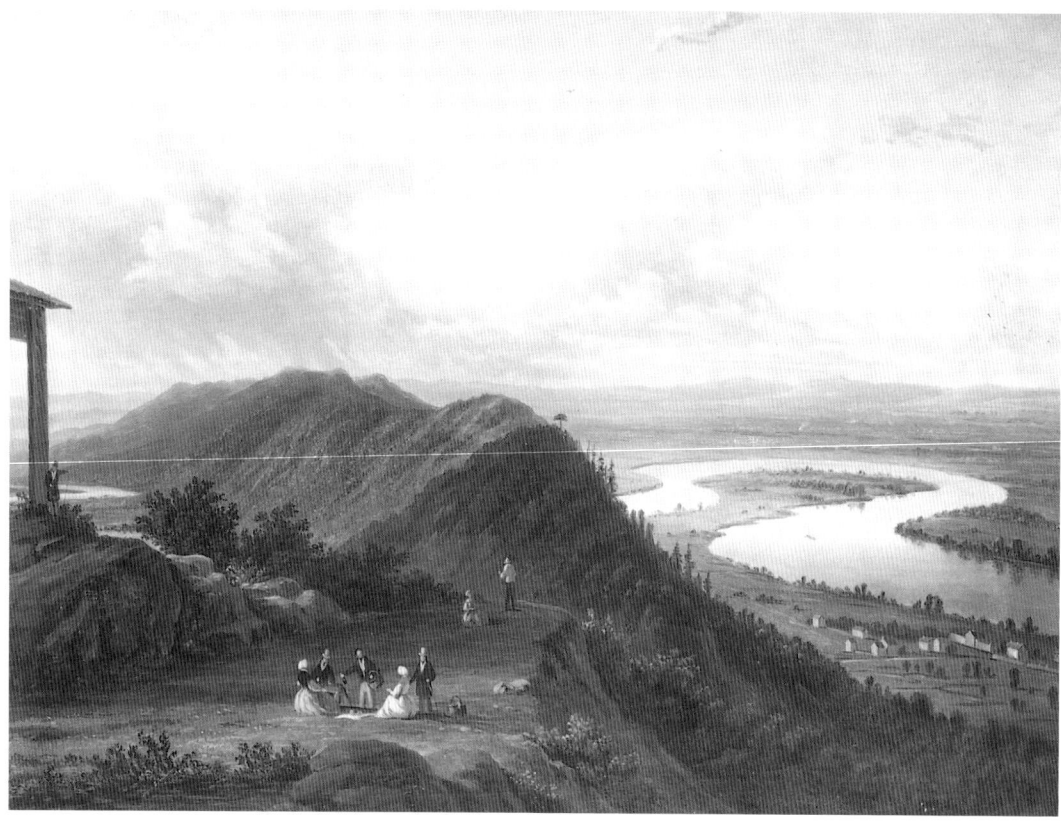

copyists room for invention. A view of the Oxbow by folk artist Thomas Chambers (figure 26), for example, exaggerates peaks and curves but essentially follows the lines of his model.[13] French artist Victor de Grailly made the most extensive use of Bartlett as a source. De Grailly operated something of a workshop in Paris producing views from many of Bartlett's engravings, presumably for export to an American public.[14] *The Oxbow of the Connecticut from Mount Holyoke* (figure 25) shows how closely de Grailly followed Bartlett's model. He painted many similar versions of this subject, always stressing its benign, pastoral quality.

Valley of the Connecticut (figure 23), Bartlett's second view, north towards Hadley, contrasts untamed nature on the mountain with tidy development along the winding river beyond. In the foreground he included rocky outcroppings, writhing tree trunks, and a hunter firing a gun. The vast distance contains a sprinkling of orderly towns. The two main streets of Hadley distinctively parallel each other — as they do today — from one bend in the river to the next.

FIGURE 24. Anonymous, *The Oxbow of the Connecticut River*, ca. 1850, oil on canvas. Mead Art Museum, Amherst College, Amherst, Massachusetts, Gift of Professor Charles H. Morgan

FIGURE 25. Victor de Grailly, *The Oxbow of the Connecticut from Mount Holyoke*, ca. 1840–45, oil on canvas. Smith College Museum of Art, Northampton, Massachusetts, Purchased 1975 (not in exhibition)

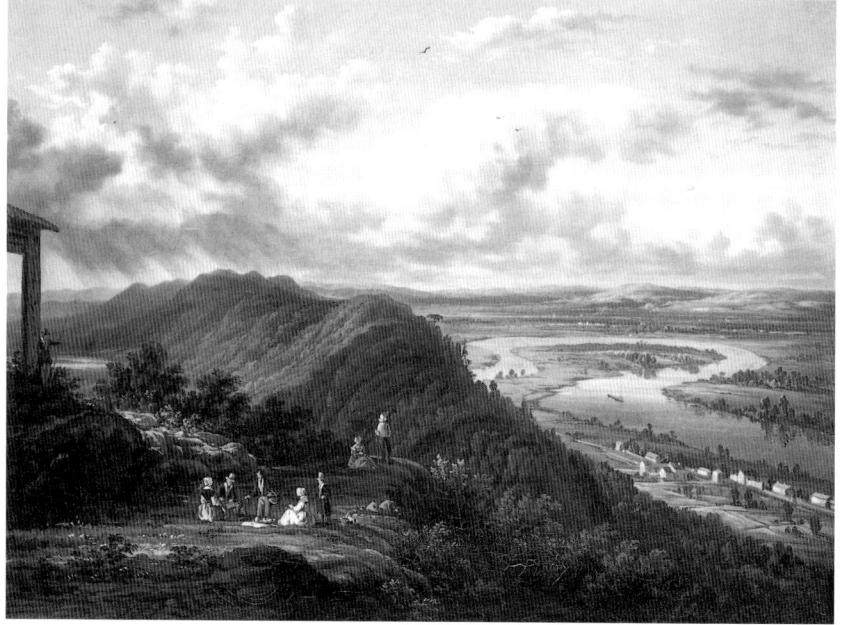

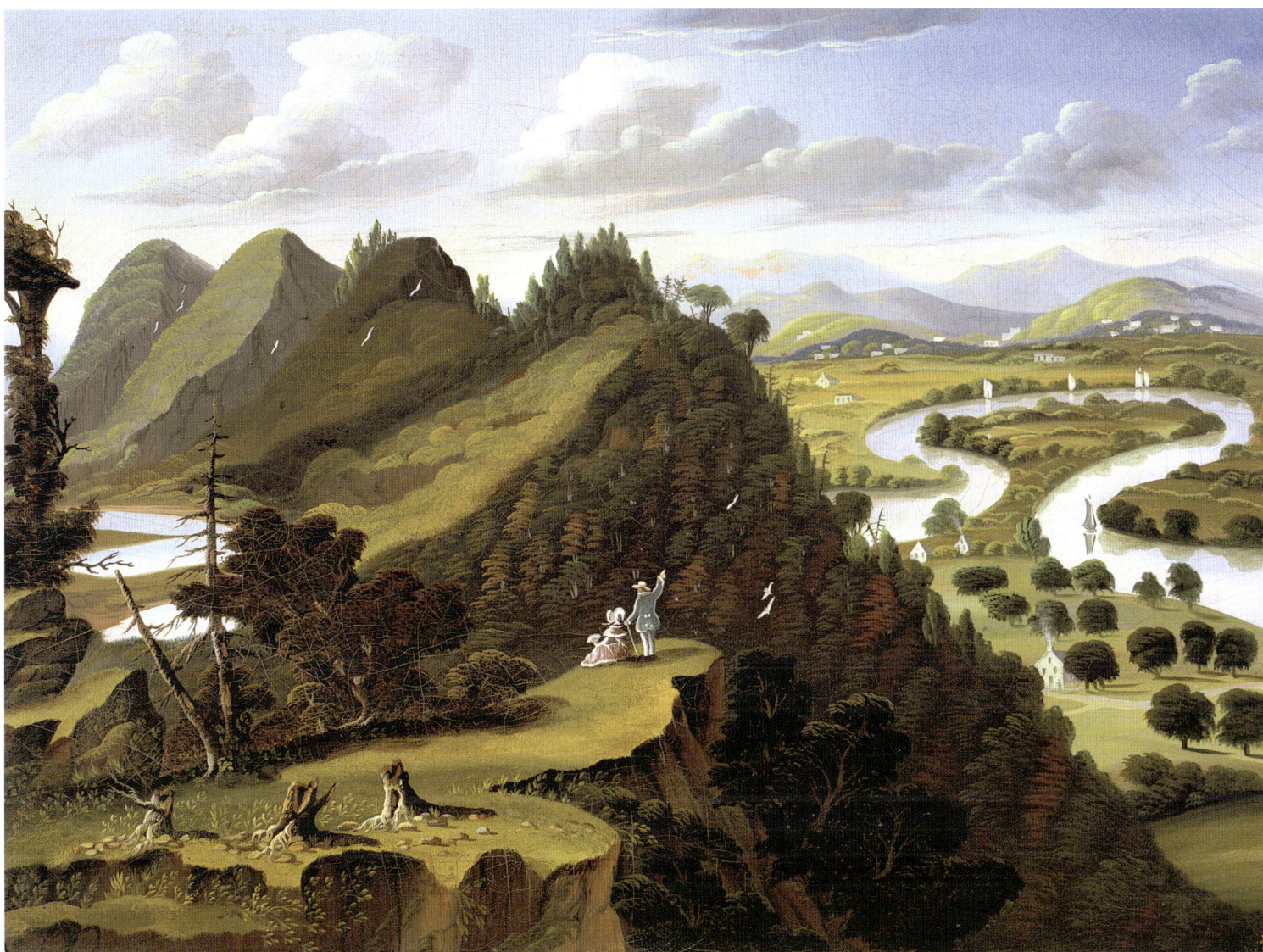

FIGURE 26. Thomas Chambers, *View from Mount Holyoke*, ca. 1845, oil on canvas. Fruitlands Museums, Harvard, Massachusetts

This Hadley view appealed to copyists for its promise of prosperous civilization. Victor de Grailly's *The Valley of the Connecticut from Mount Holyoke* (figure 27), which also exists in multiple versions, reveals some changes to the foreground of Bartlett's engraving, but retains its composition and details. De Grailly restrained the foreground foliage to a greater degree, moving Bartlett's partially blasted tree from center to side and adding a party of well-dressed sightseers. Other artists also emphasized the valley's domesticated features and calmed the unruly nature of Bartlett's mountaintop. Edmund Coates, for example, in his spectacular *The Connecticut River from Mount Holyoke*, dated 1855 (figure 28), greatly expanded the concept of peace and prosperity by dotting the landscape with many signs of settlement. He also suffused the whole with glowing color and light emanating from a sun setting in the north. Coates usually painted from print sources, and he produced at least three additional versions of this scene.[15] In the hands of copyists who had had less academic training than either de Grailly or Coates, the town of Hadley received most emphasis, its parallel streets sometimes resembling airport runways in the middle distance.[16]

Prominent artists of the Hudson River School

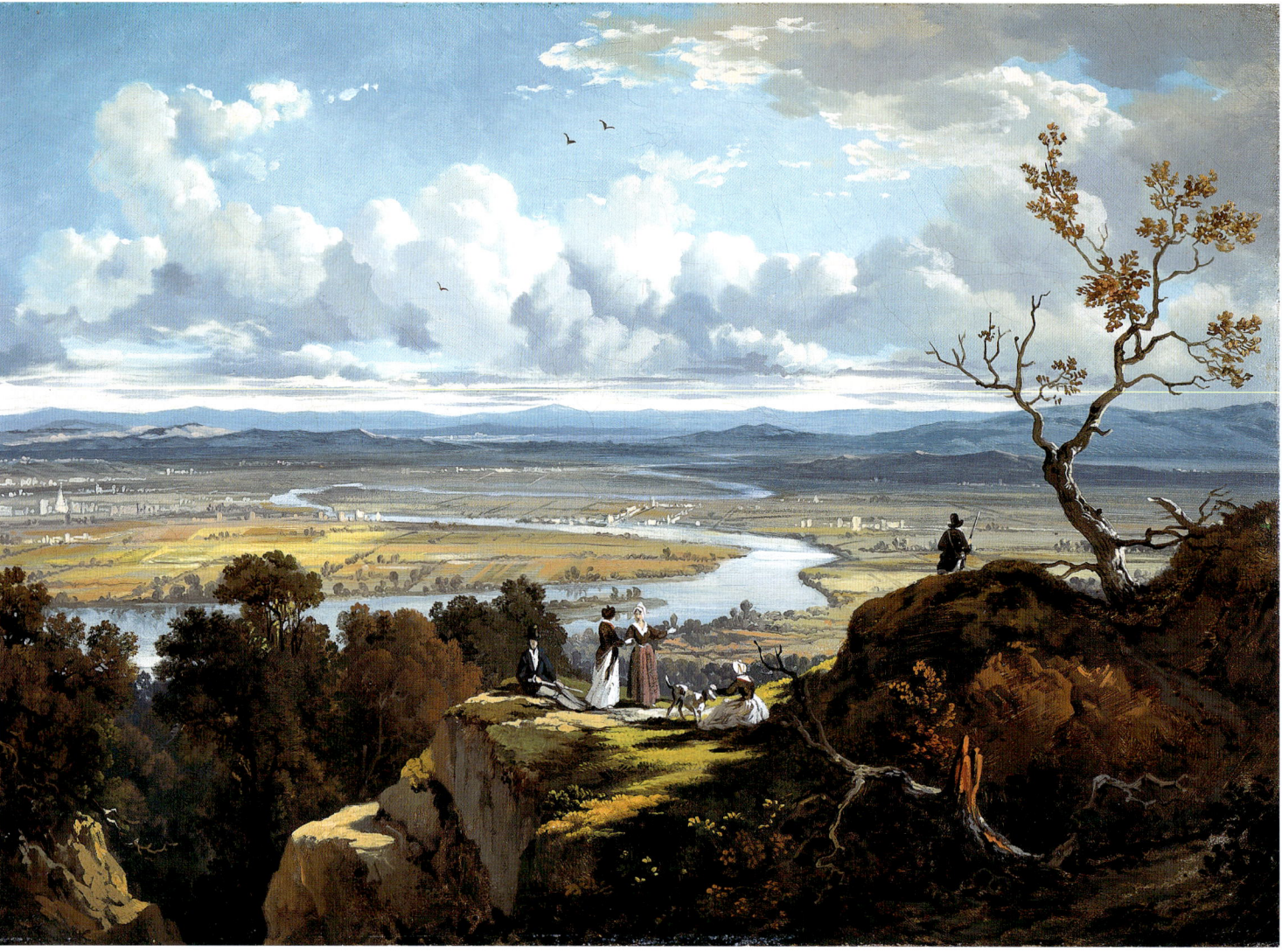

seem not to have painted the view from Mt. Holyoke, most likely because Cole had established such a definitive one or perhaps because the new shape of the Oxbow did not appeal to them. Perhaps also they sought more dramatic wilderness landscapes further north. Jasper Cropsey and Sanford Gifford visited the Summit House in 1853. A drawing by Cropsey of the Oxbow and another of farms along the river directly below the mountain house (both in the collection of the Newington-Cropsey Foundation) attest to his general interest, but no finished paintings of either view have been located.[17] T. Addison Richards, a lesser landscapist who wrote and illustrated an account of his travels along the Connecticut, referred deferentially to Cole's example in his 1856 article for *Harper's Monthly*: "The painter Cole has left us a bold chronicle of the wayward humors of the waters here. A hint at their odd caprices will be found in our own budget of pencilings."[18] Two of Richards's pencilings that indicate the Oxbow's altered formation were reproduced in the magazine, including one that also shows the mountain house (figure 29).

Documentation exists of a forty-foot, moving panorama of the Connecticut River painted by New York artist Nicolino Calyo about 1849, although nothing of it survives. Shown in Boston at Boylston Hall in the spring of 1850, the panorama included a view from the top of Mt. Holyoke

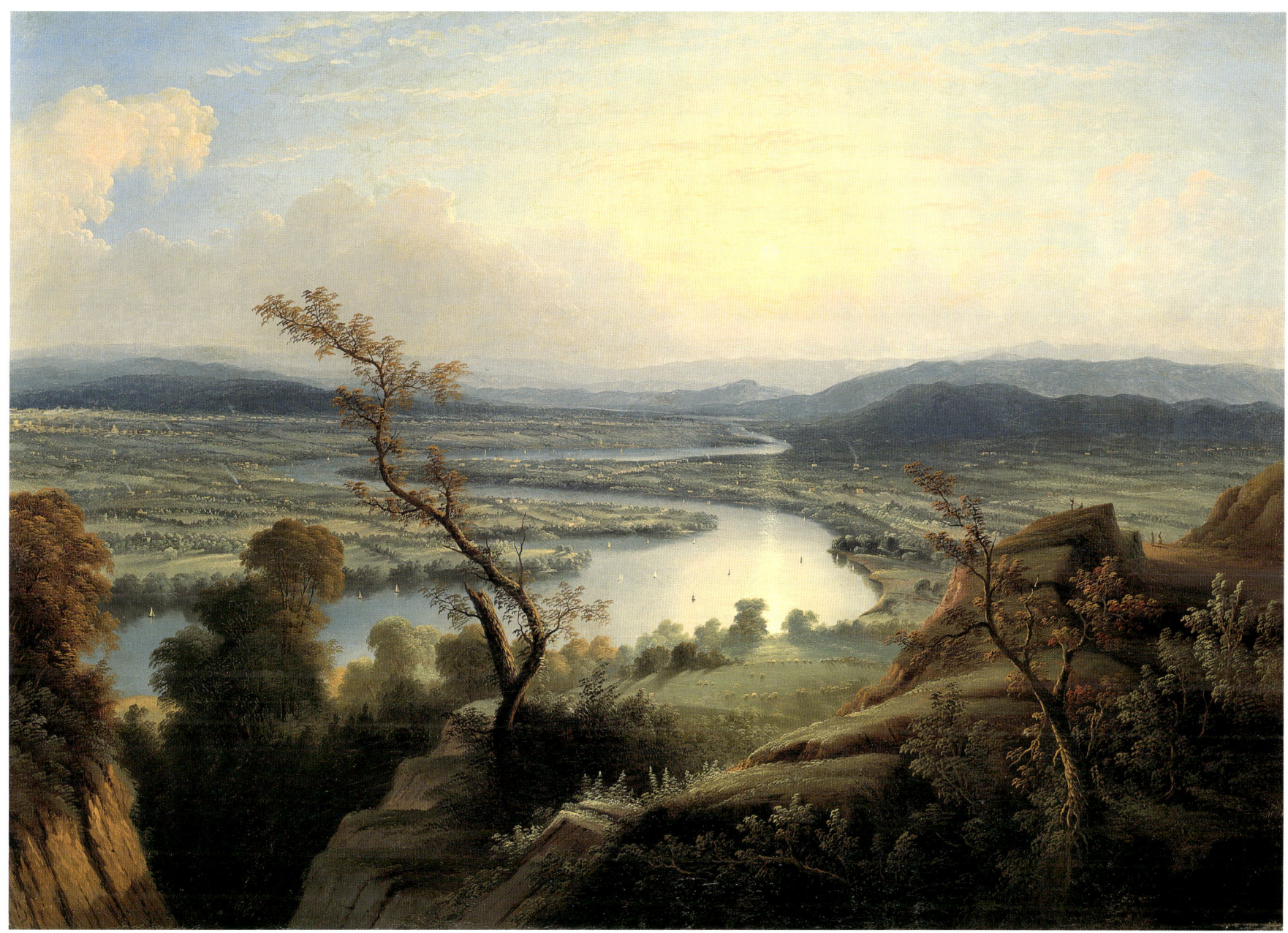

FIGURE 28. Edmund Coates, *The Connecticut River from Mount Holyoke*, 1855, oil on canvas. Mead Art Museum, Amherst College, Amherst, Massachusetts, Purchase

which was described in advertisements as "a splendid spectacle, embracing a wide area of lovely landscape," and as "the richest landscape probably in the world."[19] The spectacle most likely embraced both northern and southern views. Lost also is Robert Havell's painting *Valley of the Connecticut from Mount Holyoke*, from about 1847, which the artist presumably executed from nature since he is known to have traveled in the area.[20] Painting of panoramic views from Mt. Holyoke reached its peak in the mid-1800s; later in the century such expansive, detailed views had fallen out of fashion.

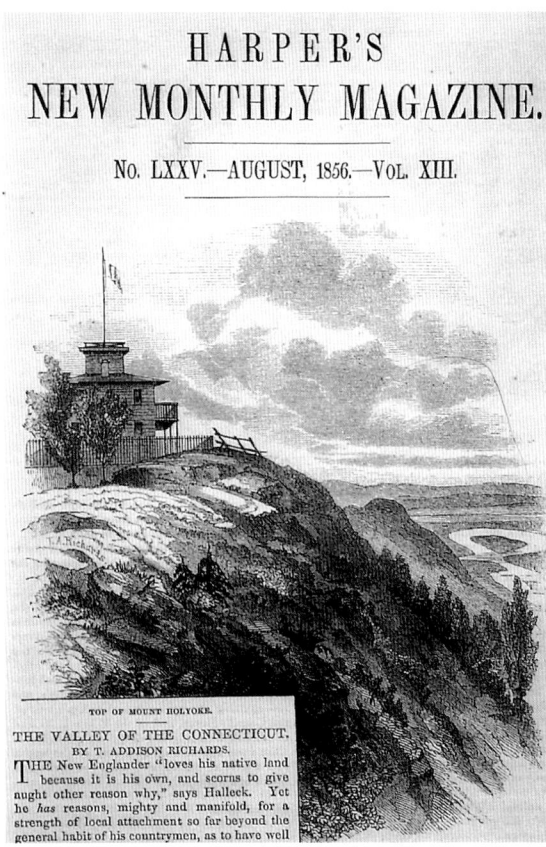

FIGURE 29. T. Addison Richards, *Top of Mount Holyoke*, wood engraving, reproduced in *Harper's New Monthly Magazine*, August 1856

Contemporary Artists and the Oxbow

It remained for the later twentieth century to rediscover Thomas Cole's vision of the Oxbow and accord it icon status. This odyssey began in 1908 when the painting passed from private ownership into the collection of the Metropolitan Museum of Art. Until about 1950, nineteenth-century American art attracted little notice, but after that, scholars, collectors, and the general public took a growing interest in American landscape painting and in Thomas Cole's career. *The Oxbow* was reproduced with increasing frequency; its steady rise in esteem can be charted in the many books on American art published since 1950, and especially in the last thirty years.[21] In some surveys, it is the only example of Cole's pure landscape work.[22] It has been reproduced in diverse ways that reach a mass audience: on postcards, in high school history texts, and as slides used in teaching art history across the country. Scholars have called it "the artist's most celebrated work," "one of the outstanding works in the American landscape tradition," and "the greatest landscape painting of the era."[23] Cole's painting has remained prominent partly because its ambiguities encourage varied interpretations. It has been regarded as epitomizing the message of harmony, as well as political dominance, central to nineteenth-century American landscape painting; as extolling the virtues of American over European scenery; as warning against the destruction of nature; and, conversely, as advocating the advance of civilization.[24]

Landscape painters today desire to recapture the spirit of Cole's arcadian, pre-industrial world. They pay homage to his painting in order to show that they belong to a tradition and that they embrace continuity with the past. By referring to Cole they establish another level of meaning for their own work. These artists also find particular inspiration in the formal underpinning of Cole's composition — the graphic impact of his reduction to diagonal line and circle — and in the boldness of his spatial organization. Reinterpretation necessarily involves change. Changes in features such as sky and vantage point — the elimination of Cole's storm or the shift to a higher horizon line — alter the meanings of today's works. Comparisons of contemporary depictions of the Oxbow to Cole's authoritative version point out not only the continuities, but also the new concerns specific to modern times.

Renewed interest in Cole's painting began with realist artist Alfred Leslie. While teaching at Amherst College in 1972, he painted *View of the Connecticut River as Seen from Mount Holyoke* (figure 30), his rejoinder to Cole's idealized vision. Considerably larger than Cole's work, it formed the first in a projected series devoted to major landscape sites made popular by artists of the nineteenth century. Seeking to "refresh" views that had become "discredited," Leslie planned to show these sites in the present.[25] For practical reasons he focused on destinations in the northeast.

Although Leslie was clearly aware of Hudson River School landscape painting, he worked "from nature, not art history." For his initial drawing, *View from Mt. Holyoke of the Oxbow Oct 17–71* (see exhibition checklist), he hiked along a trail south of the Summit House and sat at the very edge of the ridge. He recalled finding the Oxbow difficult to decipher because trees had grown to obstruct the view. Guided by this and later drawings (he did not work from photographs), he developed the painting in his Amherst studio. Leslie regards his paintings not as documents of reality but as "collages" of real and fabricated elements. He modeled the distant trees, for instance, on those he could see from his studio window, combining early and late fall seasons in their foliage. He also brought materials into the studio, such as the leaves and tree in the foreground. Leslie purposely allowed these foreground elements to retain the look of studio props, in order to invest the painting with two levels of meaning: the reality of nature and the reality of artistic creation. In this fashion he

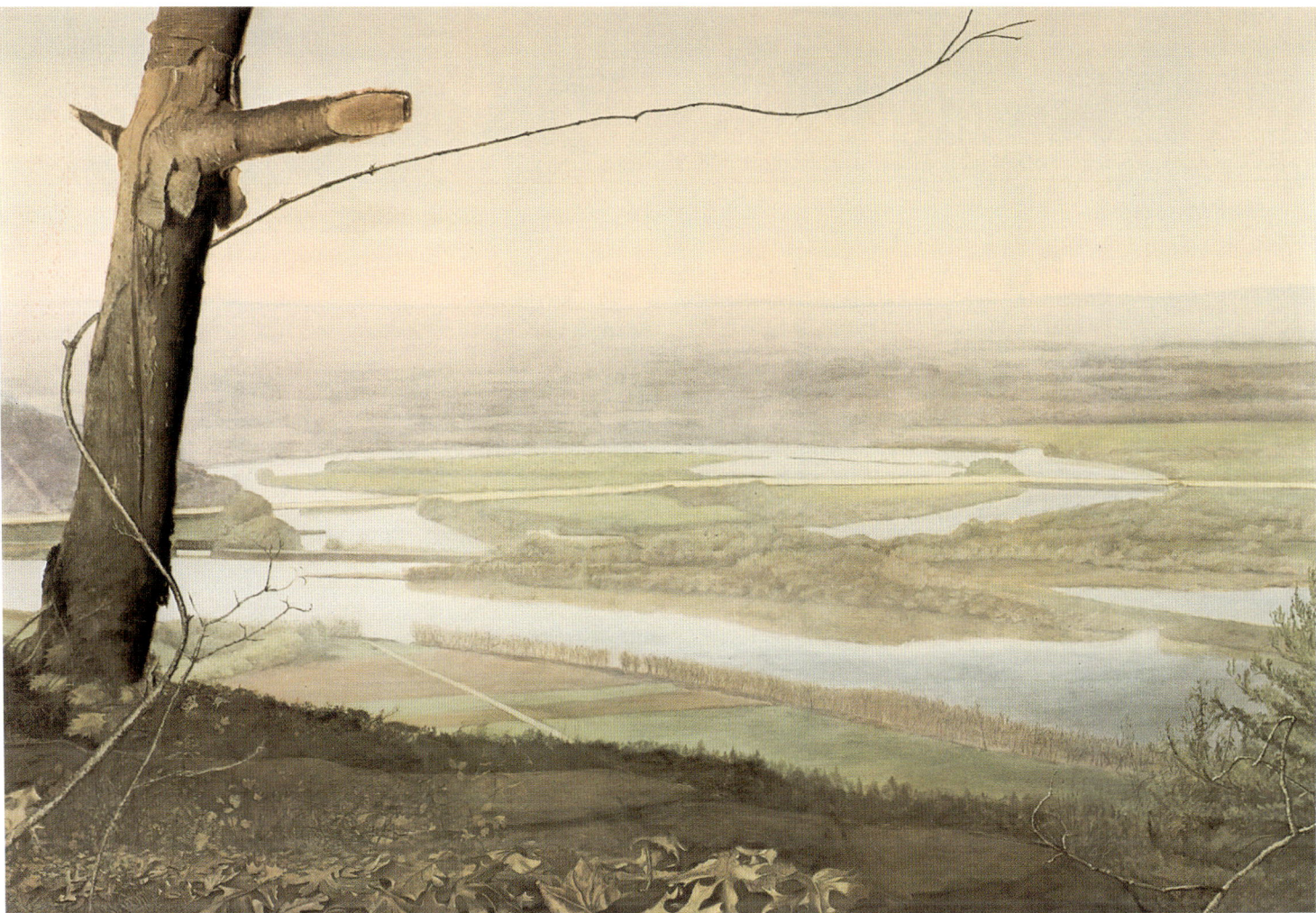

FIGURE 30. Alfred Leslie, *View of the Connecticut River as Seen from Mount Holyoke*, 1972, oil on canvas. Museum Moderner Kunst, Stiftung Ludwig, Vienna (not in exhibition)

put himself in the painting, as Cole had put the figure of an artist in his picture.

While the composition has direct links to Cole's, Leslie also introduced some important features that give his work a new meaning. He converted Cole's hillside to a nearly level stage and limited the distant view with atmospheric haze. As a result the Oxbow forms a horizontal zone between dark and light bands. The nearly dead tree in the left foreground of the Cole finds its counterpart in Leslie's sharply rendered, bare trunk in the same position. Leslie's tree, however,

has had its branches cut, rather than ravaged by nature, and the branch or vine twisted around it resembles barbed wire. In Leslie's revisionist interpretation, the balance of man and nature has shifted. Where nature had the upper hand in Cole's painting, man has aggressively intruded in Leslie's view, which shows twentieth-century modifications to the Oxbow itself: a major highway now crosses it and a large bite of land is missing from its center.

The Oxbow underwent significant changes even in the nineteenth century. After the

Connecticut River broke through its neck in 1840, the natural process of erosion and deposition began to fill in the Oxbow's north entrance. By the next year, enough soil had built up to make it possible to pass "from Middle Meadow, to the island formed by the new cut of the river, *on dry land*," according to the *Hampshire Gazette*.[26] Additional filling of the north and south arms of the Oxbow must have occurred when the railroad was built over it in 1845 (see map, figure 31). The railroad further necessitated rerouting the Mill River to run parallel to the rail tracks and empty

FIGURE 31. L.E. Neuman, *Northampton and Easthampton.* Detail of engraving from *County Atlas of Hampshire, Massachusetts, from Actual Surveys by and under the Direction of F.W. Beers*, New York, F.W. Beers and Co., 1873. Historic Northampton, Northampton (not in exhibition)

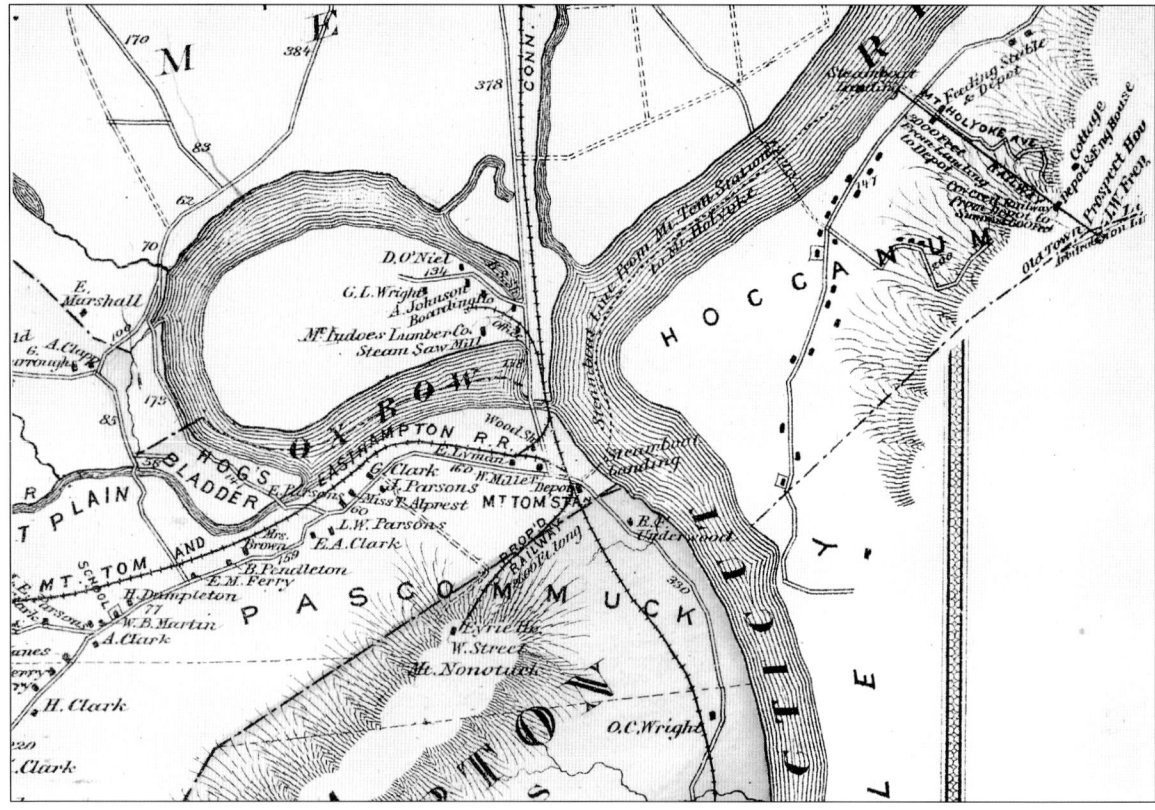

into the Connecticut directly. When seen from Mt. Holyoke today, the entire area at the former mouth of the Oxbow appears as a muddled, indeterminate shape covered with foliage. The most visually striking addition to the scene came in the mid-1960s, when Interstate 91 bisected the center of the Oxbow. The "Save the Oxbow" campaign in 1964 protested unsuccessfully the closing of access to the river from a northern section of the Oxbow. Two small bridges visible in Leslie's painting — over the Oxbow's south arm for the railroad and for Route 91 — allow water and boats to pass to the Connecticut River. As another consequence of building the interstate highway, a large area of topsoil between the river and the Oxbow was removed for fill, creating a rectangular pond that appears at the lower right in Leslie's painting. Also visible is the circular pond in the center of the Oxbow resulting from the removal of additional fill land for the highway.

In depicting the new prospect, Leslie focused on Interstate 91. It was the highway that originally impelled him to choose this site. "When I found out that they had built 91, I knew I wanted to paint it," he recalled. To emphasize the highway's path, he reduced the Oxbow to its essential form and the road to a light stripe that cuts across the middle of the canvas, its line echoed by the river's banks. To reinforce the contrast between man and nature, he established a visual link between the straight line of the highway and the twisted line of the foreground branch. Despite the bleakness resulting from such spare forms and stark foreground, his distant landscape still holds beauty. He continued the tradition of showing rich farm-land by including the near shore of the river with its cultivated fields. He achieved a peaceful mood through the simplification of landscape features, absence of buildings, gently sloping foreground, and repeated horizontal lines. Because he more accurately plotted the perspective, the Oxbow assumes a flattened, horizontal shape. In place of Cole's dynamic diagonal lines and sense of energy, Leslie emphasized restraint. He eliminated Cole's storm clouds and thus much of the drama of Cole's work.

Leslie replaced Cole's religiosity with an elegiac mood. He also avoided the nationalist sentiment of his predecessor's painting. Where Cole envisioned future agricultural abundance and plentiful natural resources — both implied by the Oxbow's configuration — Leslie rejected any implication of manifest destiny. His realism in-volves a symbolic level, however: his foreground tree, standing straight like a sentinel, surveys the changed scene below. Leslie shows instead that modern civilization has compromised the unique historical, geological, and aesthetic significance the view once held.

At the opposite pole from Leslie's realist view of the Oxbow is Stephen Hannock's idealist painting of the same vista. More than any other contemporary artist, Hannock has made the Oxbow a central, defining subject of his work. His paintings of this theme summarize the influence on his art of nineteenth-century American landscape painting traditions, the roots of his deep attachment to landscape, and his overriding preoccupation with light. To date Hannock has produced seven views of the Oxbow as seen from Mt. Holyoke and is currently completing two more. The first of these,

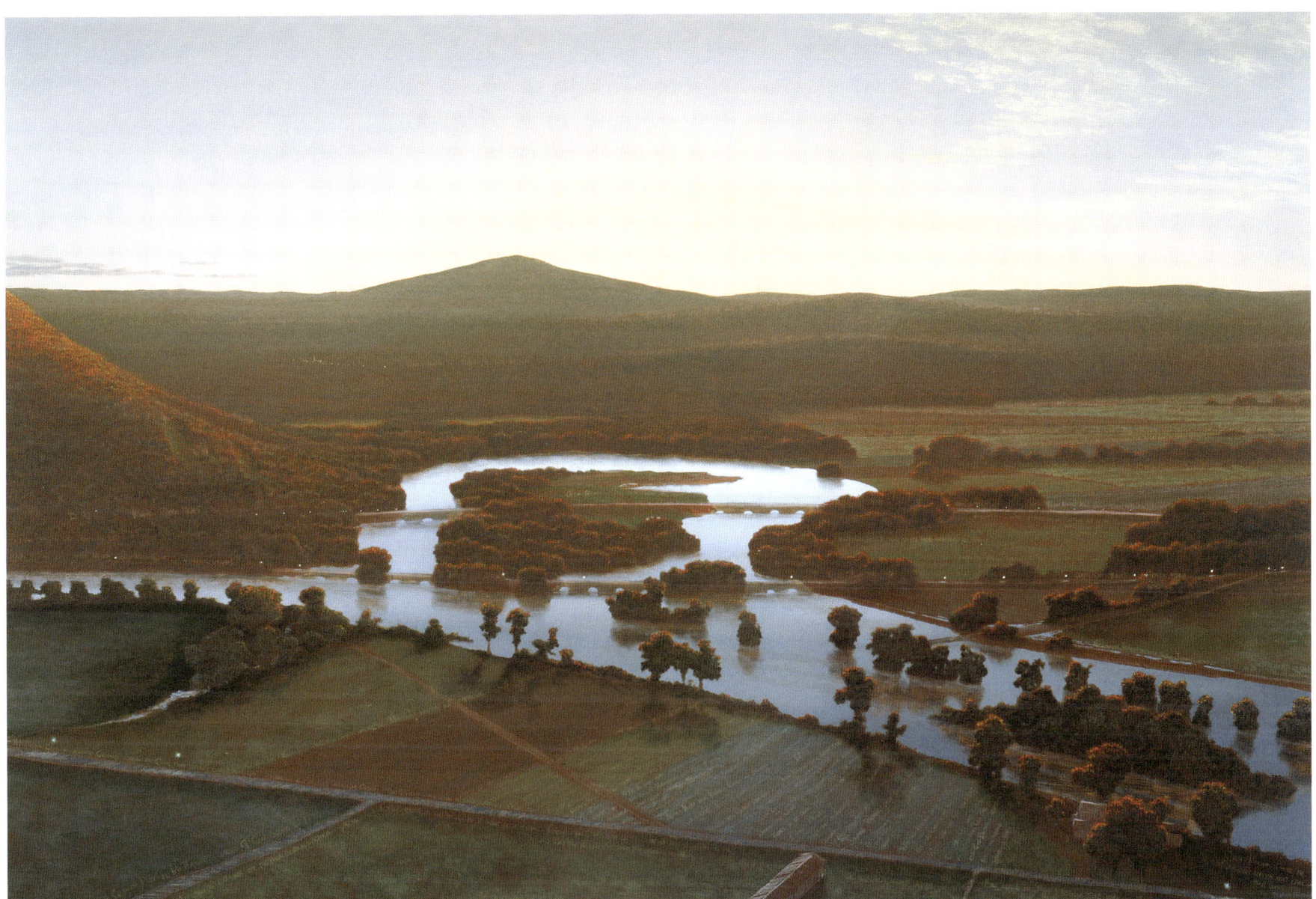

FIGURE 32. Stephen Hannock, *The Oxbow, After Church, After Cole, Flooded, 1979–1994 (Flooded River for the Matriarchs, E. and A. Mongan)*, 1994, polished oil on canvas. Smith College Museum of Art, Northampton, Massachusetts, Gift of Irene Mennen Hunter (class of 1939), 1995

The Oxbow, After Church, After Cole, Flooded, 1979– 1994 (Flooded River for the Matriarchs, E. and A. Mongan), was painted in 1994 (figure 32) and is in the collection of the Smith College Museum of Art.[27] His title announces his knowledge of Cole's precedent, as well as a general allegiance to the Hudson River School. It also refers to the years Hannock lived in Northampton, from 1971 to 1986, where he studied art with Leonard Baskin and met sisters Elizabeth and Agnes Mongan, prominent art curators who became mentors for his career. Hannock's interest in depicting the Oxbow began in 1979 and culminated with this painting in 1994.

Accepting the challenge of Cole's work, Hannock said he tackled the subject of the Oxbow "because I thought I could paint a better painting."[28] Influenced by Cole's example, he nevertheless departed from it in ways that change the overall feeling of the work. He made his painting a few inches larger than Cole's in order to underscore his own act of reformulation. He eliminated

Cole's foreground mountain and plunged the viewer over the precipice immediately, establishing a bird's-eye vantage point that let him tip up the Oxbow as Cole had. He raised the horizon line significantly, increasing the importance of the land even more, and he exaggerated the scale of Cole's mountain. Above all, he replaced Cole's dramatic thunderstorm with calm skies and Cole's sunshine with early evening light.

Light is Hannock's primary subject. "I'm obsessed with light," he admits, "I'm obsessed with everything light does. With how powerful it is and yet how fragile, how intense and yet how fleeting. One minute it's overwhelming, unbelievable, and the next minute, gone. The work is about what the paint can do to create the illusion of luminosity."[29] Hannock's obsession led him to also appreciate the art of Cole's pupil, Frederic Church,[30] who depicted the effect of light as it radiated to all corners of a scene, touching the edges of forms and bathing the landscape with glowing color.

Hannock's first painting of the Oxbow shines with the soft light of dusk, which accentuates the golden reddish cast of ground and trees. The river takes on a special luminescence. Hannock always paints the river at flood stage because it provides him a greater surface for reflected light. Flooding changes the river's shape as well, allowing Hannock to suggest the Oxbow formation but establish new patterns against the dark form of the land. Although flooding occurs annually in the spring, Hannock varies both season and time of day, and thus light and color, in his different approaches to the composition. For example, in the Museum of Fine Arts, Boston's *The Oxbow: After Church, After Cole, Flooded (Flooded River for Fran)* from 1999, he portrayed the river at sunset, lit by a flaming orange sky, and in *Evening Oxbow: Flooded (for Rockwell Kent at the Smith College Museum)* from 1996 (private collection), he used cool light to illuminate a river at a higher flood stage. Hannock's floods, like Cole's thunderstorm, renew the land; they bring alluvial deposits to enrich the soil in an annual cycle.

Hannock admires the work of nineteenth-century Luminists like Martin Johnson Heade and Sanford Gifford. Their concern with light is an obvious tie, but more than that, their tendency to present the landscape as serene and still, usually composed in terms of strong horizontal forms, also finds expression in Hannock's Oxbow paintings. Hannock's mood is one of reverie induced by breathtaking beauty. Contributing to this sense of idyllic calm is the conspicuous absence of modern life. Except for an occasional house and small lights that animate the few roads, the landscape belongs to another century. The Oxbow has returned almost to its pre-railroad and highway shape, and those modern features have been turned into aqueducts. Rejecting what he calls the nineteenth century's "baggage about being true to nature," Hannock blends that century's romanticism with the twentieth century's concern for the formal elements of painting — color, value, shape,

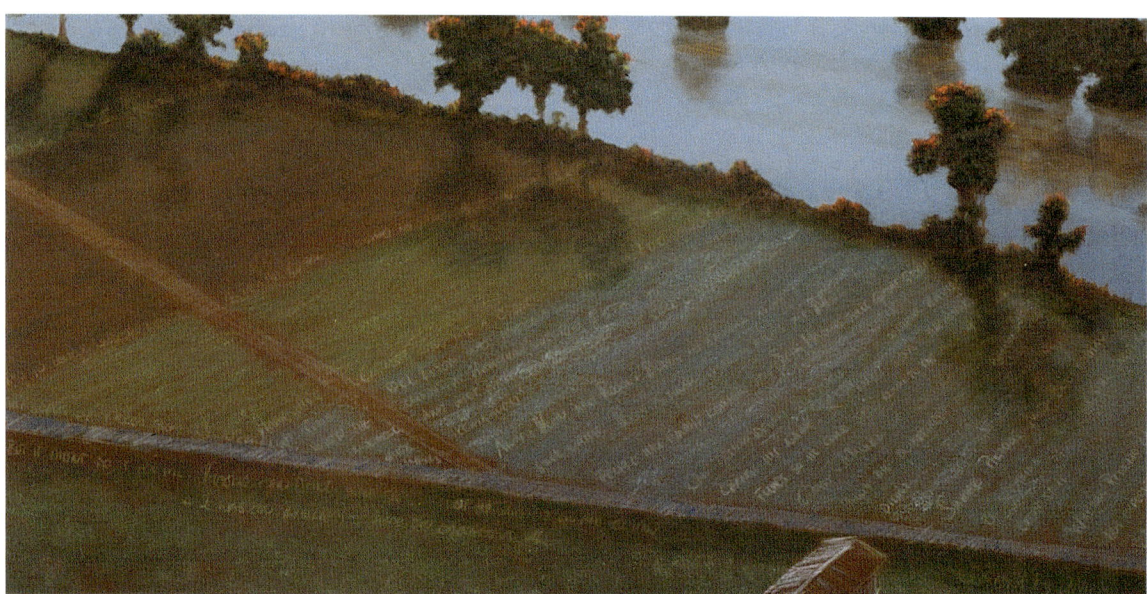

FIGURE 33. Stephen Hannock, *The Oxbow*, detail, see figure 32

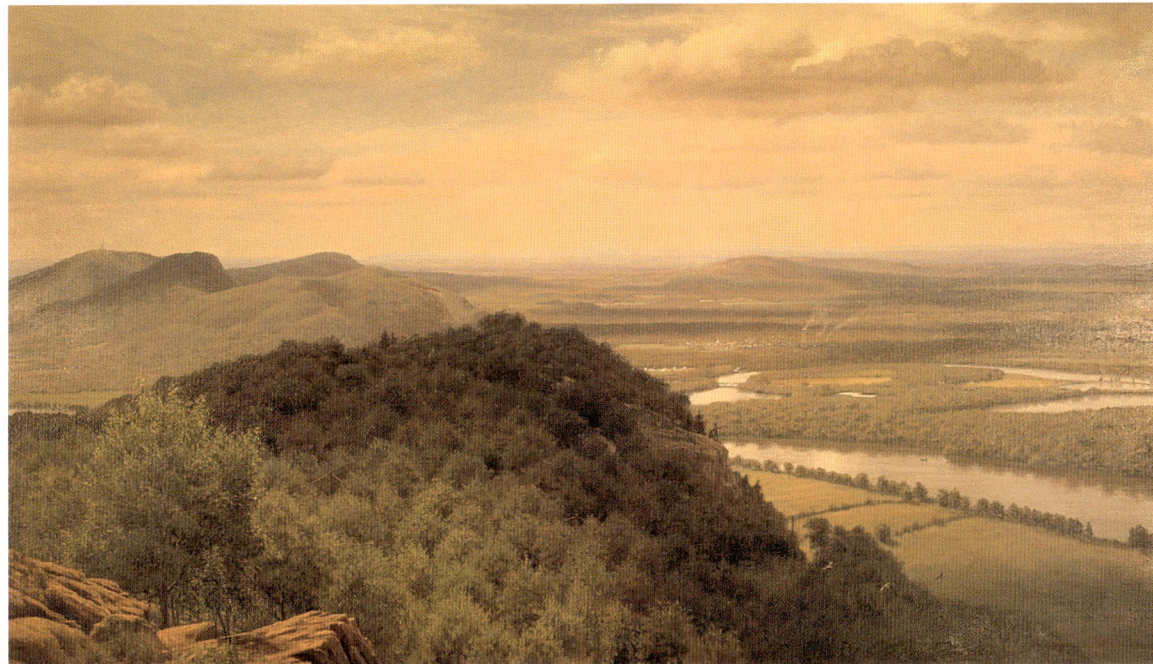

FIGURE 34. Joseph McGurl, *Homage to Thomas Cole (Oxbow of the Connecticut)*, 1992, oil on canvas. Property of Houghton Mifflin Company (not in exhibition)

It was quite stark and real . . . very flat light. It really didn't appeal to me when I first started studying the Oxbow at Smith. But I've grown to appreciate it for its total disregard for any sense of Romanticism. I'm really surprised that none of the other New England painters have sunk their teeth into the composition. Just the light is enough to rattle any painter's cage. Gregory, or Fran Gillespie, Scott Prior, Jane Lund, Randy Deihl, Greg Stone." Hannock's own position is unabashedly romantic.

Many other artists have painted the Oxbow with degrees of realism and romanticism that would locate them between the two poles of Leslie and Hannock. Cape Cod artist Joseph McGurl's *Homage to Thomas Cole (Oxbow of the Connecticut)*, dated 1992 (figure 34), is probably the most straightforward and accurate, although McGurl also suppressed evidence of modern changes to the Oxbow. No highway is cut into its center and a marina constructed in 1976 is not present; barely visible are a road at the far right and a bridge over the Oxbow's south arm. However, one telling detail from contemporary life has been invented by the artist: a power line crossing the mountain in the foreground. Two hikers view the scene from a rocky ledge, in the fashion of onlookers found frequently in nineteenth-century landscapes. McGurl followed Cole's composition in the general sense, including the mountain's slanted line and bands of light and dark on foliage reflecting clouds overhead. Like Cole and Bartlett before him, he portrayed the river as it emerged from behind the mountain to continue its course on towards Holyoke at the left edge of the canvas. Mt. Tom, identified by towers on its crown, lies in the distance. McGurl depicted a large area of shoreline below the mountain, however, and

and the picture's surface.[31] The many oil studies he made for the Smith College work, for instance, show his fascination with the abstract qualities of the river's unusual shape as he reduced it to an irregular omega pattern on different background colors.

Hannock adds a definite modern note to his paintings in the way they are executed. Using alternating layers of oil and resin, he polishes the oil down with a power sander between coats. He developed this highly personal technique to trap light; by creating a translucent surface, light is visible through the layers but the surface does not produce too much distracting glare. He does not try to remove the traces of the sander but incorporates its patterns and "accidents" into his work.[32] Unlike the tight brushwork of Luminism, his paint is remarkably broad and visible.

Hannock also includes an autobiographical dimension in his Oxbow paintings, writing whole sentences under and on the layers of paint (figure 33). His canvas serves as a diary, and in this way

he inserts himself in the painting as Cole did in his. On the Smith College painting, for example, Hannock identified his location: "My view is 100 yards off the hang-gliding launch" (on the ridge south of the Summit House). Other notations refer to his associations with the places, as in "Buz and I put in some serious time with the Frisbee," or "Gordo the wacko almost blew Jimmy's head off with an M-80." Sometimes he indicates directions, such as "this way to the Berkshires."

He typically comments on other artists. Aware of Alfred Leslie's painting of the Oxbow, Hannock inscribed on Smith's 1994 painting, "Alfred did a nice piece in the 70s, but it didn't do it for me." Hannock modified this assessment in 2000 with an observation written on his largest version of the subject (measuring 96 x 144 inches), *The Oxbow: After Church, After Cole, Flooded (Flooded River for the Matriarchs E. & A. Mongan), Green Light* (Metropolitan Museum of Art). Referring again to the Leslie painting, he noted, "Alfred did a huge piece in '73 . . . I think it was bigger than this painting.

positioned himself so that the curve of the Oxbow extends almost to the right edge of the canvas and the far side of the bend is not visible at all. Most striking is his new ratio of trees to open land on the Oxbow's center. In place of trees scattered over open fields shown in views by Cole and Bartlett, few fields and mostly forests characterize McGurl's landscape.

McGurl embraces the nineteenth-century aesthetic, also finding inspiration in Luminism. He calls his art "New American Luminism."[33] Applying the approach of the past to the present, he paints the "sublime" in the modern era through the quiet, reflective, selfless style of past Luminists. This means restoring verisimilitude as a goal and minimizing the traces of brushwork, although McGurl's soft edges and visibly brushed forms depart from the sharply focused clarity of his predecessors. As a New American Luminist he seeks out the sublime in totally and relatively unspoiled nature. McGurl also wants to restore the earlier Luminists' intimations of Divine presence in nature. "There is a spirituality in the landscape and a purity in being out in the field," he has said.[34] He paints small oil studies on the spot and then constructs his paintings in the studio, as Hudson River School painters, including Cole, typically did.

In his monumental *Kindred Spirits* of 1987 (figure 35), Richard Crozier acknowledged Cole in more unusual ways. First, his title refers to Asher Durand's famous work, *Kindred Spirits* (New York Public Library), painted in 1849 to memorialize Cole just after his death. It shows Cole and poet William Cullen Bryant standing on a rock ledge in the pristine wilderness communing with nature. Alluding to Durand's composition, Crozier depicted two people gazing out at the prospect from Mt. Holyoke. Second, taking Cole as a starting point Crozier focused not on the Oxbow, which is barely recognizable at the far right of his canvas, but on the concept of the panorama.

Crozier's painting is a triptych, made up of three canvases joined together to form an exceptionally long work, measuring 140 inches. In the central panel he depicted the two spectators on a rocky ledge in the foreground, Mt. Holyoke in the middle ground, and Mt. Tom further in the background. In the right wing Crozier represented the Oxbow, while in the left, the river meandering south along Mt. Tom to Holyoke. Unlike other artists who have painted the view, Crozier made the mountains his central focus, relegating the river to a subordinate role.

Crozier's interest in brushwork and color balances his interest in topography. His painting is foremost a landscape, with a variety of greens and brushstrokes, and secondarily a view of a specific place. "I was after the same grandeur and sublimity that Cole and Durand were looking for, adding my own sense of the importance of the ordinary in the scheme of things," he wrote.[35] The "ordinary" enters in his emphasis on the varied trees, with their loosely brushed foliage patterns, in the foreground, rather than on the vastness of the space beyond. Crozier composed *Kindred Spirits* in large blocks of texture and tone, capturing through his panoramic format and sheer size the feeling of being on top of the world without controlling it. His simplifications exclude reference to contemporary life below, except for the vague suggestion that those are cleared, farmed fields. When he created this work, Crozier was experimenting with introducing the figure without adding a narrative content, having been influenced by Bay Area figurative painters such as Elmer Bischoff and Richard Diebenkorn, as well as by Wayne Thiebaud, his teacher at the University of California at Davis.

Although Crozier normally paints and teaches in Virginia, for much of 1986 and 1987 he lived in South Hadley. "One of the striking features of the landscape in this area," he recalled, "is the Mount Holyoke Range, a series of abrupt and dramatic hills that rise up out of a more-or-less flat landscape. When I arrived in South Hadley, they immediately caught my attention as something I was

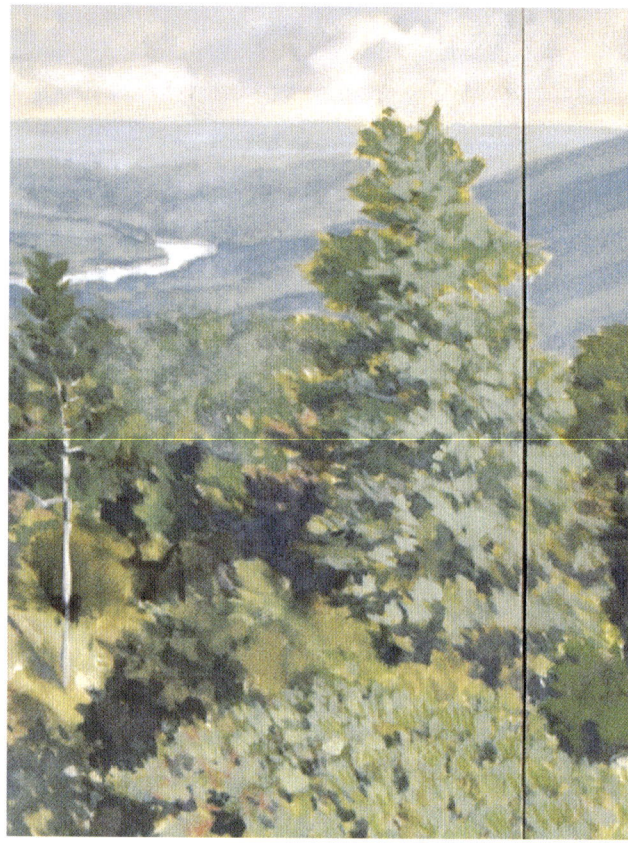

going to involve myself with."[36] Following his usual practice of beginning with small, on-the-spot oil studies, he sketched the scene on a cardboard composed of three smaller boards joined together.[37] He also made a number of studies of the mountain from below. Referring to a sketch of the mountain in winter from the flat fields of Hadley, he noted, "I was looking at a lot of lighting conditions in different seasons, and I did a number of paintings of this and other similar motifs."[38] Using his studies, but drawing also from memory, he composed the large work in his studio. Prior to painting *Kindred Spirits*, Crozier had seldom worked on such a large scale, but in the same year he was inspired to paint three more panoramic views: *Penobscot Bay Viewed from Mount Battie* and *St. George's River*, as well as what he

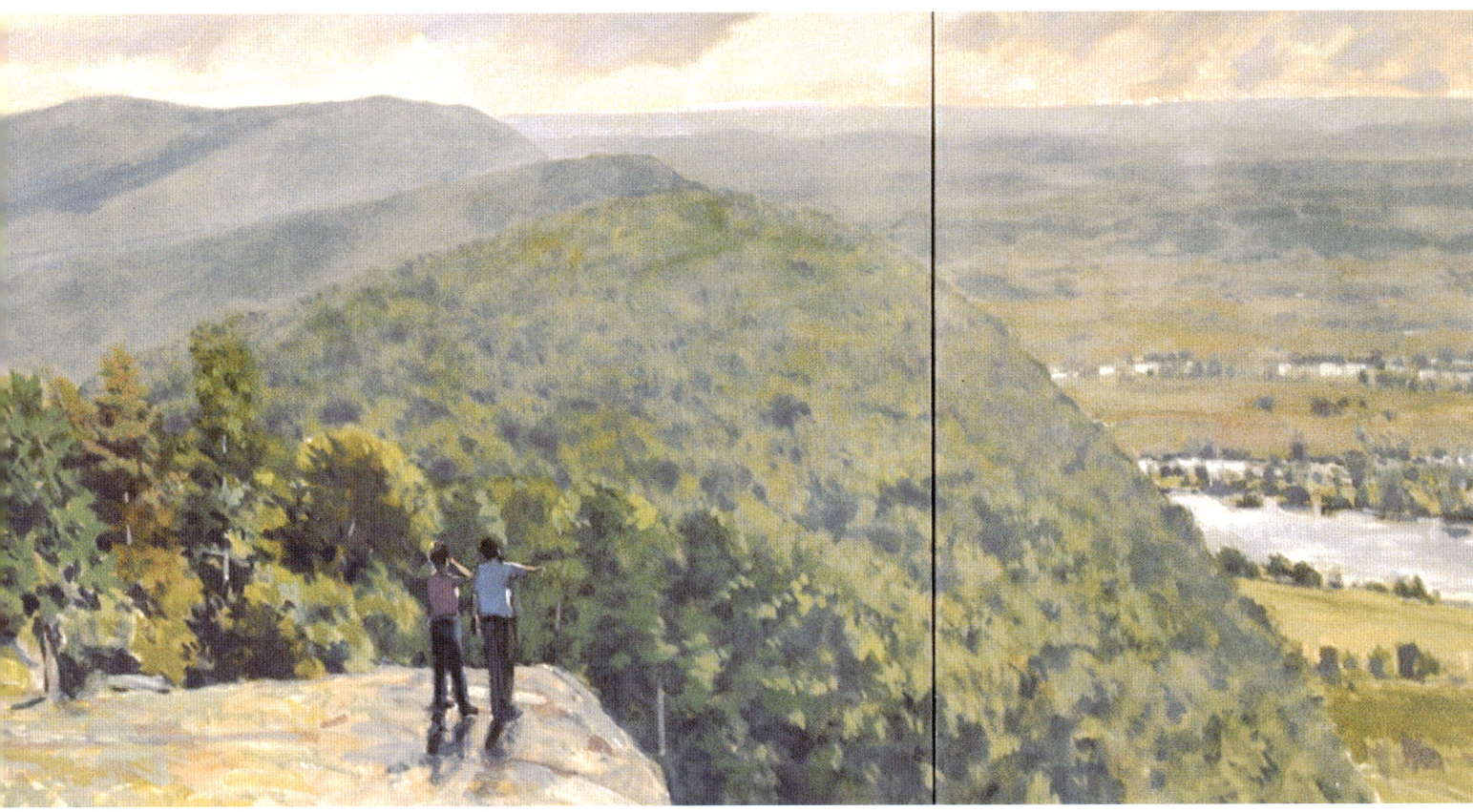

FIGURE 35. Richard Crozier, *Kindred Spirits*, 1987, oil on canvas. Collection Citigroup

called his "most ambitious painting to date," *Gardening in Maine*, a triptych even longer than his painting from Mt. Holyoke.[39] He has continued to paint panoramas sporadically since then.

In 1993, a group of Northampton area artists decided to reinterpret Cole's painting of the Oxbow, choosing to portray the view in winter and exhibiting their results that same spring at the Northampton Center for the Arts. The nine artists involved were: Martha Armstrong, David Gloman, Charles Kanwischer, Elizabeth Meyersohn, Marion Miller, Gary Niswonger, Cathy Osman, Lorna Ritz, and Robert Sweeney. All started with a reproduction of the Cole painting. Some climbed the mountain in the snow (the road to the Summit House is closed to cars in winter); some hiked into the fields below. Several of the

artists drew or painted sketches on the spot; some worked from photographs. They produced drawings, prints, and paintings, and they responded to varying aspects of the subject. Gary Niswonger, for example, in his painting *View from Mount Holyoke* (collection of the artist), concentrated on the inherent geometry of the fields under snow and the pattern of the river. He included Interstate 91 as a line crossing the Oxbow, but otherwise retained the integrity of the Oxbow's crescent shape. Elizabeth Meyersohn in *Connecticut River from Mount Holyoke* (collection of the artist) barely indicated the Oxbow, focusing instead on the sloping edge of the mountain, painting the whole with loose strokes that resemble the pastel drawing she made on the site.

Cathy Osman, who ascended the mountain to

draw with Meyersohn, first made a small oil copy of a reproduction of the Cole painting, in order to get herself thinking about it (she has never seen the actual painting).[40] Typically Osman works from memory rather than from direct observation, so she found being out in nature and collaborating to be an exciting "expedition." It reminded her of the "freedom of responding directly to landscape," she noted, but added that she was interested less in the Cole painting than in placing herself in the environment. In the landscape tradition of John Marin and Marsden Hartley, Osman's canvases are expressionistic, concerned with, as she has said, "mark and nuance of surface." In Cole's painting she especially noticed the yellow color of the fields, and the "intensity of the yellow glow is what I painted." In her large-scale *Oxbow Revisited*

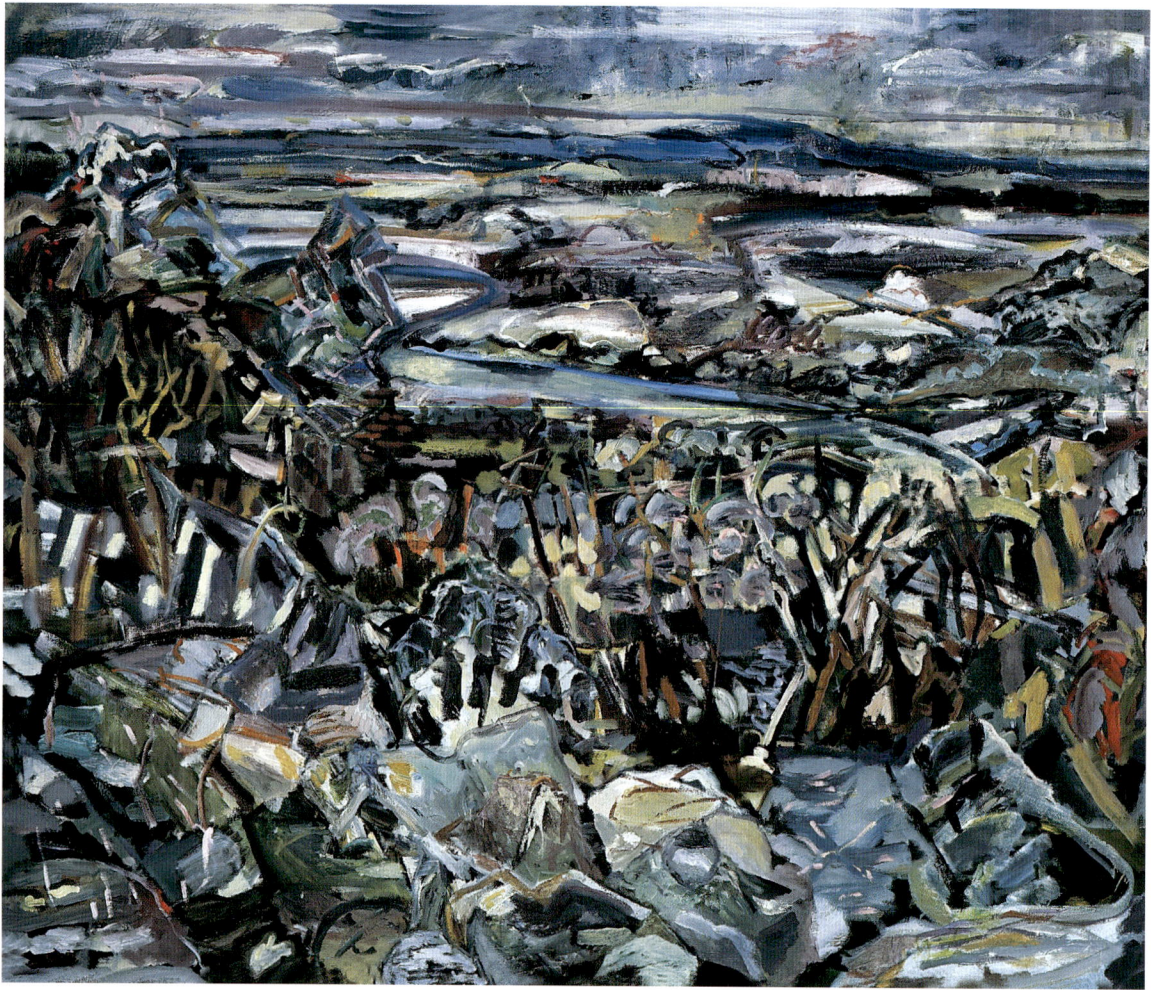

FIGURE 36. Cathy Osman, *Oxbow Revisited*, 1993, oil on canvas. Collection of the artist

she reduced Cole's composition to the essential intersection of line and paddle shape and started a large canvas based directly on his painting. In the end she abandoned this approach and painted entirely on site, returning the Oxbow to its actual shape as seen from the summit and opposing its geometry to the hillside and snowy fields in *Oxbow from the Summit House* (figure 37). Armstrong typically paints landscapes in a semi-abstract style using bold broad strokes of color and strong contrasts of horizontal and vertical. For this winter view she emphasized the horizontal patterns of land and river, breaking up the scene into arc and wedge-like segments fitted together.

In addition to participating in the group exhibition, Robert Sweeney has painted from Mt. Holyoke many times. In 1990 he produced two large views on commission for Heritage Bank. In *Oxbow, Dusk* (figure 38) he approximated Cole's vantage point, and in *Connecticut River* (private collection) he looked directly south along the river to Holyoke and South Hadley, not a traditional subject. *Oxbow, Dusk* shows Sweeney's awareness of the Cole painting in his deliberate emphasis of the diagonal mountainside in the left half, but otherwise he manipulated the actual prospect very little. A late afternoon haze settles on much of the far distance, rich fields occupy the middle distance, and small buildings below indicate peaceful settlement. The scene as a whole is orderly and manicured. Nature is also subdued on the mountain, with some bare trees tucked into the foreground so as not to interrupt the view.

Sweeney conveyed the vastness of the distance by accurately rendering the unpronounced shape of the Oxbow with its roads and bridges largely hidden by foliage. The season is early fall, indicated by the line of lacy branches along the river. Sweeney came to Cole's painting through the intermediary of Alfred Leslie's work, which he saw when Leslie exhibited it at Boston University in 1972. Then Sweeney arrived to teach at

(figure 36), her swirling brushstrokes suggest a sense of perspective, aerial position, and specific place that link her work to Cole's.

Martha Armstrong began by drawing directly from Cole's *Oxbow* in the American galleries of the Metropolitan Museum, and then making small oil studies from her drawings. Cole's construction of his view fascinated her; she found it "baffling," she said:[41] "He did not compose his paintings in the traditional European manner but made up a way that was convincing and looked perceptual." She finally concluded that "Cole relies on perceptual detail to be convincing." In her oil sketches

Amherst College just when Leslie was finishing his visiting professorship. For Sweeney, Leslie's example "validated" the process of drawing on past artistic conventions while representing the modern landscape.[42] Compared to Leslie's severe, highly constructed realism, however, Sweeney's interpretation of the subject is naturalistic.

More recently, in a similar spirit of naturalism, Chesterfield artist Robert Aller photographed the view from Mt. Holyoke. Approaching the subject as he imagined Cole would have, he made photographic "sketches" of the details of nature that he saw on his walk up the mountain.[43] Cole and other landscape painters of his time, in fact, made drawings of closely observed natural forms — a tree, a tree trunk, a plant — in order to become so familiar with the minute workings of nature that they could automatically create seemingly accurate detail in their studio paintings. In addition to his "sketches," Aller took panoramic photographs from the mountaintop. In *Mt. Holyoke*, a silver print from 2001, he tried to duplicate Cole's perspective on the scene (figure 39). With his panoramic format he could include a rock ledge at the left, evoking the presence of tourists or picnickers, as well as an extended view of the river on the right. Although a slight haze obscures some details in the distance, Aller captured a sense of the vastness of the space. His photograph also reveals the difficulty of identifying the lines of the Oxbow today. Some key features do stand out: the Interstate 91 bridge over the river, the white roof of a large corrugated box factory on Oxbow land, and the marina basin. Though signs of development lie in the distance, the scene in the foreground is remarkably similar to painted views of both centuries. The wooded mountain slope, the river passing close to it, the sprinkling of farm buildings on the near shore, and the fields bordered by trees look almost unchanged from the time of Cole and Bartlett.

Other Connecticut Valley artists have been attracted by the prospect from Mt. Holyoke and

by the example of Thomas Cole, attesting to the steady market for paintings of the subject. Over the past ten years Jeff Kern has painted the Oxbow from many angles, including a view framed by the window of the Summit House (R. Michelson Galleries, Northampton). Lewis Bryden in *The Oxbow from Mt. Holyoke* from 1999 (R. Michelson Galleries) showed the formation almost totally masked by thick summer foliage and atmospheric haze. Charles Malzenski in *The Oxbow*, painted in 1997 (private collection), returned Cole's scene to a primeval state, covering every surface with a dense carpet of trees. Robert Masla painted his 1996 *View from the Summit — Homage to Thomas Cole* (figure 40) using the same dimensions and

general compositional arrangement as the Cole. He even placed the figure of an artist sketching in the right foreground. He included Cole's storm clouds, but they arc over the right half of the composition. His bolt of lightning in the distance alludes to the possibility that Cole represented Hebrew lettering on the furthest hillside.[44] In great contrast to Cole's sophisticated technique, however, Masla imparted a folk quality to his work. He changed Cole's blasted trees to truly anthropomorphic ones. He used an artificially intense green for foliage and covered mountain and fields with lush rounded trees. He also added a personal spiritual dimension by hiding within the swirling clouds various figures such as Jesus

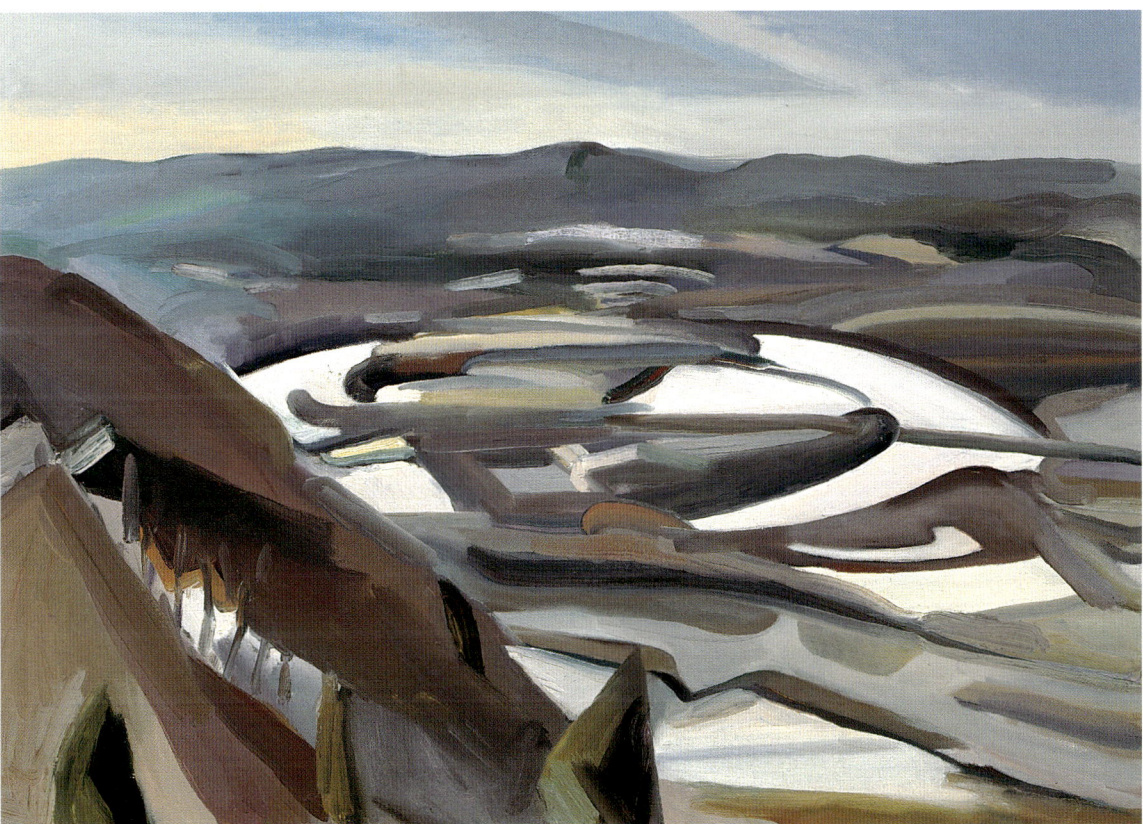

FIGURE 37. Martha Armstrong, *Oxbow from the Summit House*, 1993, oil on canvas. Collection of the artist

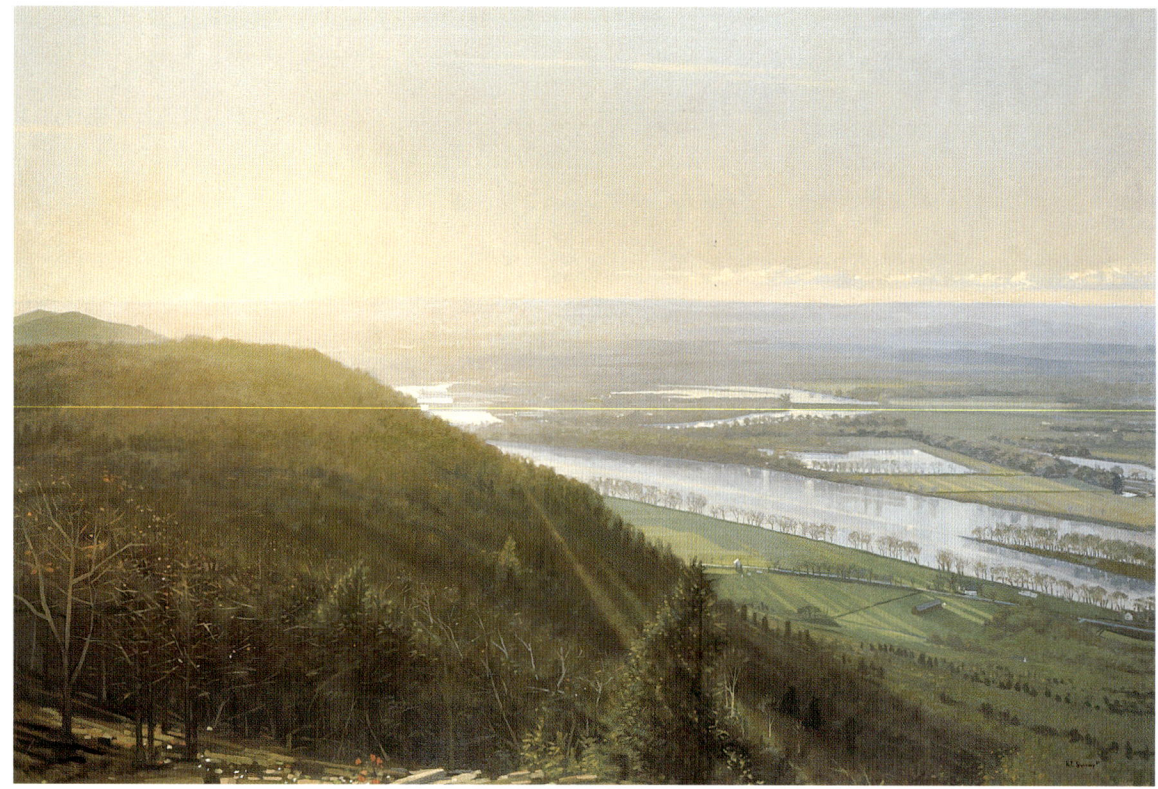

Christ and God the Father from Michelangelo's Sistine Ceiling.

David Moriarty has taken one of the most inventive approaches to the theme of the Oxbow. Intensely aware of art history and nineteenth-century landscape traditions, Moriarty nevertheless used Cole only as a point of departure for his own fantasies. He was attracted to the Cole painting by what he called the "eccentricity of that form — the flat frying pan" and by the "large game-board" of the surrounding fields.[45] In *New World: Red*, painted in 1996 (figure 41), he explored the essence of the Oxbow's shape, changing it to a completed circle and connecting the interior island by a bridge. Within the island he placed architectural towers inspired by Erastus Salisbury Field's vast structure in his *Historical Monument of the American Republic* of about 1865 (Springfield Museum of Fine Arts). On a mountain ledge above the prospect, Moriarty depicted two Native American children looking at the towers of modern civilization. He layers all of his paintings with such meanings, enjoying the resulting ambiguity and

FIGURE 38. Robert Sweeney, *Oxbow, Dusk*, 1990, oil on canvas. Private collection (not in exhibition)

FIGURE 39. Robert Aller, *Mt. Holyoke*, 2001, silver print photograph. Collection of the artist

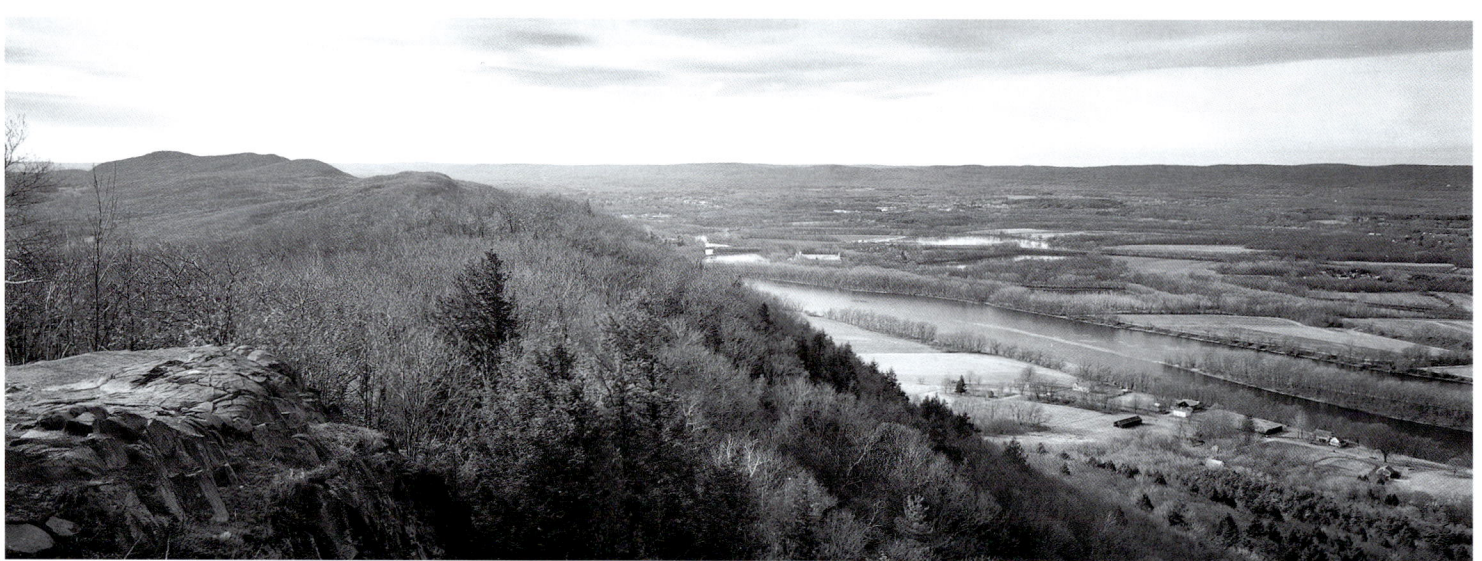

intending the ironic edge of his images. In 1991 Moriarty moved from Brooklyn to Holyoke, choosing this location partly because of Cole's painting. He did numerous sketches from the top of the mountain and then painted *New World: Red* from memory. He has since abstracted the shape of Cole's Oxbow even further and combined it in several recent works with various kinds of figures and moods. He has no interest in realism as an end in itself and sees landscape as a "theater for morality plays" and his own "docu-dramas."

Contemporary Artists and the View of Hadley For most of the twentieth century few painters chose the second view from Mt. Holyoke, the one looking in the direction of Hadley. Over the last two decades, however, there has been a resurgence of interest in this prospect. In *Connecticut River Near Northampton*, dated 1987 (figure 42), James Winn dramatized the northern bend of the river as it heads towards Hadley, suggesting a second oxbow by accentuating the pattern of its curve. Executed in his usual medium of acrylic on paper, and with his usual dimensions of 24 x 72 inches, this painting recasts the conventions of the panoramic view.

Winn has always lived and worked in the Midwest, choosing its flat farms and prairies as his subject. When he came to Northampton in 1986 for a commission to paint a typical New England scene for Arthur Andersen & Co., he settled on the northern view from part way up the mountain.[46] His lower vantage point allowed him to concentrate on the fields in the foreground and on the first turn of the river. He emphasized a side-to-side panoramic sweep over deep space, as he had in his midwestern scenes, using the length of the river to establish his wide-angle view. He also extended the river almost to the edge of the picture, organizing the neatly plotted fields to complement its stretched shape. In all his paintings he exaggerates horizontal forms, as he did here with river, fields, low hills beyond, and clouds.

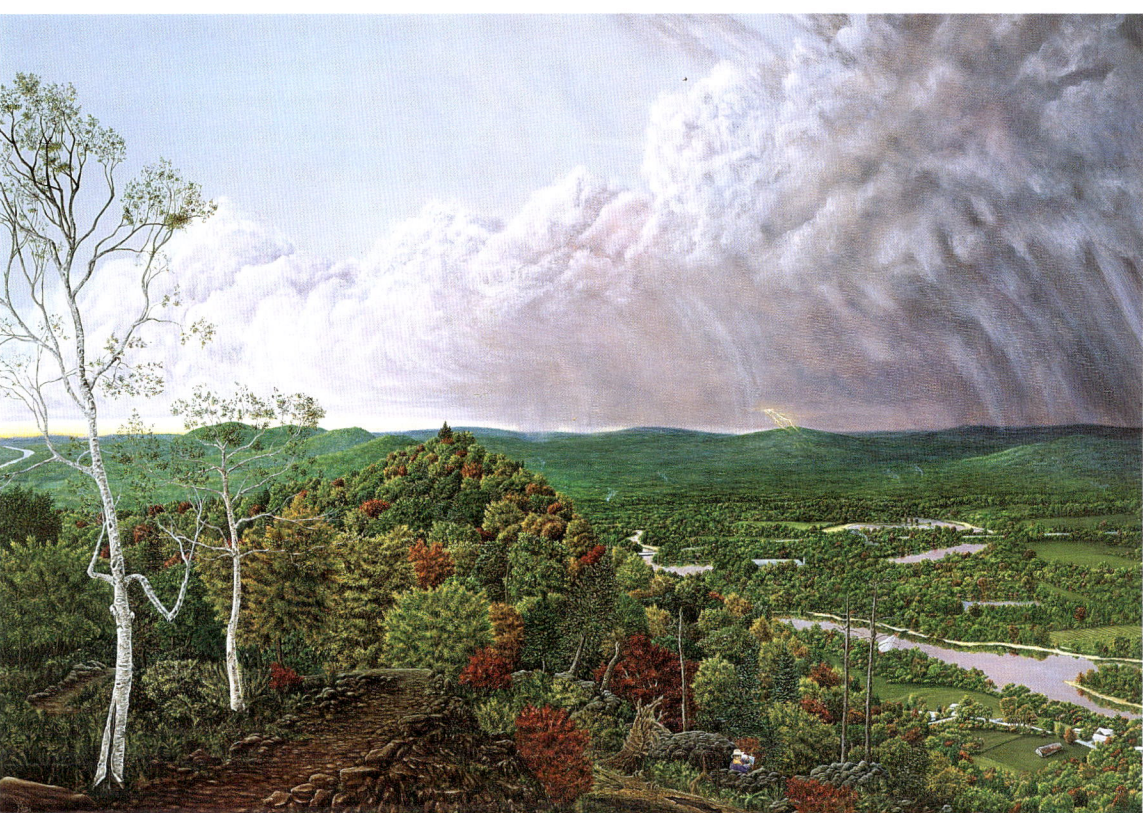

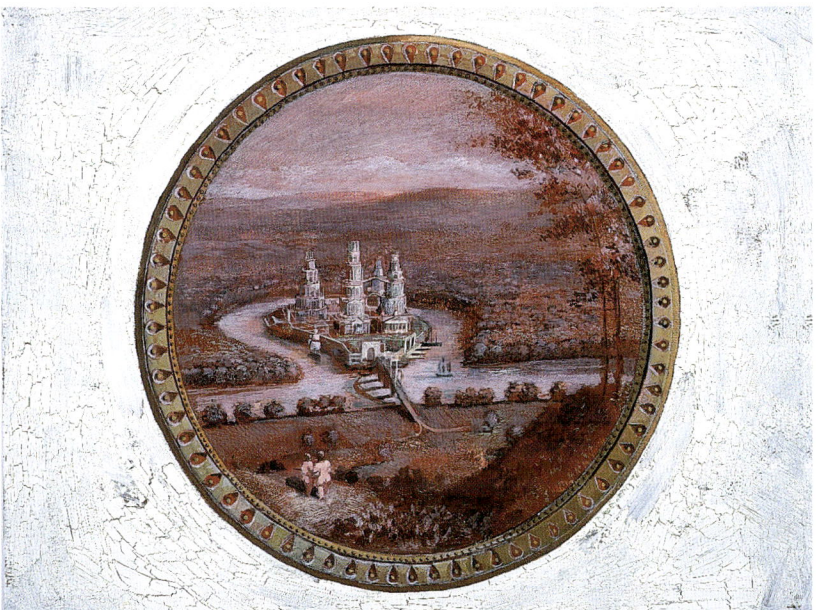

FIGURE 40. Robert Masla, *View from the Summit — Homage to Thomas Cole*, 1996, oil on canvas. R. Michelson Galleries, Northampton (not in exhibition)

FIGURE 41. David Moriarty, *New World: Red*, 1996, acrylic on prepared paper. Holyoke Community College Collection, Holyoke

Invariably Winn devotes at least half — and usually more — of his composition to skies or clouds, his true subject. First establishing cloud color, light, and formation, he then correlates ground to sky. Usually he takes color slides of his sites at different times of day and "mixes and matches," so that ground from one site might wind up with sky from another. He does this, he says, "because they are compositions," not photo-realist records.

Since he climbed Mt. Holyoke on an overcast day in April when the Connecticut River was flooded, Winn essentially invented the light and color of his painting. His desire to capture light has led him to prefer certain times of day, especially dusk or sunset. For this depiction of the Connecticut River, Winn chose sunset — causing the sun to descend in the north, like Edmund Coates before him — and set the horizon ablaze with warm oranges. Softer peach-orange tones reflect the spectacle in the surface of the river and blue clouds stand out against the complementary color

of the sky. Winn's remarkable technique heightens the painting's luminosity. He has achieved a transparency, particularly obvious in his treatment of the river's surface, and a subtlety that resemble watercolor. At the same time individual strokes of paint visible in foreground elements lend an additional freshness to the image.

When he chose to paint the Hadley view, Winn was not avoiding the Oxbow. "I'm not worried about Thomas," he said, noting that he was aware of the Cole painting but that Cole is not among his favorite painters. He is more interested in the Luminists, whose work he first encountered at *American Light*, the 1985 exhibition devoted to the subject at the National Gallery of Art. What leads so many contemporary landscape painters to the Luminists is the shared preoccupation with light. Luminism's horizontal emphasis and contemplative mood must have appealed to Winn as well. The stillness of his Hadley view is unbroken by elements of modern life. He suggests the parallel streets of Hadley by the line of trees, but omits

cars, power lines, and roads, even removing Route 47 from the foreground. Winn is inspired by Luminism's reverential description of the details of nature, although he is also impressed by the mysticism of Scandinavian painters whose work he saw while living in Finland for several years. In his paintings Winn seeks to imbue nature with a spiritual dimension. His open spaces and spectacular skies intimate the presence of a higher power.

The view from Mt. Holyoke offered Northampton area artist Randall Deihl a deep perspective and a motif — the river — that would lend themselves to the circular composition he wished to explore. Looking out over the meadows toward Northampton and Hadley in *View of the Valley* of 1985 (figure 43), Deihl, like Winn, emphasized the straight line of the river in the foreground and the pronounced curve it makes on its way to Hadley. From his vantage point lower down the mountain at the Half-way House, he did not show the river meandering into the distance. Accuracy has never been Deihl's goal. He started with an on-the-spot

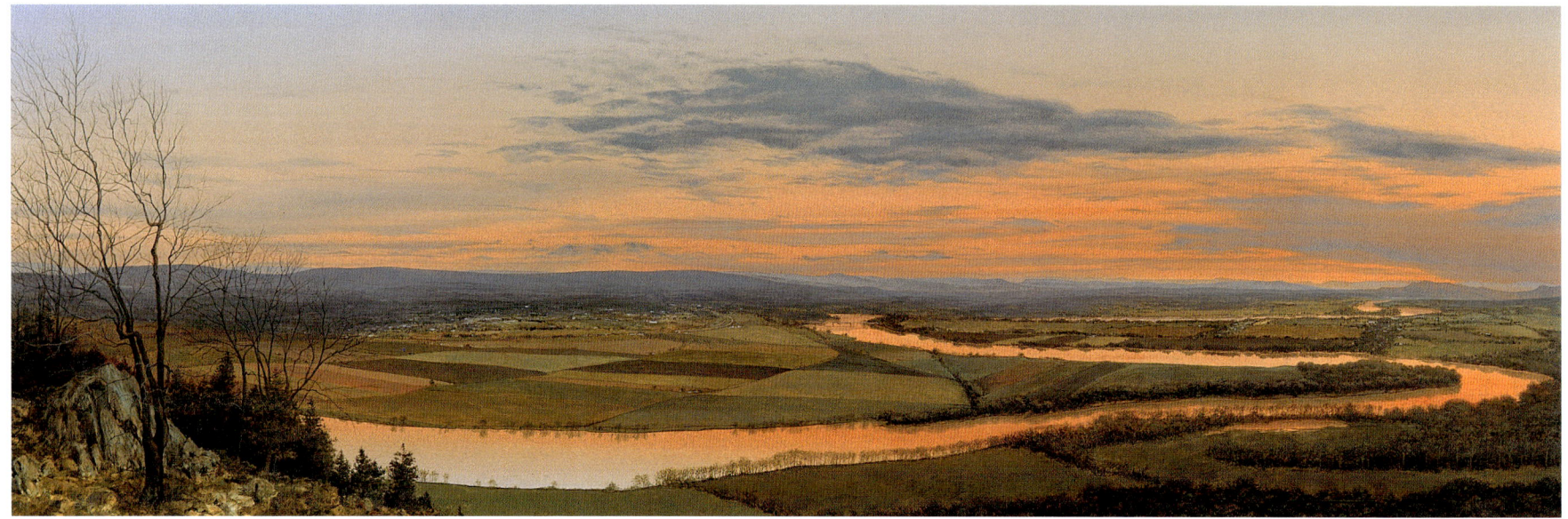

FIGURE 42. James Winn, *The Connecticut River Near Northampton*, 1987, acrylic on paper. Boston-Andersen

— 52 —

drawing and then invented portions of the land-scape as he worked in his studio. With its precisely painted forms, brilliant green fields, and bright blue sky, his painting has the dream-like quality characteristic of much of his work. Typical also is his witty inclusion of human activity in the tin can at the viewer's feet, the posted sign at the edge of the ledge, and the airplane streaking across the sky. Although Deihl admires Cole's painting today, he was not aware of it then; he was, and still is, most influenced by Dutch seventeenth-century art.

As before, the view of Hadley continues to symbolize agricultural richness and the values of rural New England life. Today's artists, however, have tended to shift their angle of vision to express these ideas. Winn and Deihl turned towards the west for their paintings; others like Lewis Bryden and Mark Meunier have depicted a narrower slice and cut off the far curve of the river as it loops back around Hadley. By making the river's first curve the prominent feature of the landscape, all these artists evoke the evolving form of an oxbow, perhaps further testimony to the power of Cole's image.

Lewis Bryden directed his eye north in two similar paintings done in 2000. *An Higher View* (R. Michelson Galleries, Northampton) and *Mid-Summer in the Valley* (figure 44) represent essential-ly the same scene at different times of day.[47] Bryden usually employs a dark foreground wedge of foliage to enhance the feeling of vast space. In the distance lush forests overwhelm the landscape, indicating the denser forestation, as well as the shift away from farming to residential use of the land, in the present. By contrast, in David Gue's 1903 *View from Mount Holyoke* (figure 15), stands of trees dot the open fields and Hadley's parallel streets provide a clear focal point. Bryden typically begins his paintings out of doors, closely observ-ing conditions of light and air. When painting *Mid-Summer in the Valley*, he incorporated the hazy conditions, which cast the distant mountains in mist. He makes very slight shifts in color, in order

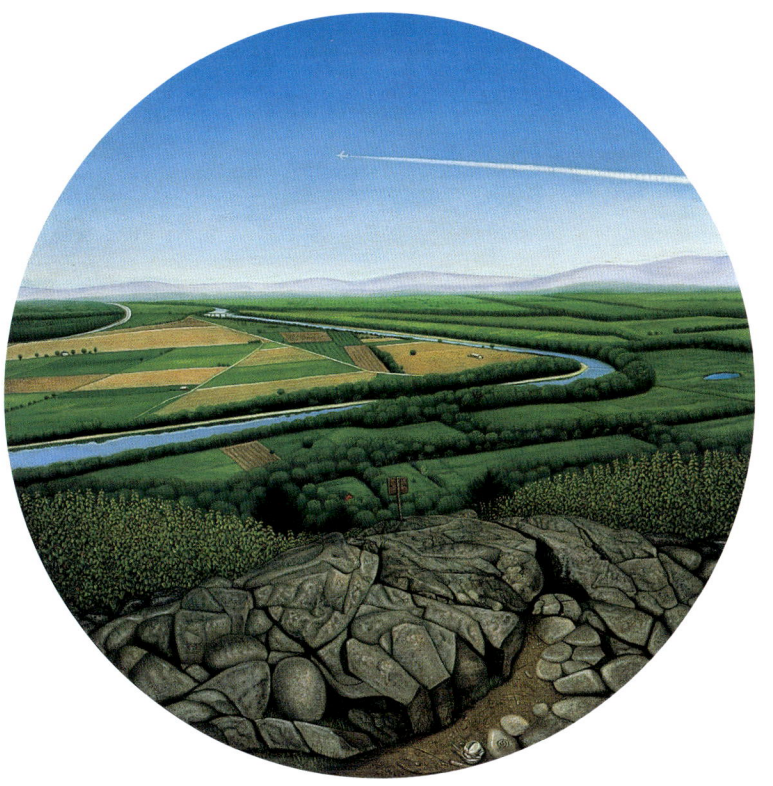

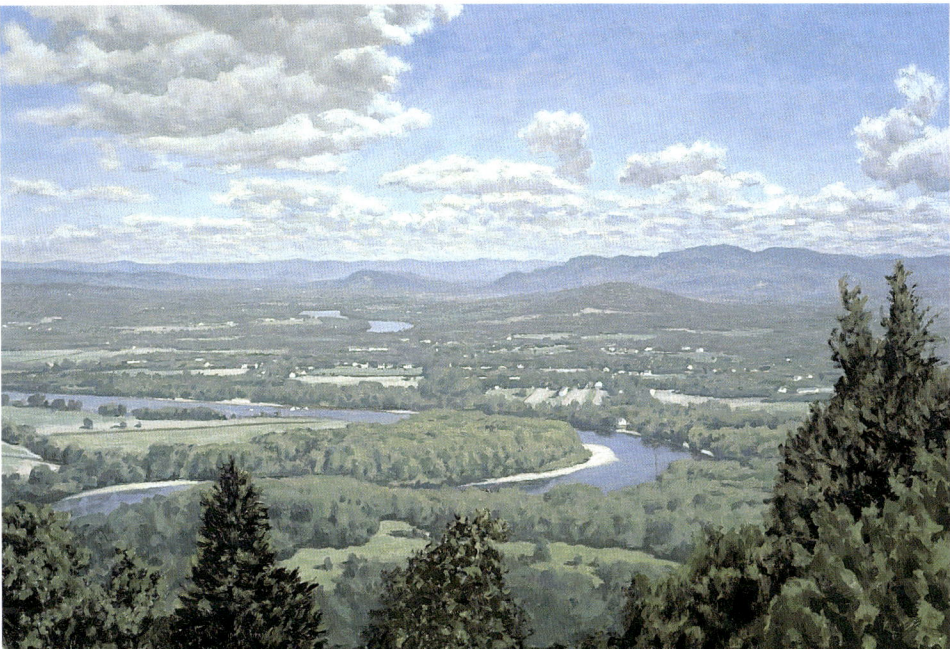

FIGURE 43. Randall Deihl, *View of the Valley*, 1985, oil on board. Private collection (not in exhibition)

FIGURE 44. Lewis Bryden, *Mid-Summer in the Valley*, 2000, oil on canvas. R. Michelson Galleries, Northampton

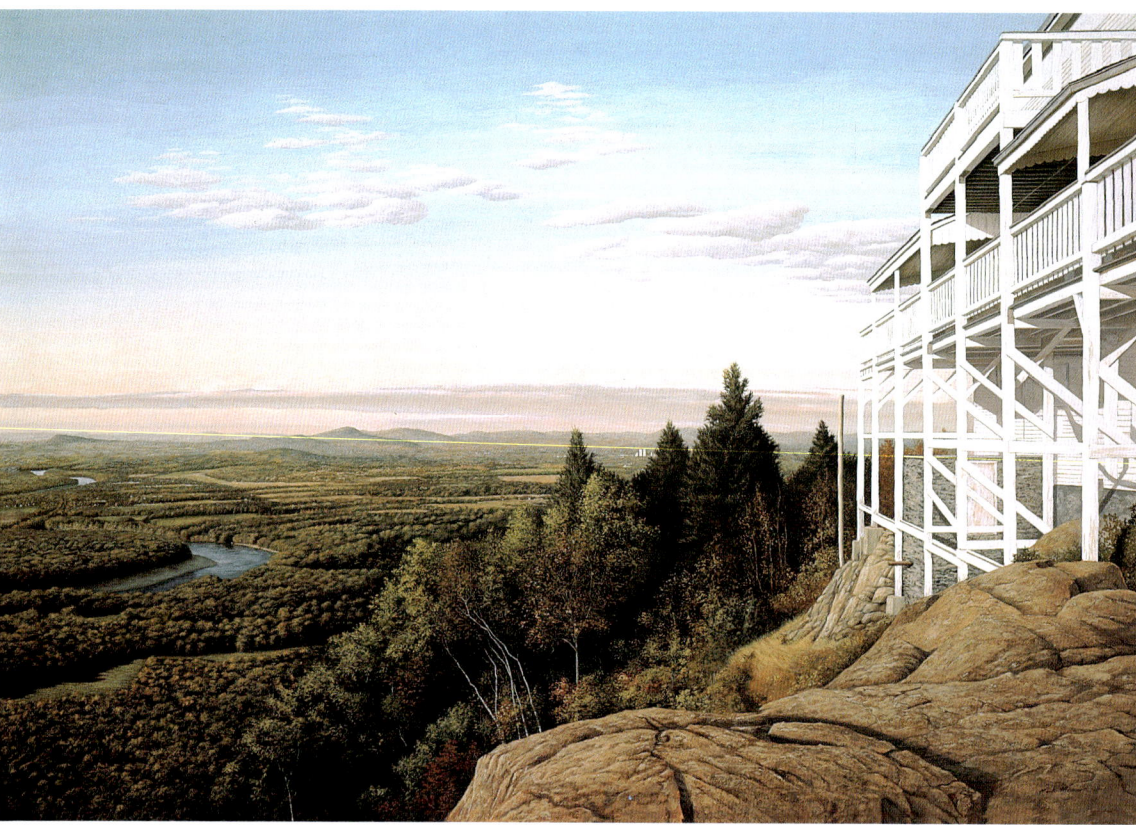

to suggest, as he noted, "the presence of air."[48] For *Mid-Summer in the Valley* he used vivid blues and rich greens; for *An Higher View* he changed the color tone to soft greens and faded blues.

It is also common for contemporary artists to include some part of the Summit House in a picture's foreground to establish a sense of distant space and to contrast past and present, nature and man. Mark Meunier's 1995 *Valley View* (figure 45), opposes green, irregular, verdant nature with the geometric, hard, white supporting trusses of the Summit House. Jeff Kern makes the Summit House an important part of many compositions he paints at the top of Mt. Holyoke. In his *Summit House* from 2001 (R. Michelson Galleries, Northampton), for instance, he took a position on the building's long porch, using its railing and floor to lead rapidly into space. In these works both Meunier and Kern focused on the near curve of the river. Meunier moved his viewpoint around to the east enough to catch a glimpse of the University of Massachusetts at Amherst. In his 1996 *View from Mt. Holyoke* (figure 46), Scott Prior purposely looked east to the university because its Alumni Association commissioned the work. He invented one important aspect of his view: he moved the truncated curve of the Connecticut River, the graphic symbol associated with Hadley, to a spot in front of the university.

As they did in the nineteenth century, market forces dictate both subject matter and style to a great degree. Cole painted his view of the prospect from Mt. Holyoke because he was confident he could sell it. The many copyists of Bartlett's prints, notably Victor de Grailly, painted for a public that was hungry for realistic, detailed pictures of specific tourist sites. Art collectors today, typically, want the same, and views from Mt.

Holyoke sell steadily in the Connecticut Valley region. Reproductions of several of these — Mark Meunier's *Valley View* and Lewis Bryden's *Northampton from Mt. Holyoke* (private collection), for example — always bring good prices at the local public broadcasting station's annual art auction. Both paintings were commissioned by the television station and auctioned as featured works in 1996 and 1999. During the last decade a miniindustry of producing views of and from Mt. Holyoke has developed in the Northampton area.

Mt. Holyoke from the Meadowlands The legacy from the past also extends to the third type of image of Mt. Holyoke: the mountain seen from the fertile fields below. In the second half of the nineteenth century, the view from Mt. Holyoke attracted fewer

artists than did the view from ground level. The image of the garden, so prevalent in writing about the valley, dominated later in the nineteenth century as artists emphasized abundant lands, rather than mountain scenery, up and down the Connecticut River. New York artist Edward Nichols painted several canvases in 1864, including *Northampton Meadows* (Historic Northampton).[49] During his summer in Northampton in 1865, New Yorker Thomas Farrer painted *Mount Holyoke* (figure 18), a view from inside the Oxbow that features both railroad and mountain house and emphasizes the forest line above cleared pastures on the mountain's lower slopes.[50] David Gue's *View of Mount Holyoke*, dated 1890 (figure 16), shows Mt. Holyoke and surrounding meadows from the base of Mt. Tom. In general, however, the later nineteenth century favored more intimate

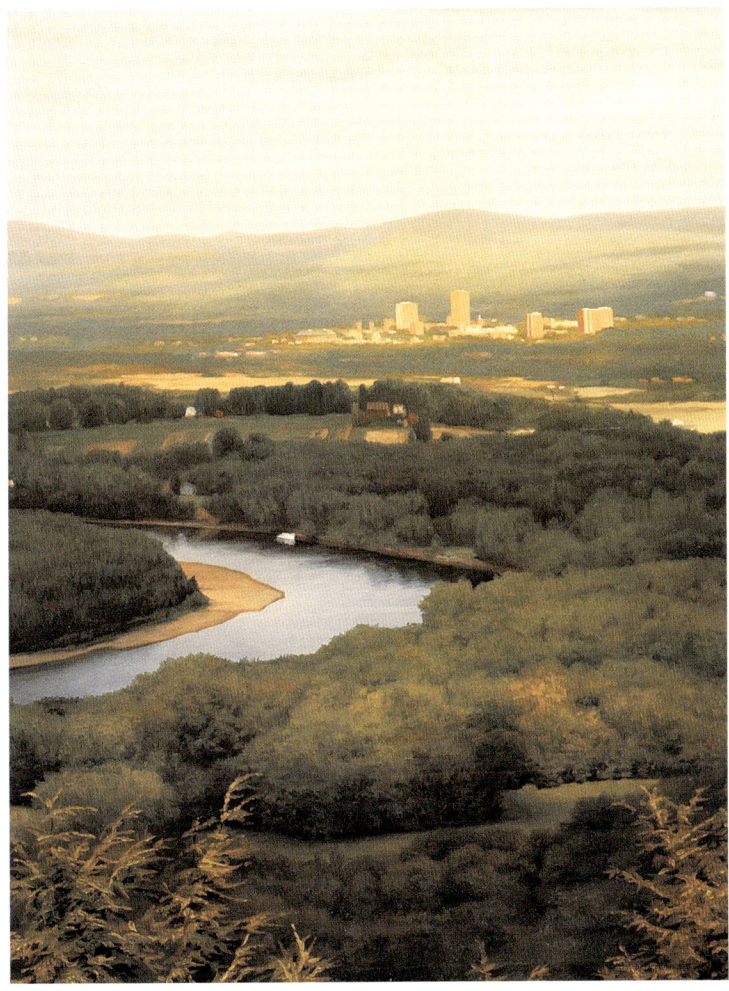

FIGURE 46. Scott Prior, *View from Mt. Holyoke*, 1996, oil on canvas. Collection of David K. Scott

FIGURE 47. Edward Corbett, *Mt. Holyoke*, 1962, oil on canvas. Whitney Museum of American Art, New York. Purchase, with funds from the Friends of the Whitney Museum of American Art 62.54

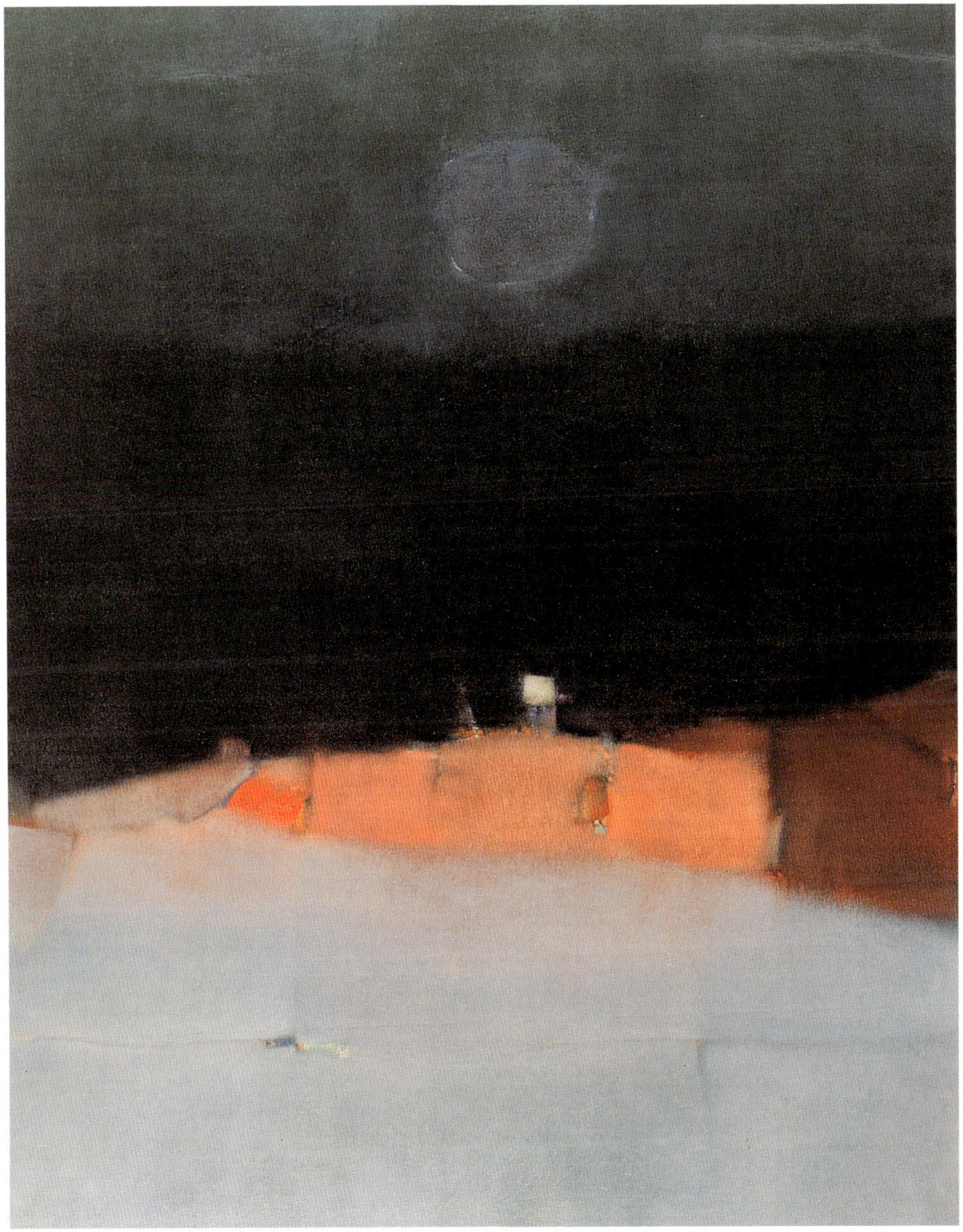

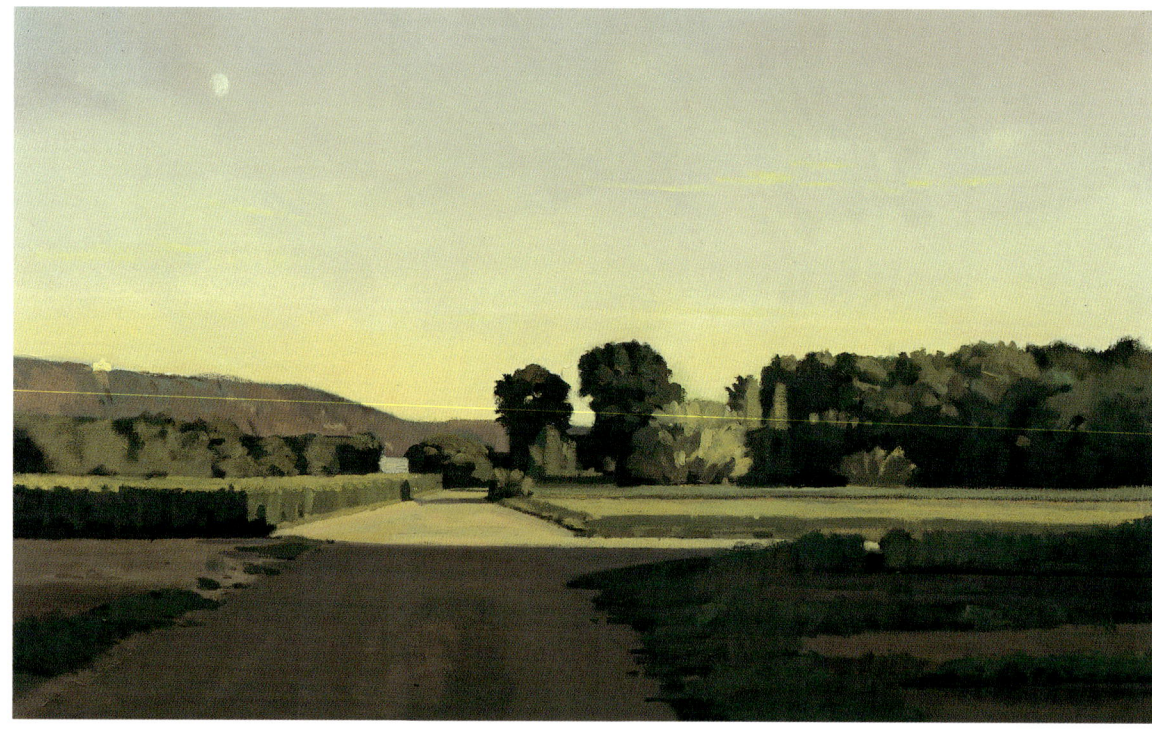

landscapes over panoramic views, and topographical detail gave way to suggestive impressionistic renderings of nature.

Artists of the later twentieth century have shown particular interest in depicting the mountain's profile and its agrarian setting. Edward Corbett, who taught for many years at Mount Holyoke College, created *Mt. Holyoke* (figure 47) in 1962. The canvas is unusual for its highly abstract vocabulary influenced by Abstract Expressionism. Painted from the foot of the mountain, it presents an arrangement of simplified mountain forms. A brilliant peach-orange passage in a deep green field would seem to represent the Half-way House, while a circle hovering at the crest of the mountain must be the moon. In more recent times, David Gloman has used broad blocks of color and rich paint to represent the flat farmland surrounding Mt. Holyoke. In *Hockanum Road* of 1996 (figure 48), a view of Mt. Holyoke from the Northampton meadows, he employed his usual low

FIGURE 48. David Gloman, *Hockanum Road*, 1996, oil on canvas. Collection of the artist

FIGURE 49. Elizabeth Meyersohn, *Flooded Fields*, 2001, oil on canvas. Private collection

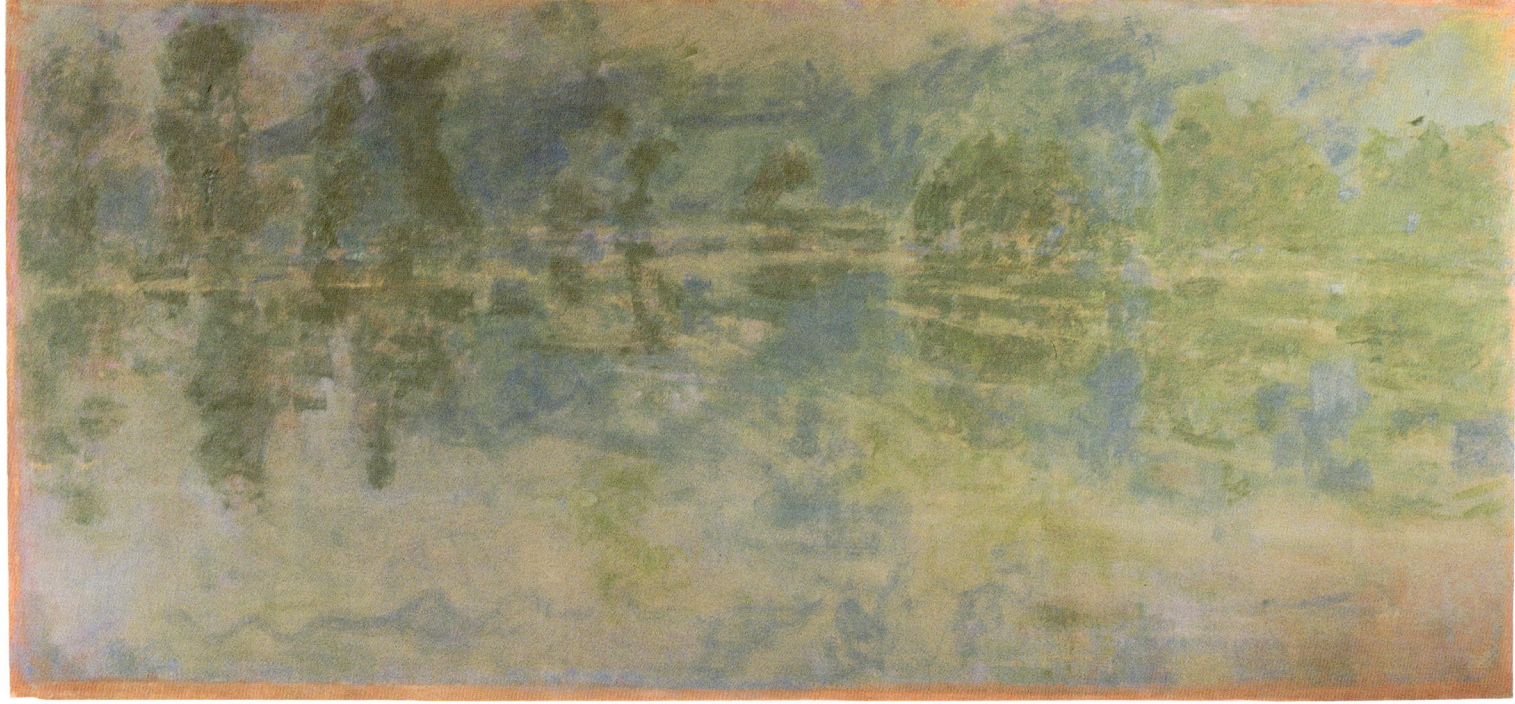

vantage point and road leading into space to suggest deep recession and wide-angle view. Elizabeth Meyersohn, on her 1993 excursion to the top of Mt. Holyoke along with her artist colleagues, produced a painting that differed from her more typical use of the mountain as background. For example, in *Flooded Fields* dating from 2001 (figure 49), she painted it as a veil of color behind a screen of hazy trees standing in flooded fields. She sees the mountain out her studio window in Northampton. Finding it a beacon at every point, she judges her location relative to it. As she has observed, "It is hard to be a landscape painter and not be aware of the mountain."[51]

Area photographers have also portrayed the mountain from the surrounding fields. In *The Meadows from Rt. 91* from 1989 (figure 50), Stephen Petegorsky photographed a road and rows of corn leading directly into the distance, with Mt. Holyoke and its Summit House visible on the horizon. Petegorsky was attracted by the inherent structure of the forms and the density of the agriculture, but he also chose the scene for the presence of an old billboard in the middle distance. In 1996 Jerome Liebling photographed the profile of Mt. Holyoke from the Northampton meadows as light caught the white Summit House on its perch above the dark trees (figure 51). John Marcy captured the Holyoke Range rising out of early morning mist on the river in his 1985 photograph *Houseboat on the Connecticut River* (figure 52).

As in his 1972 view from Mt. Holyoke, Alfred Leslie introduced the modern industrial world into the pastoral image of the mountain. His large black and white watercolor, *Holyoke Range, Near Oxbow, Easthampton, Massachusetts* from 1983 (figure 53) depicts the dark silhouette of the mountains against a light-streaked sky as seen, not from rich meadows, but from Interstate 91. The highway is clearly indicated, and prominent in the middle of the picture are the white lines and rectangles of two highway signs. Leslie reserved a horizontal zone of white paper along the bottom edge

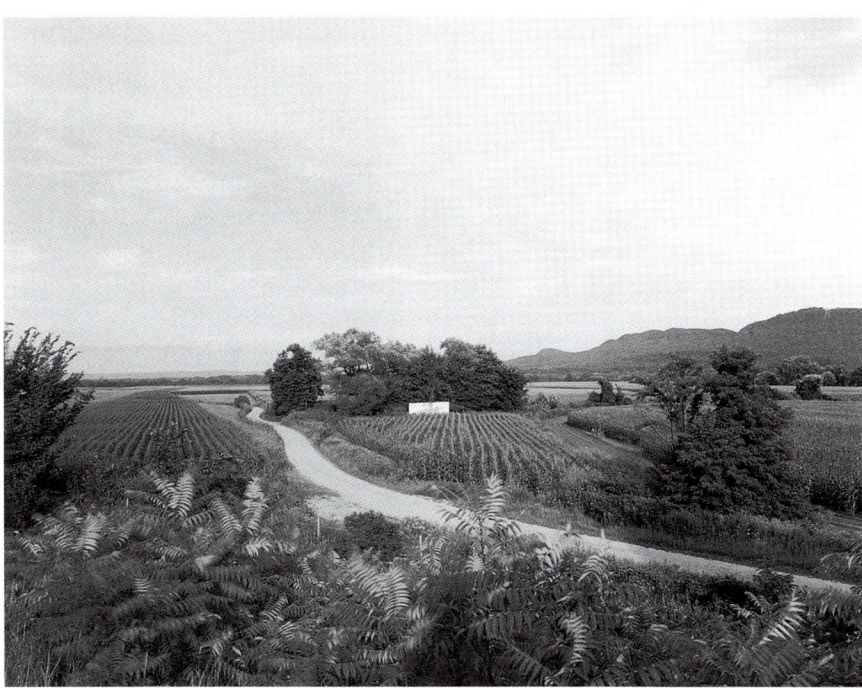

FIGURE 50. Stephen Petegorsky, *The Meadows from Rt. 91*, 1989, gelatin sliver print photograph. Collection of the artist

FIGURE 51. Jerome Liebling, *Summit House, Mt. Holyoke*, 1996, Type C color photograph. Collection of the artist

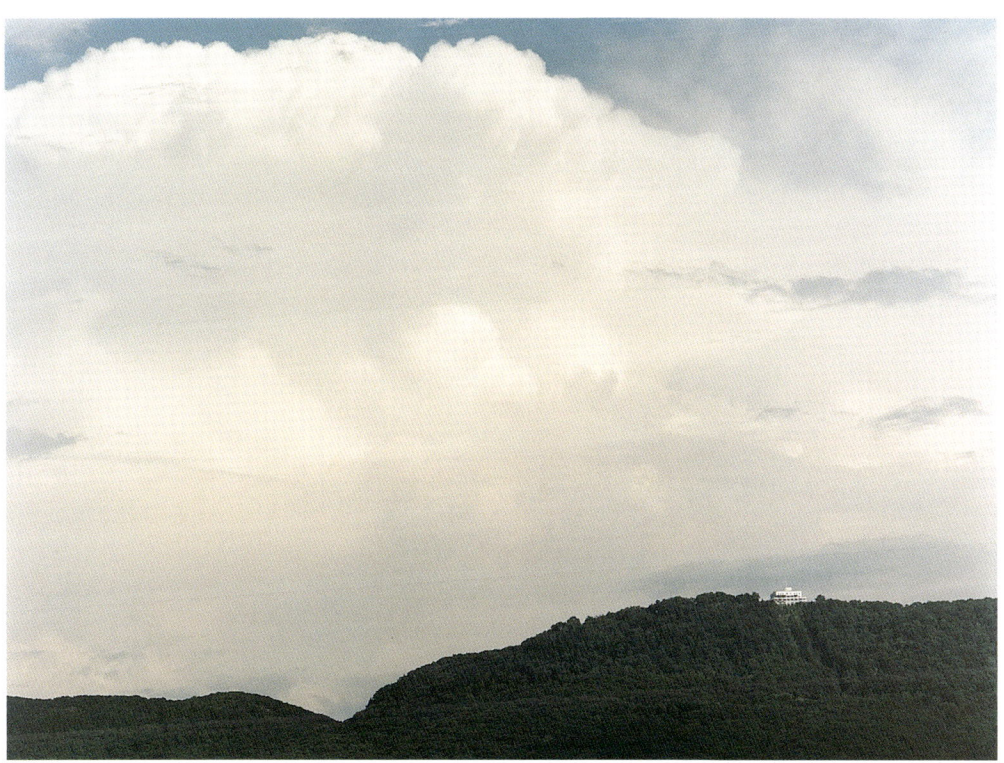

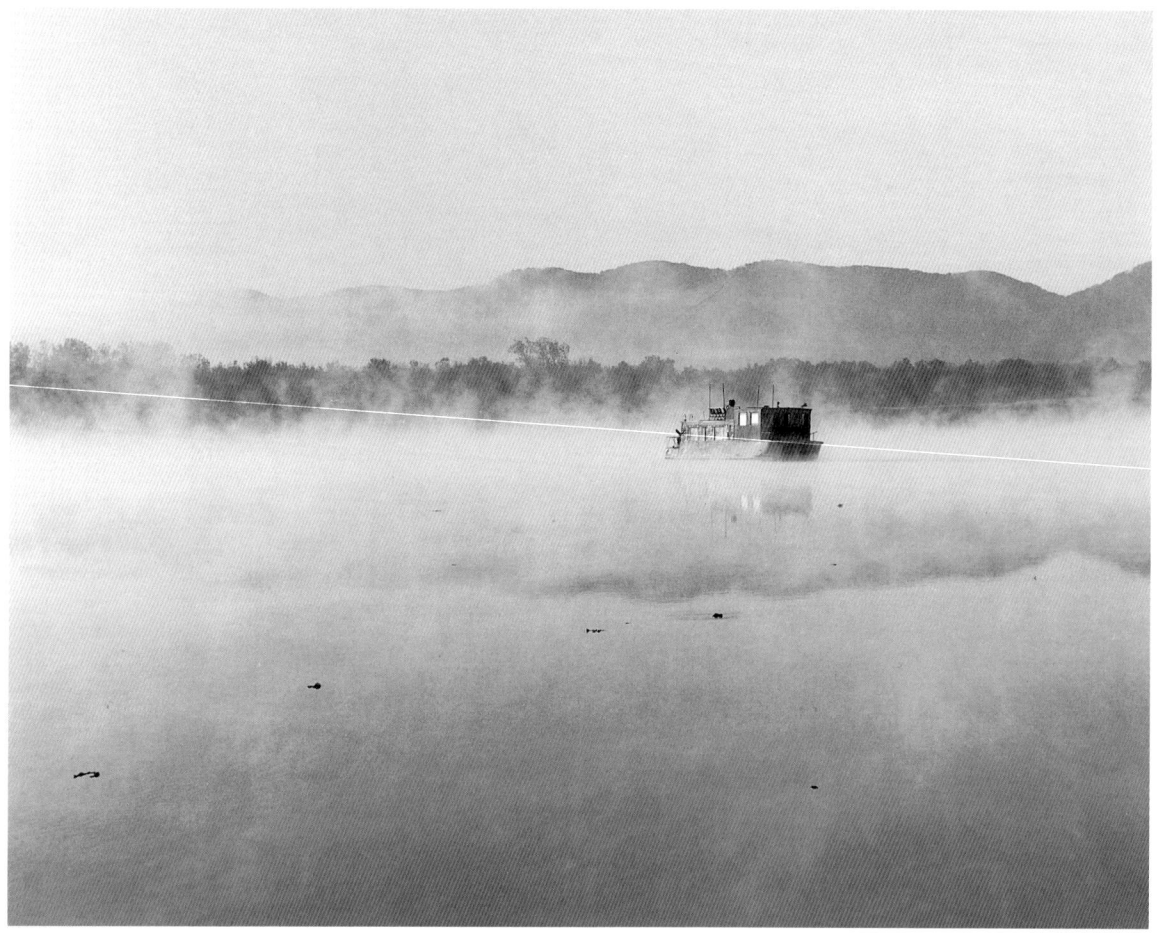

FIGURE 52. John Marcy, *Houseboat on the Connecticut River*, 1985, platinum/palladium photograph. Collection of the artist

mountain. Aside from Armstrong and Gloman, who have made oil studies of it, most artists avoid depicting the large coal power plant that looms along the river at the base of Mt. Tom. From the Summit House porch looking out toward the Oxbow, the power plant is not visible. Standing at the plant, it is possible to see the mountain rising behind modern machinery and even to glimpse a corner of the Summit House. Driving along Route 47 beneath the Summit House, it is also possible to see the high smokestack of the power plant between the two mountain ranges.

Ongoing dialogue with the past has strengthened the work of present-day artists, whether they paint from the top or the bottom of the mountain. They pick and choose elements from the more overtly dramatic Hudson River School painters, in particular ingesting the grand compositions of Cole and the colored light of Church. Many have preferred the quiet scenes of domesticated landscape by core Luminists like John Kensett and Martin Johnson Heade. Freed from the nineteenth century's need to express a nationalist agenda, artists who depict Mt. Holyoke today convey their personal response to the beauty of the landscape, one that almost all have lived in at some point. The majority softens, minimizes, or even eliminates traces of modern civilization in a return to Arcadia. They suppress roads, cars, railways, industry, and housing in favor of bucolic fields and verdant forests. Inherent in their nostalgia is a plea to preserve the present balance of man and nature.

Interest in painting the mountain has coincided with state and local concern for preserving it. First came restoration of the Summit House in the 1980s and, more recently, the effort to turn

of the watercolor to signify both earth and paper, foreground and artifice at the same time. Leslie's watercolor is one of 100 similar views of such places as Gallup, New Mexico, and Youngstown, Ohio, that he saw while driving across the country. He exhibited and published them together as *100 Views Along the Road* in 1988.[52] Inspired by the Japanese technique of notan (composing in terms of balanced blacks and whites), Leslie stressed broad shapes and patterns animated by ragged edges and luminous skies.

Contemporary artists who depict Mt. Holyoke from ground level exhibit a wide range of styles. Edward Corbett's *Mt. Holyoke* is recognizable only by its silhouette; with soft-edged, amorphous

forms and glowing color Corbett conveyed not how the mountain looks, but what it feels like to be at the base of the mountain at night. Meyersohn works very broadly as well, using thin washes and soft edges. In contrast, artists who paint from Mt. Holyoke usually work in a more traditional, realist style, which depends on lifelike detail and specifics of the view itself. They interpret and suggest, but they do it in a language of accurate observation. Their subject lends itself to factual presentation. Less circumscribed or predictable, on the other hand, the view of Mt. Holyoke allows greater freedom in approach. Yet few artists have chosen to represent commercial or industrial development within sight of the remaining private land into state land. Two years ago a local real estate developer's plan to build luxury homes on the slopes of Mt. Holyoke sparked a successful campaign to "Save the Mountain." Concerned citizens from all over the Connecticut Valley voiced outrage over what they saw as desecration of a sacred site. Using flyers, bumper stickers, yard signs, public hearings, and fundraising campaigns, they reiterated the importance of the site historically, economically, aesthetically, socially, and environmentally. Repeatedly they invoked the image of the mountain as it was created by nineteenth century landscape painters. Such a passionate outpouring testifies to the power of past images and words to shape the imagination — and the public policy — of the present.

As for Thomas Cole's inescapable painting, contemporary artists have found ways to do what Cole did on their own terms. They insert themselves in the picture by writing diarist notations across it or emphasizing their brushwork. They present the cycle of nature by choosing times of sunset or flood. They recast the panoramic format, enlarging the canvas dimensions or widening the angle of view. They qualify optimism by eliminating dramatic storms, showing alterations to the landscape, or implying the need for responsible development over uncontrolled expansion. For those who paint or photograph the view naturalistically, the Oxbow formation is a subtle feature of the landscape; for those who paint the concept of the view, the Oxbow remains a focal point. Artists today continue to search for the exact spot from which Cole painted his spectacular scene — concluding it was near the hang-glider launch or it was below the Summit House porch or the trees have grown taller and obscured his vista or he made a composite of two views. No one can exactly duplicate Cole's view because in fact he altered reality.

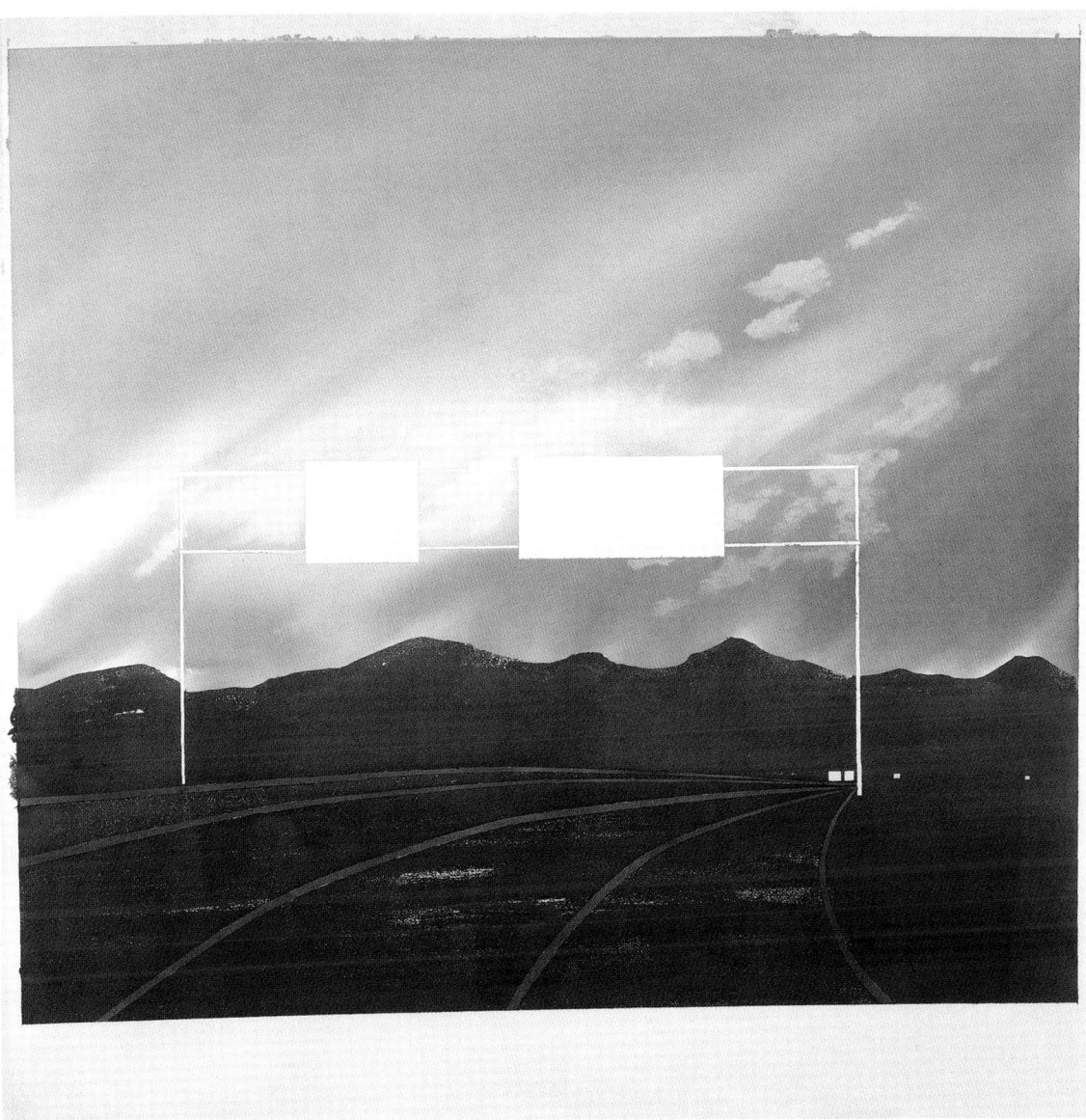

FIGURE 53. Alfred Leslie, *Holyoke Range, Near Oxbow, Easthampton, Massachusetts*, 1983, watercolor on paper. Collection of the artist

1. Erwin Panofsky, *The Life and Art of Albrecht Dürer* (Princeton: Princeton University Press, 1943 [1971 edition]), p. 59.

2. For the most complete discussion of Cole's drawings for the painting see Alan Wallach, "Making a Picture of the View from Mount Holyoke," *Bulletin of the Detroit Institute of Arts* 66 (1990), pp. 35–46, revised and reprinted in *American Iconology*, ed. David C. Miller (New Haven: Yale University Press, 1993). Oswaldo Rodriguez Roque lists all Cole's notations on his 1833 drawing in "*The Oxbow* by Thomas Cole: Iconography of an American Landscape Painting," *Metropolitan Museum Journal* 17 (1982), p. 65. For additional literature on the painting, see Susan Danly's endnote, no. 30.

3. Quoted in Roque, "*The Oxbow* by Thomas Cole," p. 64.

4. Quoted in David Graci, *Mt. Holyoke, An Enduring Prospect* (Holyoke: Calem Publishing, 1985), p. 9. Graci presents a full history of Mt. Holyoke's mountain house. On landscape tourism and Mt. Holyoke see also Wallach, "Making a Picture of the View from Mount Holyoke," pp. 35–37.

5. Timothy Dwight, *Travels in New-England and New-York*, 4 vols. (London: William Baynes and Son, 1823) I, p. 318, and II, pp. 314–15.

6. Theodore Dwight, *The Northern Traveller* (New York: A.T. Goodrich, 1826), p. 255.

7. Margaret Hunter Hall, *The Aristocratic Journey: Being the Outspoken Letters of Mrs. Basil Hall Written During a Fourteen Months' Sojourn in America 1827–1828*, ed. Una Pope-Hennessy (New York: G.P. Putnam's Sons, 1931), p. 80. Only a few published images of the Oxbow preceded Cole's painting. Theodore Dwight included a simplified rendering by C.H. Throop in *The Northern Traveller* in 1826, and Orra White Hitchcock drew the view as *West View from Holyoke*, plate V in Edward Hitchcock's *Report on the Geology, Mineralogy, Botany, and Zoology of Massachusetts* (Amherst: J.S. and C. Adams, 1833). Basil Hall illustrated it in *Forty Etchings, from Sketches Made with the Camera Lucida, in North America, in 1827 and 1828* (Edinburgh: Cadell and Co., 1829). Cole's tracing of Hall's etching is in the collection of the Detroit Institute of Arts. On the relation of Cole's painting to Hall's book, see Roque, "*The Oxbow* by Thomas Cole." Roque argues that Cole deliberately produced a grand rejoinder to Hall's negative remarks about America.

8. Dwight, *Travels*, II, p. 314.

9. The Manhan River, which flows into the Oxbow south of Hulbert's Pond, does not appear in Cole's painting.

10. The events are described in "More About the Freshet," *Hampshire Gazette*, March 4, 1840, p. 2. The author feared that should the Oxbow suffer future changes, "the Prospect from the summit of Mt. Holyoke will also be marred, for this graceful turn of the river afforded one of the most delightful scenes which met the eye, at that distinguished place of public resort."

11. Nathaniel P. Willis, *American Scenery* (London: George Virtue, 1840). The volume was published in either 1838 or 1840; it is traditionally cited as 1840.

12. On the painting's provenance see Roque, "*The Oxbow* by Thomas Cole," p. 63, note 1, and A.T. Gardner and S.P. Feld, *American Paintings: A Catalogue of the Collection of the Metropolitan Museum of Art* vol. I (New York: Metropolitan Museum of Art, 1985), p. 229.

13. In *The Connecticut Valley*, a second view of the Oxbow from Mt. Holyoke in the collection of the National Gallery of Art (illustrated in Deborah Chotner, *American Naïve Painting* [Washington: National Gallery of Art and Cambridge University Press, 1992], p. 50), Chambers further simplified his decorative mountain and river forms but rendered the river's post-1840 configuration. He may have based this painting on the reworked Bartlett print published in Edward Hitchcock's *Final Report on the Geology of Massachusetts* (Northampton: J.H. Butler, 1841), vol. 2, plate 2 (see fig. 2).

14. See Sheree Jaros, "The View from Mt. Holyoke," *Arcadian Vales, Views of the Connecticut River Valley*, ed. Martha Hoppin (Springfield: George Walter Vincent Smith Art Museum, 1982), pp. 53–59, and her catalogue entry, Ibid., pp. 73–74. See also William N. Banks, "The French Painter Victor de Grailly and the Production of American Views," *Antiques* 106 (July 1974), pp. 89–90; and "*West Point*: A Painting in Context," *The Register* 5 (Lawrence: Museum of Art, University of Kansas, 1976), p. 52.

15. Wrongly titled as views of the Oxbow, they include: *The Oxbow of the Connecticut River at Northampton*, dated 1864, offered by Sotheby-Parke-Bernet, Los Angeles, March 4–5, 1974; *The Oxbow on the Connecticut River*, dated 1852, at Berry-Hill Galleries in the 1970s; and *The Oxbow*, ca. 1855–59, auctioned at Christie's, May 22, 1991. Coates also painted views of Mt. Tom based on Bartlett's engraving.

16. See, for example, *The Valley of the Connecticut* by an unknown artist illustrated in *Arcadian Vales*, p. 57.

17. Gifford and Cropsey signed the mountain house register (Historic Northampton) on July 7, 1853. William S. Talbot reproduced Cropsey's account book in *Jasper F. Cropsey, 1823–1900* (New York and London: Garland Publishing, 1977). The account book lists the sale of two paintings titled *Connecticut River Scenery* in 1858 and a third one in 1863. One of these brought a sufficiently high enough price ($500) to have been fairly large.

18. T. Addison Richards, "The Valley of the Connecticut," *Harper's Monthly* 8 (August 1856), p. 294, illustrations pp. 289, 290.

19. *Boston Post*, April 26, 1850; *Boston Courier*, May 11, 1850. Calyo signed the Mt. Holyoke mountain house register (Historic Northampton) on August 2, 1848. The panorama rolled across the stage, allowing only sections of it to be visible at one time. For a fuller discussion, see Martha Hoppin, "Arcadian Vales: The Connecticut Valley in Art," in *Arcadian Vales*, pp. 40–41.

20. The painting was shown at the American Art Union in 1847. See Mary Bartlett Cowdrey, *American Academy of Fine Arts and American Art Union: Exhibition Record, 1816–1852* (New York: New-York Historical Society, 1953).

21. For example, Oliver Larkin, *Art and Life in America* (New York: Holt, Rinehart, and Winston, 1949), p. 202; Richard McLanathan, *The American Tradition in the Arts* (New York: Harcourt, Brace, & World, 1968), p. 243; Barbara Novak, *American Painting of the Nineteenth Century* (New York: Praeger, 1969), p. 76; Matthew Baigell, *A History of American Painting* (New York: Praeger, 1971), p. 114; Daniel Mendelowitz, *A History of American Art* (New York: Holt, Rinehard, and Winston, second edition 1973), p. 203; John Wilmerding, *American Art* (New York: Penguin, 1976), fig. 93; and Wayne Craven, *American Art and Culture* (New York: Abrams, 1994), p. 202.

22. For example, see Craven, *American Art*, p. 202.

23. Wallach, "Making a Picture of the View from Mount Holyoke, p. 42; Roque, *"The Oxbow by Thomas Cole,"* p. 63; John Driscoll, *The Artist and the American Landscape* (Cobb, CA: First Glance Books, 1998), p. 9.

24. William Cronon in "Telling Tales on Canvas: Landscapes of Frontier Change," *Discovered Lands, Invented Pasts* (New Haven and London: Yale University Press, 1992), pp. 40–44, and Angela Miller in *The Empire of the Eye, Landscape Representation and American Cultural Politics, 1825–1875* (Ithaca: Cornell University Press, 1994), pp. 39–49, discuss Cole's attitude toward progress and conclude that in *The Oxbow* Cole condensed into one canvas the first two paintings of his five-part series, *The Course of Empire*, which move from wilderness to Arcadia. See also Alan Wallach, "Thomas Cole, Landscape and the Course of American Empire," *Thomas Cole, Landscape Into History*, ed. William H. Truettner and Alan Wallach (New Haven: Yale University Press, 1994), pp. 76–77; Roque, *"The Oxbow by Thomas Cole"*; Matthew Baigell and Allen Kaufman, "Thomas Cole's 'The Oxbow': A Critique of American Civilization," *Arts Magazine* 55 (January 1981), pp. 136–39; and Albert Boime, *The Magisterial Gaze, Manifest Destiny and American Landscape Painting c. 1830–1865* (Washington and London: Smithsonian Institution Press, 1991), pp. 48–57.

25. All quotations by the artist were drawn from the author's conversations with him in June 1981 and January 2002.

26. *Hampshire Gazette* (June 9, 1841), p. 3.

27. The others are in the Museum of Fine Arts, Boston, illustrated in Duncan Christy, *Luminosity: The Paintings of Stephen Hannock* (San Francisco: Chronicle Books, 2000), plate 18; the Houston Museum of Fine Arts; the Metropolitan Museum of Art; and three private collections, two of which are illustrated in *Luminosity*, plates 19 and 20, and the third in Robert Atkins, *Stephen Hannock* (New York: James Graham & Sons, 1996), fig. 13. A finished study for the Smith College painting (24 x 36 inches) in the collection of the artist is illustrated in John Arthur, *Green Woods & Crystal Waters: The American Landscape Tradition (*Tulsa: Philbrook Museum of Art, 1999), p. 144.

28. Quoted in Christy, *Luminosity*, p. 17.

29. Ibid.

30. Hannock referred in his title, *After Church, After Cole,* to a specific painting, *The Ox-bow,* a view from Mt. Holyoke once thought to be by Church (illustrated in John Wilmerding, *American Light, The Luminist Movement 1850–1875* (Washington, DC: National Gallery of Art, 1980), p. 30, but painted after Bartlett, not Cole. Hannock wrote on his 2001 painting in the Metropolitan Museum of Art, *The Oxbow: After Church, After Cole, Flooded (Flooded River for the Matriarchs E. & A. Mongan), Green Light:* "The concept of Church after Cole for this specific piece is not true. The student painting of the Oxbow attributed to Church was not by him after all. It really does suck...." He continues to include Church's name in the titles of his Oxbow paintings to refer broadly to the Hudson River School.

31. Quoted in Christy, *Luminosity*, p. 16.

32. For a full discussion of Hannock's technique, see Christy, *Luminosity*, pp. 11–15.

33. McGurl joined with Donald Demers and William R. Davis to form the "New American Luminist" group in 1998. See Julian Baird, *The New American Luminists, Landscape as Sacred Space* (Orleans, MA: Tree's Place Gallery, 2000).

34. Quoted in Julian Baird, *The New American Luminists Revisit the Native Landscape* (Orleans, MA: Tree's Place Gallery, 1998), p. 2.

35. Richard Crozier with Thomas Bolt, *Inventing the Landscape* (New York: Watson-Guptill, 1989), p. 141.

36. Ibid., p. 107.

37. Author's conversations with the artist, January 2002.

38. Crozier, *Inventing the Landscape*, p. 107.

39. Ibid., p. 143. All three are illustrated in Bolt, *Inventing the Landscape*, pp. 8–9, 108–9, 142–43.

40. All quotations by Osman from the author's conversation with the artist, December 2001.

41. All quotations by Armstrong from the author's conversations with the artist, October 2001.

42. Author's conversation with the artist, January 2002.

43. Ibid.

44. Matthew Baigell and Allen Kaufman detect the Hebrew words "Shaddai" or "Noah" written on the large hill in the distance. See their article, "Thomas Cole's 'The Oxbow': A Critique of American Civilization," pp. 136–39.

45. All quotations by Moriarty from the author's conversations with the artist, January 2002.

46. All quotations by Winn from the author's conversations with the artist, December 2001 and January 2002. I thank John Arthur for calling my attention to Winn's painting. Arthur helped arrange the commission and accompanied the artist on a trip up the mountain. He discusses Winn in *Green Woods & Crystal Waters*, p. 129.

47. *An Higher View* is illustrated in Martha Hoppin, *The Search for Light, Landscape Paintings by Lewis Bryden* (Northampton: R. Michelson Galleries, 2001), p. 4, as is *View of the Marina*, his painting of the Oxbow from Mt. Tom, p. 12.

48. Lewis Bryden, statement for R. Michelson Galleries, Northampton, 2001.

49. See Hoppin, *Arcadian Vales*, p. 43, for a discussion of Nichols and an illustration of his unlocated painting *Mt. Holyoke*, a view from the slopes of Mt. Tom above the south arm of the Oxbow showing the railroad's path and covered bridge.

50. Notices in the *Hampshire Gazette*, September 26, 1865, and *Northampton Free Press*, October 13, 1865, indicate that Farrer exhibited in Northampton a number of paintings of the area, but few are known today. In addition to *Mount Holyoke*, these include *View of Northampton from the Dome of the Hospital* (Smith College Museum of Art) and *Mount Tom* (private collection). Both are illustrated in Linda Ferber and William H. Gerdts, *The New Path: Ruskin and the American Pre-Raphaelites* (New York: The Brooklyn Museum, 1985), pp. 164–65. Gina Greer and Andrea Smith, *American Paintings 1860–1940* (New York: Vance Jordan Fine Art, 2000), p. 46, suggest that Farrer intended this painting of Mt. Holyoke as a companion piece to his view of Mt. Tom. Farrer also exhibited an unlocated watercolor, *Mt. Holyoke at Sunset*, in the 1867–68 annual exhibition of the American Society of Painters in Water Colors (see James Yarnall and William H. Gerdts, *The National Museum of American Art's Index to American Art Exhibition Catalogues From the Beginning through the 1876 Centennial Year* [Boston: G.K. Hall, 1986], p. 1220).

51. Author's conversation with the artist, December 2001.

52. Alfred Leslie, *100 Views Along the Road* (New York: Timken Publishers, 1988).

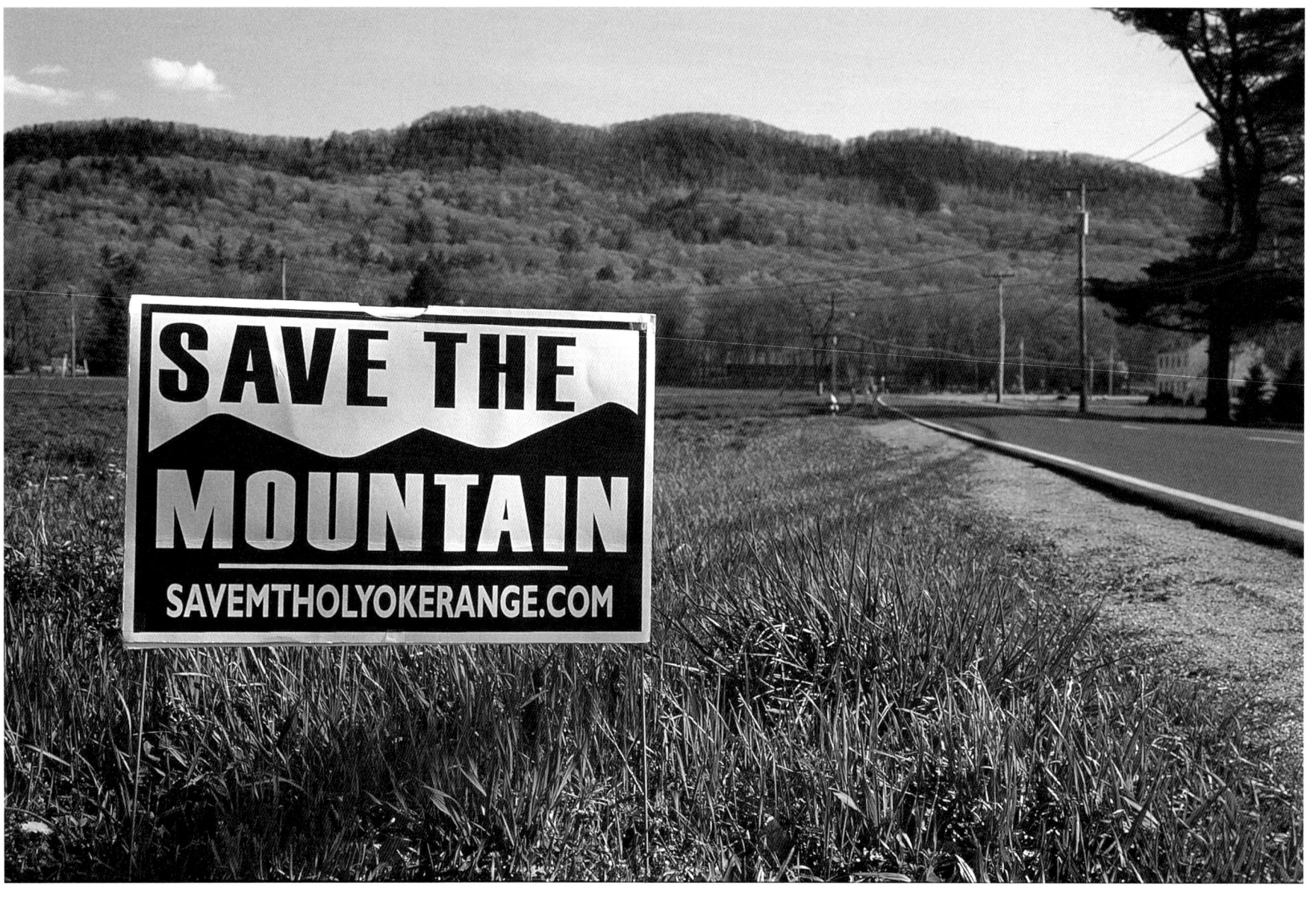

FIGURE 54. Allison Bell, *Save the Mountain Sign*, 2002, gelatin silver print photograph. Collection of the artist (not in exhibition)

Preserving Mount Holyoke

Ethan Carr

After 100 years as the cynosure of tourism and scenic sensibility in the Connecticut River Valley, Mt. Holyoke remained central to the formation of fresh concepts of regional identity and natural beauty in the twentieth century. If the Summit House itself suffered a period of neglect, Mt. Holyoke was more visited than ever, as the post–World War II interest in outdoor recreation swelled into the backpack boom of the 1960s and 1970s.[1] This new and numerous public (and the mountain was a public park after 1940) inevitably reinvented its mountain, even as the Summit House itself declined. State park officials and federal recreation planners often failed to appreciate the value of the old hotel and tramway. These vestiges of nineteenth-century tourism did not easily find a place in postwar models for managing "natural" landscapes, and only gradually were they recognized as significant historic resources in their own right.

In the 1960s and early 1970s, the Mt. Holyoke Range became the subject of ambitious "national recreation area" schemes that called for extensive acquisition and management of land but offered little vision of how the Summit House could be adapted for a new generation of visitors. Eventually it was not the federal government, but area residents, historical societies, preservation advocates, and property owners who provided the impetus and creativity necessary to save the structure. Over the last twenty years, in collaboration with state and local governments, they have defined the appropriate preservation of the hotel and the Mt. Holyoke Range itself. This flexible and responsive partnership approach has featured a wide range of participants and strategies — as well as successes and failures — and continues to the present day.

The changes that the twentieth century brought to Mt. Holyoke extended and altered aspects of earlier ideas and imagery of the region. Appreciation of the Connecticut River Valley landscape had been guided since the late eighteenth century by the notion of an "American arcadia."[2] The compositions of nineteenth-century painters and engravers, as numerous historians have suggested, reflected the larger balance of a landscape composed of rich agricultural lands framed by forested hillsides and rock ledges. But this delicate balance of land uses shifted in the second half of the nineteenth century when regional manufacturing increased and the relative economic importance of farming declined. New England industrial towns grew quickly, even as much farmland was abandoned, creating a stronger and in some ways more hostile contrast between what was increasingly seen as "Man and Nature." In his 1864 book of that title, George Perkins Marsh observed that arcadia had also featured an insatiable appetite for resources that now threatened the destruction of society as well as nature. The harmonious balance rendered by Thomas Cole had been shifted, probably disastrously, by the relentless advance of modernization. By the 1870s, a movement to salvage and regenerate the nation's remaining forests indicated a broad desire for forest conservation, which in itself belied the pastoral ideal of a benign human presence in the landscape.[3] By the end of the century, the arcadian prospect from Mt. Holyoke had become more difficult to apprehend. Although much of agricultural New England began to be reforested through succession, the reality of mill towns, industry, and the shifting economics of agriculture presented a new landscape that opposed and contrasted a threatened nature with the spreading effects of industrialization and population growth.

Shifting perceptions of landscape inevitably guided how Mt. Holyoke was seen and managed in the twentieth century. Mountain houses (epitomized by the 1823 Catskill Mountain House, the

1851 Mt. Holyoke Summit House, and the 1853 Tip Top House on Mt. Washington) had been a popular sensation, linked to the contemporary, thriving market in Hudson River School imagery. Changing tastes and patterns in public recreation eroded the popularity of both phenomena in the twentieth century. In the years immediately before and after World War I, motor vehicles rapidly eclipsed trains, river launches (and even dramatic inclined and cog railways) as the preferred means of accessing and enjoying scenery. The new form of transportation directly affected the profitability of many older resorts. Visiting scenic areas by rail and steam launch, nineteenth-century tourists were the paying customers of railroad and hotel entrepreneurs, who might also provide livery services and even handle the logistics of elevating their clients to their hotels. Automotive tourists not only moved themselves, but also showed a tendency to care for themselves as well, either by camping or finding less expensive and more convenient (roadside) accommodations. Their machines allowed the pleasure of visiting mountaintops as part of a scenic drive, and their mobility soon spelled difficulties for businesses that depended on a more captive group of patrons.

More significantly, automotive tourists were not customers at all. They were the "public," in the same sense that the people who used urban public parks in the nineteenth century had been. Automobiles encouraged expanding the concept of the public park — supported with public funds and administered by a park commission — to regional, state, and national level by giving the general public (defined, of course, mainly as the middle class) more affordable and pervasive mobility. Once scenic areas were more accessible, they could be transformed into public places, in this specific sense. Hundreds of county, state, and national parks were established in the early twentieth century, and almost all were developed (or redeveloped) for improved automobile access with scenic drives, picnic areas, campgrounds, and new

"rustic" lodges and museums. While dozens of mountain houses built on northeastern mountaintops in the nineteenth century declined, new regional and state parks flourished and were visited by millions in the early twentieth century.[4]

Early Preservation Efforts Massachusetts was a particularly important center for developing new types of twentieth-century regional landscape reservations. Mt. Greylock State Reservation, the first of its type in the Commonwealth, was established in 1898. Wachusett State Reservation followed the next year.[5] In 1900 landscape architect Charles Eliot began the campaign to pass state legislation that established the Trustees of Reservations in 1901, an unprecedented private land trust that facilitated the preservation of threatened areas. That same year, Eliot and other advocates again convinced the state legislature to take an unprecedented step in land preservation by creating the Metropolitan District Commission. This regional park commission acquired and developed a system of what Eliot called "scenic reservations" in Boston's suburbs.[6]

In the Connecticut River Valley as well, concerned citizens had organized to preserve threatened scenery by 1900. That year Christopher Clarke, a successful businessman and music promoter in Northampton, organized a campaign to have Mt. Tom established as a state reservation. (Clarke had been responsible for bringing Swedish soprano Jenny Lind to Northampton for a concert in 1851. During her stay she visited Mt. Holyoke.) His prodigious efforts to organize support for public ownership of scenic areas around Northampton bore fruit in 1903 and 1906, when Mt. Tom and Mt. Sugarloaf, respectively, were brought into the state reservation system.[7]

Clarke next turned his attention to Mt. Holyoke. John Dwight, owner of the Summit House, died in 1903, and his heirs put the old hotel and its surrounding 256 acres up for sale in 1905. After three years on the market, it was evident that the business was not considered a lucrative opportunity; nor had the state or county governments moved to acquire the property to expand the state's underfinanced and fledgling reservation system. In 1908 Clarke joined a group of like-minded businessmen

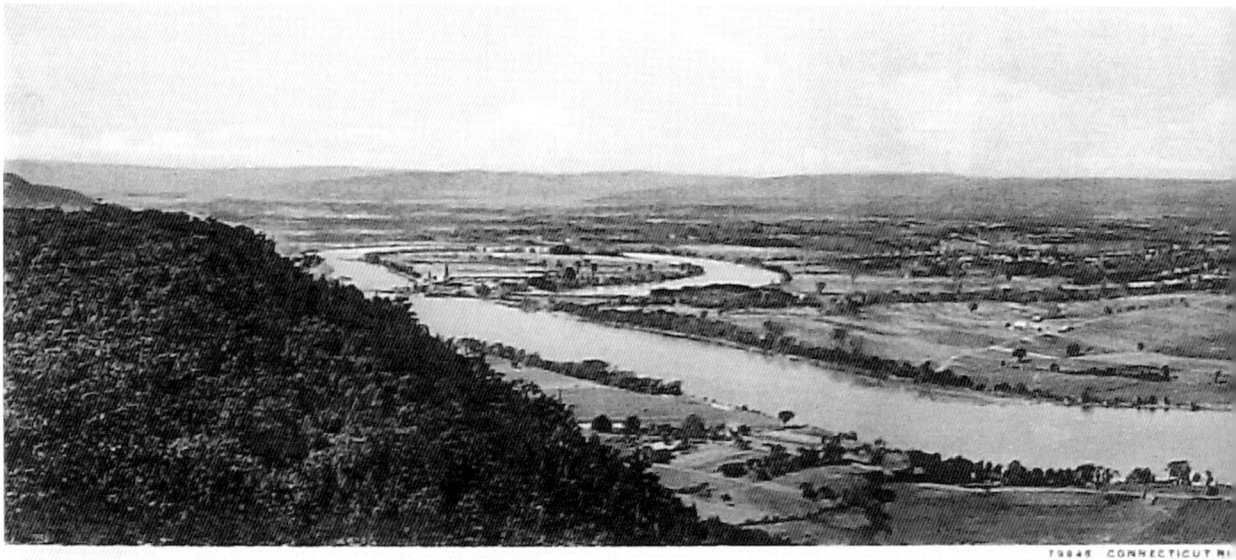

T9848 CONNECTICUT RI

and preservationists to form a corporation, the Mt. Holyoke Company, to acquire the Summit House property in order to prevent the destruction of the hotel and its surrounding forest and to modernize the resort for twentieth-century tourism. John Dwight's heirs contributed to this largely altruistic enterprise by accepting $25,000 of the company's stock as payment, a sum considered a fraction of the property's actual value.

From the outset, the company's owners, most of whom Clarke had personally recruited, were clear that their goal was, according to the *Daily Hampshire Gazette*, to "preserve the mountain with its natural beauties and furnish attractive accommodations for those wishing to visit it." They were also clear about what this would require: the construction of a (very expensive) road to the summit for automobile access. The "antique cable railway" would "probably be removed," and a garage as well as a stable would be located on top of the mountain. Besides issuing stock to the Dwight heirs, the company sold an additional $23,000 in stock in 1908 and immediately set about the construction of the new road.[8]

The inclined railroad continued to be operated as part of the hotel business (except for the 1908 season when the owners closed it), but the Mt. Holyoke Company's investment priorities clearly lay with improving access by road. Although the new summit road featured a maximum grade of ten percent, the company's directors were nevertheless dissatisfied and rebuilt it the following summer. In 1910 the road from Hockanum Ferry to the Half-way House was also rebuilt and macadamized.[9] From the beginning Clarke and the Mt. Holyoke Company's directors also shared the not unrelated vision of eventually making Mt. Holyoke a truly "public reservation" by having the state of Massachusetts assume ownership. Clarke died in 1915, but not before launching the next phase in the campaign to preserve Mt. Holyoke. In 1914 the state legislature had created a State Forest Commission empowered to buy cutover logging lands and establish forest reservations. Clarke quickly convinced the new commission that Mt. Holyoke should become such a reservation. He then lobbied the legislature to buy out the Mt. Holyoke Company for $50,000, consider-

ably less than the company had already invested in the property. Clarke did not emphasize the property's forest resources in his appeal but rather focused on its potential for public recreation, including the "fine new automobile road."[10]

The next year Frank W. Rane, a state forester, prepared a glowing report on the potential of Mt. Holyoke as a public park, noting that it was "not merely a forestry" issue, but a question of "preserving for all time to the state a beautiful spot." Rane recommended acquiring the property and dedicating it to Christopher Clarke. He also noted, however, that both Hadley and South Hadley were opposed to having the property removed from the tax roles, and that the nearby reservation at Mt. Tom made another park seem unnecessary to many.[11] Indeed the state legislature quickly rejected the proposal.

With Clarke now gone and the state in no mood to buy out the Mt. Holyoke Company, its owners convened to decide how to proceed. The company had never made money, but the goal of preserving the property remained. None of the stockholders was more committed to that goal

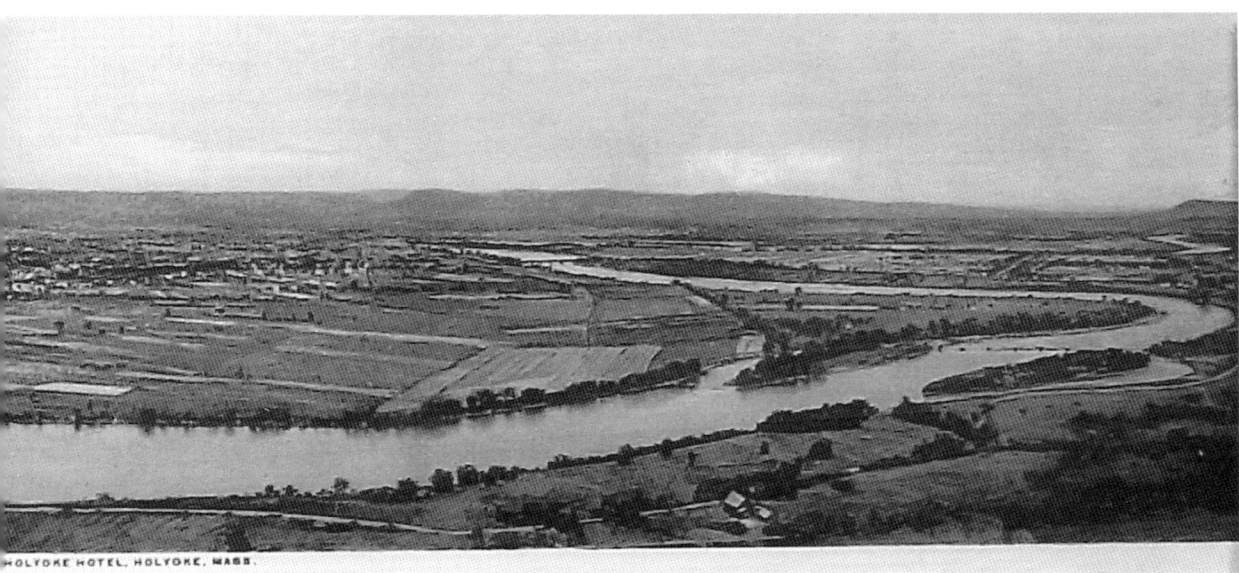

FIGURE 55. Detroit Publishing Company, *Connecticut River from Mt. Holyoke Hotel*, ca. 1903, panoramic postcard. The Florence History Project, Florence, Massachusetts

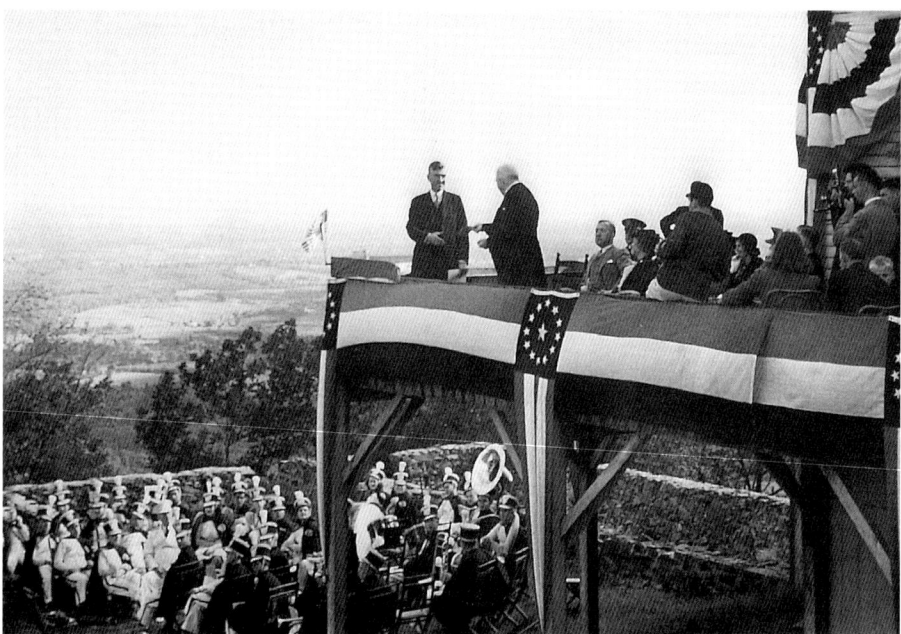

than Joseph Allen Skinner, a wealthy silk manufacturer from Holyoke, who had already served as the first president of the company between 1908 and 1910. In December of 1916 he bought out his fellow stockholders for $50,000 and became the sole owner of Mt. Holyoke and its hotel. In the coming decades Skinner served as a worthy curator of the property. On the one hand he continued to explore the possibilities of state acquisition; on the other he invested generously in improvements.

Following the advice of foresters, he logged stands of blighted chestnut (while they still had commercial value) and planted thousands of white pines in their place. The hotel was modernized with plumbing and electrical service, new rooms, and improved management. In 1927 the inclined railroad was converted from steam to electric power, and the automobile road was improved and straightened as well. Skinner seemed determined that the Summit House would survive the transition to the twentieth century, even as other northeastern mountain houses were headed into decline and disappearing.[12]

Skinner also never gave up Clarke's idea of seeing the property pass into public ownership and management. In 1919 the Massachusetts State Forest Commission was reorganized as the Department of Conservation, indicating a broader approach to land preservation by the state. By 1929 the department had acquired 100,000 acres of forests as well as some important automotive tourist destinations, such as the Mohawk Trail and Windsor state forests. Most of these state lands, however, remained largely undeveloped for recreation until 1933 when Franklin D. Roosevelt's creation of the Civilian Conservation Corps (CCC) launched the entire nation on an unprecedented era of state and national park making. FDR's "tree army" initially stressed forestry and natural resource management; but the ability of the well-supervised crews of young men to build roads, overlooks, lakes, bathhouses, and other recreational facilities soon became clear. In Massachusetts, as in most states, CCC construction established a legacy of recreational facilities that even today defines the core of the state park system.[13]

But while the CCC made improvements at nearby Mt. Tom and Mt. Sugar Loaf, Mt. Holyoke remained in private hands through the 1930s and, therefore, missed an important period of federal largesse in park development. This was due in part, ironically, to Joseph Skinner's extraordinary efforts to keep the Summit House economically viable and in good condition. During this time Massachusetts was eagerly identifying properties for acquisition as state parks, since the CCC and other federal programs would pay for their development. In 1934 a proposal to acquire Mt. Holyoke began to work its way through the state legislature. The legislation called for a new park covering 800 acres of the Mt. Holyoke Range (including Skinner's property) as a memorial to Calvin Coolidge (although local newspapers recalled that it was the venerable Christopher Clarke who had first envisioned such a preserve twenty-five years earlier).[14]

The plan was backed by the Department of Conservation, the agency coordinating most CCC and other park developments in the state. By 1936 the department and the Massachusetts State Planning Board were collaborating with the National Park Service to produce a statewide park and parkway plan that included recommendations for many acquisitions.[15] That year the Massachusetts legislature also authorized funds for the purchase of 500,000 acres of new forests to be identified by the Department of Conservation and the State Planning Board and then developed with federal funds and CCC labor. The proposal for an 800-acre park on the Mt. Holyoke Range soon made it to the floor of the legislature and began to be seriously debated. Many of the old arguments (such as loss of tax revenue) resurfaced, but clearly there was a more favorable reception of the idea than Clarke and Skinner had received in 1915.[16]

Although the Department of Conservation was in favor of a new Mt. Holyoke park, the agency recoiled at the idea of maintaining and operating the Summit House, which it saw as merely an eighty-five-year-old wooden hotel (rather than an historic resource) that would almost certainly require an enormous budget to maintain. Conservation Commissioner Ernest J. Dean made these concerns clear in 1937, when he enthusiastically endorsed buying the land but insisted that the "acquisition of a hotel and its operation is not . . . to be considered as a proper function of this department." State ownership would mean demolishing most of the hotel and ending its commercial operation. While perhaps the oldest (1851) portion of the hotel would be preserved for its historical interest, even this would depend on supplemental appropriations. The "disposal of [the] hotel on [the] summit," reported the *Springfield Union*, was Commissioner Dean's "only problem" with establishing the new park.[17] This attitude would only harden and, indeed, continue into the post-World War II era. The management of natural resources reached new levels of professionalism during the New Deal, typically in reorganized state departments of "conservation" or "natural resources." Still these agencies usually emphasized the acquisition of land, the management of natural resources, and planning for public "outdoor recreation." Historic buildings in an otherwise "natural" setting often simply did not fit into state (or federal) land management plans or budgets.

Sentiment in favor of making Mt. Holyoke a park, however, ran high at a series of public meetings in 1936 and 1937. Commissioner Dean confessed that he "had never been so swamped with letters" in favor of a park proposal, and he gave the plan his nominal support. A large delegation of western Massachusetts citizens, representing mainly business interests and civic groups, traveled to Boston to lobby for the purchase and stressed the economic importance of tourism to the region. In fact the only "real opposition," according to the *Springfield Union*, was from a small group of "Hadley farmers," some of whom apparently owned wood lots on the mountain. Although Commis-

sioner Dean and the Department of Conservation could have chosen to prioritize the purchase of Mt. Holyoke at this time, they did not. In a report to the legislature in 1937, Dean specified that it was desirable only if "a satisfactory solution can be determined upon regarding . . . the hotel situated on the summit of the mountain." That December Skinner even lowered his asking price to $30,000; but money had never been the issue. Commissioner Dean responded again by saying that his agency would not recommend acquisition until the legislature made additional appropriations specifically for the maintenance and operation of the hotel.[18]

The hurricane that devastated so much of New England in September 1938 almost solved the problem. The large 1894 addition to the Summit House was so badly damaged that Skinner decided to demolish it, with the knowledge, of course, that the state had already promised to tear down at least that portion of the building if they ever took over the property. After razing three quarters of his hotel, Skinner offered the state the entire parcel as a gift. Finally, in June 1940, the state accepted the gift which, on Skinner's request, would be named Joseph Allen Skinner State Park.[19]

A dedication ceremony was held in September, with Skinner and many other figures who played prominently in the history of the Summit House in attendance, to hear Governor Leverett Saltonstall speak on the "solemn duty of conservation" (figure 56). Raymond J. Kenney, the new conservation commissioner, announced that he hoped the CCC would be able to develop the park and build a stone museum on the summit. His parks director, Edgar L. Gillett, specified that although "plans had been drawn up" for such a stone structure to replace the Summit House, they had been changed in response to "public sentiment." The old hotel, he said, would not be razed. It remained unclear, however, what plans (if any) the state did have for it.[20] In any case, Congress discontinued the CCC early in 1942, before a new camp could be established to begin work at Skinner State Park.

Mt. Holyoke was finally a public park, but World War II, followed by the Cold War years, kept park budgets meager in Massachusetts as in the rest of the country. David Graci, the most important historian of Mt. Holyoke, refers to the next forty years as a period of steady decline for the Summit House, in which it experienced "yet another threat to its very existence . . . neglect."[21] In 1942 the electric motor for the inclined railroad burned out, never to operate again, and during the war the number of visitors went down. But the postwar years saw an almost immediate spike in visitation to Mt. Holyoke, a phenomenon familiar to state and national park managers all over the country. In 1934 Skinner had reported about 3,000 visitors, increasing to 5,200 in 1936. In 1947 the number

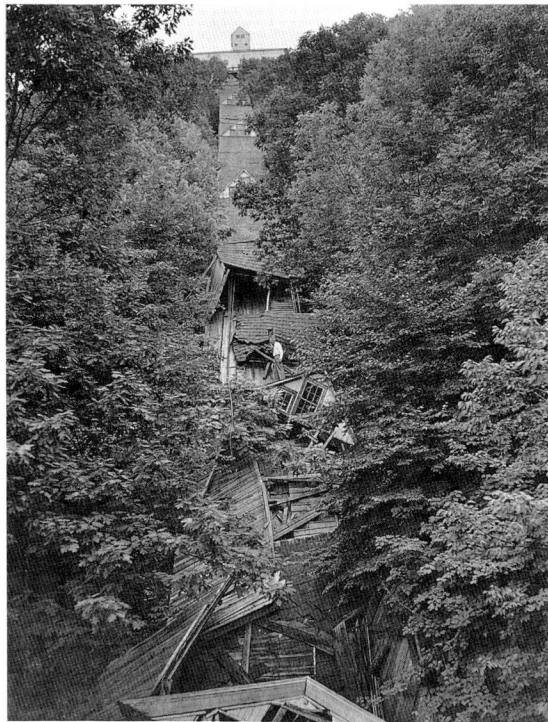

FIGURE 57. Raymond D'Addario, *Tramway Damaged by Snow in 1948*, ca. 1949, gelatin silver print photograph. Collection of the artist (not in exhibition)

was well over twice that, and every year set a new record: more than 12,000 in 1953, beyond 13,000 in 1954.[22] But low park budgets continued during these years of "wartime" priorities that emphasized defense spending and highway construction. Under a reduced maintenance budget the Department of Conservation, as it had feared, could do little except watch the Summit House deteriorate, despite increased visitation.

The one thing state park managers were willing to do was make road improvements and enlarge parking areas, desperately needed improvements since the inclined railroad was now inoperable. But rather than attempt to restore rail service up the mountain, in 1947 A.K. Sloper, the new conservation commissioner, announced that the tramway would be demolished and sold for scrap. "It has been the policy of this department," he explained, "to remove . . . any structure which is no longer usable, especially if the expenditure of state funds is required annually for its maintenance."[23] The inclined railroad subsequently became the center of a long struggle between local preservationists and the state of Massachusetts over what place and role, if any, historic structures should have in the new state park.

The response to Sloper's plans indicated that the Summit House had a fiercely loyal constituency, including the Pioneer Valley Association, a Northampton civic group that represented hundreds of local businesses and other commercial interests. One businessman, Roger Johnson, had grown up in Hockanum where his father, Clifton Johnson, had been a renowned author, painter, and photographer. The younger Johnson, acting on behalf of the Pioneer Valley Association, organized a public relations and lobbying campaign to persuade the state legislature to repair the Mt. Holyoke railroad rather than demolish it. In a furious response to Sloper (which was widely reported in area newspapers), Johnson pointed out that the railroad was in better condition than had been suggested, and that in any case it was the only

responsible means for alleviating the "dangerous" traffic situation at the Summit House. The "only covered funicular in the world," the tramway also was beloved by the majority of park visitors, who were awaiting its repair. "It is ridiculous for you to conclude," Johnson insisted, "that because it needs a few minor repairs it should be torn down."[24]

Newspapers soon reported on the "battle" to save the historic cable railroad, but Johnson suffered a setback that winter when heavy snow caused a portion of the shed covering the length of the tracks to collapse. Undeterred, Johnson managed to secure (he thought) a $20,000 appropriation from the state legislature in 1949 for repairs to begin the next year. But in what would prove to be a pattern, apparent success in the legislature never resulted in the Department of Conservation receiving or using the funds as intended. By 1951, the Summit House's centennial year, still no work had been done, although upgrades to the road and parking facilities continued. Over the next several years, as Johnson built public support and assembled estimates for the work, the Department of Conservation continued to delay. In 1953, when the estimated cost of repairs had swollen to $70,000, the directors of the Pioneer Valley Association gave up their campaign. The Department of Conservation redirected the (inadequate) funds that Johnson had already secured for the railroad to make additional improvements to the summit road and parking areas. The remains of the unique covered tramway were finally intentionally burned by the state in 1965.[25]

By the mid-1950s, concern shifted to the preservation of the Summit House itself, which according to newspaper reports was a "shambles" because "not a nickel had been spent" by the state on its upkeep, despite continued record numbers of visitors (15,000 in 1955).[26] Then in 1956, remarkably, State Senators Ralph A. Mahar and Maurice A. Donahue filed a joint bill requesting $850,000 for the restoration of the Summit House and the inclined railroad. Francis W. Sargent

(later governor), the new commissioner of the Department of Natural Resources (formerly the Department of Conservation), took on the project as one of his first priorities.

Boston architect Andrew H. Hepburn (of Perry, Shaw, Hepburn, Kehoe and Dean), who had been a central figure in the restoration of Colonial Williamsburg, was retained to develop the proposal and scope of work. For the next two years he worked on what proved to be an elaborate proposal for the complete redevelopment of Mt. Holyoke. The plan called for a new restaurant that would "preserve the historic value" of the Summit House by encapsulating the old lobby and the "Jenny Lind Room" within a larger structure. The inclined railroad, defunct and abandoned, would be completely rebuilt in a new, modernized form. After years of total neglect, the state had now proposed an almost fantastic redevelopment scheme that would replace one landmark with (they hoped) another. By 1957 newspapers reported that the "historic prospect house [was] again making headlines" as the ambitious proposal caught the public's imagination. Most remarkable of all, the state legislature passed a measure apparently authorizing the $850,000 expenditure, which Governor Foster Furcolo signed that August.[27] Just a few years earlier, Roger Johnson had been denied even the modest funding necessary to repair the tramway.

The Boston architects went to work in earnest and the next summer proposed an elegant, modernistic design for a large restaurant with a circular observation terrace and windows looking out on the valley. Presented as a model to the Department of Natural Resources and the public, it featured a second level above the restaurant with a public area, offices, and smaller circular terrace directly above the restaurant terrace. The building could best be described as an example of contemporary modernism adapted to a more "rustic" setting, mainly through horizontal massing and extensive stone cladding. The parts of the old hotel that had been incorporated were not readily

FIGURE 58. *The Case of the Holyoke Range . . . and A Proposal*, brochure, 1962. Collection of Charles M. and Dorothy A. Johnson. Cover image shows spreading gravel pit on north face of Holyoke Range. (not in exhibition)

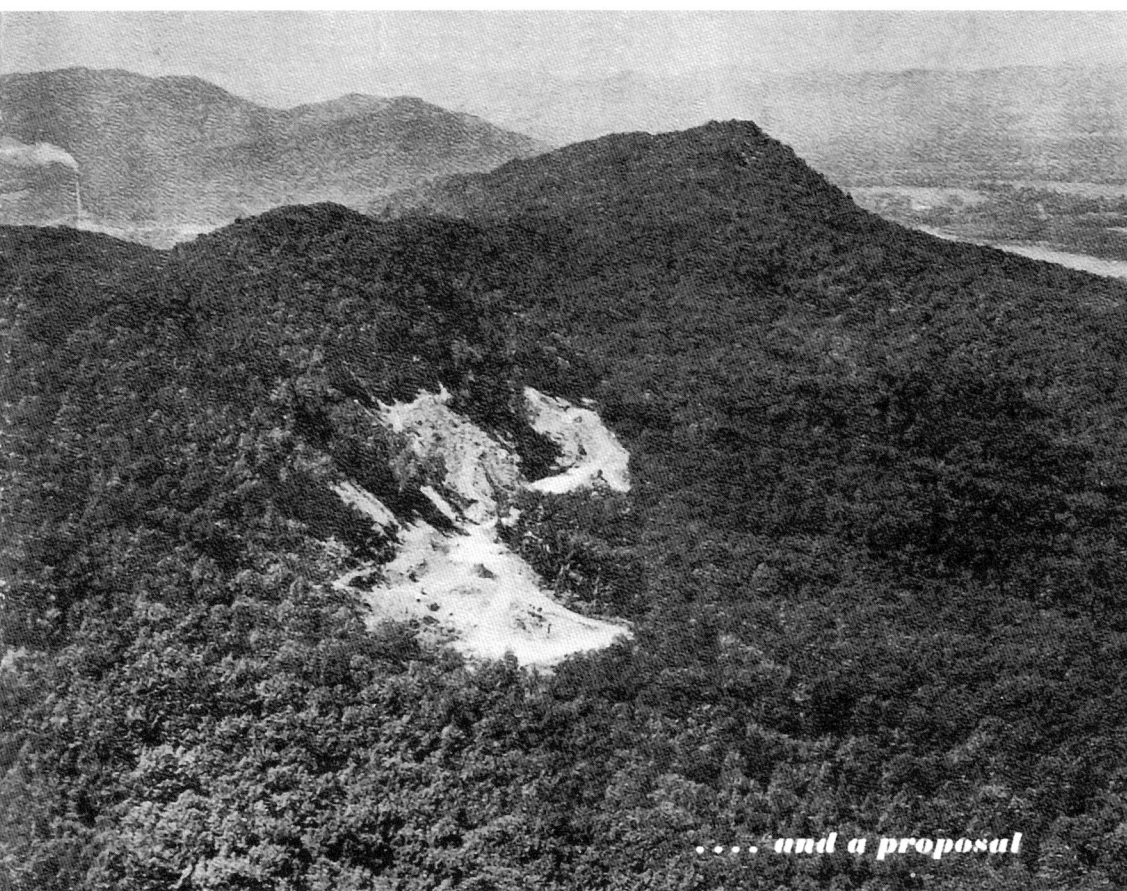

.... *and a proposal*

discernable from the exterior; but a new tramway led directly into the structure's public lobby — a unique arrangement that Hepburn revived for its particular "historical value."[28] The total cost of the building and railroad was now estimated to be one million dollars. Almost immediately it became clear that the funding was in trouble. The "measure" passed a year earlier had only authorized a bond sale, which now was unlikely to be made because of the high cost of the building. To make matters worse, $50,000 that had been appropriated for desperately needed repairs to the Summit House had been spent on the architects' fees. The unlikely proposal seems to have evaporated as quickly as it had surfaced.[29]

A New Preservation Battle

The entire movement to "preserve" Mt. Holyoke was about to take an entirely new turn, in any case. Increased numbers of visitors to the mountain in the postwar era reflected the popularity of new kinds of outdoor leisure activities, such as hiking, pursued by a new generation of the "public" who would soon begin to express their own concerns and values. And while the fate of the Summit House continued to trouble many, there were other threats to the Mt. Holyoke Range taking shape that had the potential for destroying more than just one building. In 1954, for example, the B&M Construction Company opened a gravel quarry off Route 47. Other traprock quarries soon sprang up on the Mt. Holyoke Range.[30] At the same time, the Metacomet-Monadnock (M&M) Trail was being surveyed and constructed by hikers.[31] The boom in backpacking — and the resulting public awareness of threat-

ened landscape scenery — soon came into conflict with the intensifying need for the crushed traprock that could be profitably blasted out of the ledges of the Mt. Holyoke Range.

By 1960 newspaper articles on Mt. Holyoke included characterizations of the B&M quarry's activities as "Man's Assault on Nature" and the "Giant Scar . . . being Hacked" into the Holyoke Range.[32] The source of these polemics (accompanied by convincing photographs) was the South Hadley Conservation Society, a new group of preservationists headed by Richard L. Johnson, who was ably assisted by his cousin Roger Johnson, the former champion of the inclined railroad. Johnson's new preservation battle, however, was to save the entire landscape of the Mt. Holyoke

Range from quarries, residential development, indiscriminate logging, or any other activity that promised to scar the view of the mountains from the surrounding valley. The remedy, according to the South Hadley Conservation Society, would be finding the means to put a much larger area of the Mt. Holyoke Range into public ownership. To accomplish this, in 1961 the organization involved two important partners: Charles Foster, commissioner of the Department of Natural Resources, and Ronald Lee, regional director of the National Park Service. The initial strategy was to seek funding from the state legislature to create a vastly expanded state reservation. The park service was brought in for technical assistance. Although that agency did not consider Mt. Holyoke Range to be of "national park caliber," as Foster explained, the park service had been "interested for years" in the area (at least since 1936) and had "considerable information" useful for planning a state park.[33]

The solution, Commissioner Foster felt, was not to "remove a single eyesore," but to prevent anything like it from happening again. To accomplish this, the new partners produced a brochure, "The Case of the Holyoke Range . . . and a Proposal," while simultaneously introducing state legislation that would authorize the Department of Natural Resources to acquire 10,000 acres of the range. "With the accelerated pace of land consumption," they argued, "there is danger that this beautiful region can be despoiled and robbed of the very qualities which have made it so desirable." Public ownership of the Mt. Holyoke Range would provide for recreation, preserve vital watersheds, and guarantee that this "historic and picturesque natural resource" would continue to be an "outstanding feature . . . of the Connecticut Valley."[34] Foster stressed that the proposal was the result of "local action" in response mainly to the traprock quarries that appeared in the 1950s. He also cited a study by the Outdoor Recreation Resources Review Commission (appointed by Dwight D. Eisenhower in 1960) that suggested the Connecticut River Valley was underserved in terms of recreational facilities, including parkland, campgrounds, picnic areas, and parking areas.[35]

The entire public relations and legislative effort had been carefully planned by an experienced group; nevertheless it immediately encountered serious political difficulties. Town governments were angered that they had not been involved in the planning process. In Hadley, Hockanum, and Belchertown, public meetings became forums for angry denunciations of the state park legislation, particularly the provisions that would have allowed private property to be acquired through condemnation. Even the usually supportive *Daily Hampshire Gazette* editorialized that the

"Hadley selectmen" had a point: the proposed bill included overly broad language regarding acquisition of land by eminent domain. Commissioner Foster found himself "denying rumors" that his department planned to take private homes and farmland for the creation of the park. Letters to the editor included heated polemics and accusations that the plan was being "carried out with strategy and secrecy" to subvert the rights of private property owners. The South Hadley Conservation Society and Commissioner Foster quickly offered to amend the proposed legislation and modify the eminent domain provisions, but the damage had been done.[36] By introducing the legislation simultaneously with the brochure, they had created a strong sense that town governments and individual property owners had been excluded from the planning process in an unacceptable manner. The bill failed in the state legislature.

In the meantime at the other end of the state, another effort in large-scale landscape management was playing out quite differently. The Cape Cod National Seashore, established in 1961, was a successful and unprecedented example of preservation in Massachusetts. The National Park Service had been attempting to create "national seashores" since 1939, when Cape Hatteras National Seashore was first conceived. The acquisition of land for Cape Hatteras, however, dragged on for decades because the park service could not obtain property directly but had to rely on donations of land from the state of North Carolina. (The state could either purchase land or receive it as a gift and then turn it over to the federal government.) In the case of Cape Cod, however, Congress provided appropriations for direct federal acquisition of land for the creation of the park, the first time any national park legislation contained such provisions. In what became known as the "Cape Cod Model," the legislation prevented condemnation of private land in any municipality that cooperated by implementing restrictive

zoning ordinances, meeting standards set by the Department of the Interior. The park service, local officials, and private property owners developed mutually acceptable approaches to land preservation at Cape Cod and implemented a new prototype of federal park management.

This was a busy period in recreation planning, particularly at the Department of the Interior. In 1962, following the advice of the Outdoor Recreation Resources Review Commission, Secretary of the Interior Stewart Udall created the Bureau of Recreation. This new agency took over many of the National Park Service's recreation planning responsibilities and also administered the funds for public land acquisition generated through the 1963 Land and Water Conservation Act.[37] Other national seashores followed, as well as "national recreation areas" and other ambitious and innovative federal park planning initiatives. The 1964 Ozark National Scenic Riverway, for example, incorporated two state parks and 80,000 acres of public land stretching along 140 miles of rivers and streams.[38]

It was in this context of federal activism and large-scale planning for outdoor recreation that in 1965 Senator Abraham Ribicoff of Connecticut introduced legislation in Congress to produce a study of a proposed Connecticut River National Recreation Area. The Bureau of Outdoor Recreation went to work in 1966 and over the next two years produced *New England Heritage: The Connecticut River National Recreation Area Study*, an ambitious investigation of the preservation potential along a 400-mile corridor from the source of the river near the Canadian border to the Long Island Sound. The planners recommended establishing a 56,700-acre national recreation area in four New England states. Two new state parks in Connecticut, an expansion of the Mt. Tom state reservation by 3,000 acres, a new recreation area at Turners Falls, the creation of a "Rogers' Rangers Historic Riverway" in New Hampshire and Vermont, and a "scenic automotive tourway" along the length of the entire corridor were among the additional elements of the proposal. The federal portions of the new park would be concentrated in three "units": the Gateway Unit (23,500 acres) at the mouth of the river; the Mt. Holyoke Unit (12,000 acres) covering the Mt. Holyoke Range; and the Coos Scenic River Unit (21,200 acres) along the river corridor in New Hampshire and Vermont. In all three a combination of land acquisition, easements, and restrictive zoning would be used to preserve landscapes and offer better opportunities for outdoor recreation. Perhaps because of its previous history in the area, the National Park Service was charged specifically with planning the Mt. Holyoke Unit of the new park.[39]

In January 1969 Congressman Silvio O. Conte introduced legislation in the House of Representatives to implement the Bureau of Recreation's suggestions for the Connecticut River Valley. Senator Ribicoff introduced a similar bill in the Senate that spring. But the 1968 Bureau of Recreation report had been quickly prepared by a group of professional researchers and planners, by their own admission, with little involvement from the many communities to be affected by the plan. The proposal emphasized recreational uses and public access, and many critics soon argued that preservation of resources should have been a higher priority. Other residents feared that the emphasis on recreation would mean an influx of urban populations into their relatively rural communities. The Connecticut River National Recreation Area was also proposed for a far more densely populated, urban area than earlier recreation areas had been and, therefore, would require more extensive condemnation of private property.

For all these reasons, political opposition to the plan appeared immediately. The Vermont and New Hampshire congressional delegations, ever wary of federal intervention, never supported the legislation, ending any further involvement by those states. In 1970 Senator Ribicoff introduced another piece of legislation to implement the

Connecticut portion of the recreation plan on its own. After a contentious two-year period in which different configurations for the Gateway Unit were repeatedly revised, local opposition finally ended any federal role in the Connecticut project. Planning for the preservation of the Connecticut River estuary was taken up at state and local levels, successfully resulting in state legislation in 1973.[40]

In Massachusetts, as well as in Connecticut, the 1968 federal plan precipitated widespread public opposition. The proposed 12,000-acre Mt. Holyoke Unit included the village of Hockanum, the Northampton meadows along the river, and the entire range itself. Eighty-five percent of the proposed park was privately owned land; yet those property owners had not been involved in the planning process, and neither had the municipalities that would be seriously affected by such a development. At a public meeting in Northampton requested by Senator Edward Kennedy, the Bureau of Recreation received a litany of complaints, especially regarding the potential loss of tax revenues, the taking of private farms and woodlots, and the lack of community participation in the process. As a result, the next year when the National Park Service began preparing a "master plan" for the Mt. Holyoke Unit, it did so in partnership with a newly appointed citizen advisory committee. Committee members were appointed by the state commissioner of natural resources and represented each of the towns affected, as well as a number of civic and commercial groups. The committee was chaired by State Representative John Olver.

The park service planners, led by David Kimball, at first presented plans to the committee that continued to stress outdoor recreation and public access, in line with the 1968 recommendations. The reaction of the committee, as well as the public at many meetings in 1970, made it abundantly clear that the emphasis would need to shift to "preservation," with far fewer numbers of visitors desired or accommodated. By 1971 the

park service and Olver's citizen committee had worked out a plan that anticipated 3,400 visitors a day, down from 16,000 originally planned for in 1970. The proposed park now covered 12,400 acres, only 1,100 acres of which would be zoned or developed for active use; 10,900 acres would be zoned for "preservation and conservation" and would remain undeveloped. Other aspects of the plan included access to swimming, beaches, and boating along the river, and a new tramway to the top of Mt. Holyoke, eliminating access to the Summit House by private car. About 400 acres in Hockanum and Granby would remain in private hands, subject to local zoning.[41]

Although local complaints continued to be heard in public meetings, the process had been relatively open, produced specific recommendations, and reached at least a limited consensus among the often fractious towns that surround the Mt. Holyoke Range. The citizen advisory committee had worked closely with the park service planners; and Senator Kennedy, who introduced legislation in 1971 to implement the plan, had been involved as well. State Representative Olver led a local campaign to emphasize how earlier concerns about the creation of a federal park had been addressed.[42] But the legislation for the park, rechristened the Mt. Holyoke Unit of the Connecticut Historic Riverway, nevertheless languished in Congress and continued to be a contentious issue locally. In the end, the 1971 park plan was tied to the fate of the Connecticut Gateway Unit that Senator Ribicoff was sponsoring at the same time; when the latter effort was abandoned in 1972, the Massachusetts advocates were on their own. Whittled down to just the Mt. Holyoke Unit, the Connecticut Historic Riverway proposal was not of "national park caliber," as the National Park Service had pointed out in 1961. By the end of 1972, seven years of federal efforts to establish a national recreation area in the Connecticut River Valley had effectively come to an unsuccessful end.[43]

Continuing Preservation Efforts

In a familiar pattern, state agencies and officials now attempted to implement their own version of what had proven to be overly ambitious federal recreation planning. In 1973 Commissioner Arthur Brownell of the Department of Natural Resources organized a revised effort to acquire 5,175 acres of the Mt. Holyoke Range, mostly at higher elevations. The state would also assist local towns in drafting protective zoning ordinances for another 15,000 acres. The plan emphasized cooperation with town governments and property owners, and flexibility in methods of "preservation," including acquisition, easements, revenue sharing, tax incentives, and conservation zoning. Response to public concerns raised over the previous eight years helped re-shape the planning process. The proposal specified that the citizen advisory committee would continue to play an influential role, that only "passive recreation" would be allowed on the range, and that the Summit House would be "improved and made a historical feature" of the new park.[44]

A spate of newspaper reports on the public meetings organized by Commissioner Brownell, however, revealed that the new state plan was only slightly less controversial in surrounding towns than the federal plans had been. One headline, "Holyoke Range Park Is Praised in Amherst, Criticized in Hadley," perhaps sums up much of the general public reaction.[45] While Granby and South Hadley appeared to have mixed feelings, Amherst and Hadley were at loggerheads, strongly for and against any park proposal, respectively. Perhaps anticipating difficulties in the state legislature, Brownell then worked with John Olver to devise a new legislative package later that year that linked the fate of the Mt. Holyoke Range to that of the Boston Harbor Islands. In an attempt to enlist powerful eastern Massachusetts politicians to the cause, Olver's new legislation proposed a "Bicentennial Corporation" that would be funded to acquire both the western mountain range and the eastern islands. The corporation would be run by an appointed board, and would not be allowed to condemn land in any town without prior approval of its selectmen. Otherwise, the legislation reflected the same goals and arrangements as Commissioner Brownell's proposal. But again the legislation was doomed, defeated by the lack of unity among local governments around Mt. Holyoke (Hadley continued to oppose the plan) and a parsimonious legislature that chose not to see what the acquisition of the Mt. Holyoke Range and the Boston Harbor Islands had to do with celebrating the nation's bicentennial.[46]

In the meantime the Summit House, all but forgotten in these grand "recreation area" schemes, continued to deteriorate. In 1967 (two years after the state burned the inclined railroad) the barn near the Half-way House burned, taking with it a trove of objects, photographs, guest registers, and furnishings from the hotel, all of which had been stored there for safe keeping. By the late 1960s, the condition of the Summit House itself was a scandal, described as a "shell of its former glory," or simply "falling apart."[47]

In 1963 the State of New York's Department of Environmental Conservation had intentionally burned the grandest summit house of all, the 1823 Catskill Mountain House. The reason given for that destruction was that it had fallen into a dangerous and irreparable condition. The Mt. Holyoke Summit House, perhaps now the most significant of the remaining mountain hotels, seemed destined for the same fate. All it would take was a few more years of neglect, and the Commonwealth might free itself of the old hotel that it had never wanted in the first place. As plan after plan for the wider preservation of the Mt. Holyoke Range had failed, the precarious and abysmal condition of the Summit House in the mid-1970s seemed to symbolize the fate of the mountain itself.

By 1975, however, the state legislature had finally appropriated funds for the acquisition of 5,200 acres of land and easements on the ridge of the Mt. Holyoke Range. Acquiring these forested, higher-elevation areas apparently caused less controversy, and this more limited expansion of Skinner State Park was finally approved. Commissioner Bette Woody, of what was now known as the Department of Environmental Management, also decided that the moment of truth had arrived for the dilapidated Summit House. At a public hearing in South Hadley, she sought opinions and suggestions for the management of the hotel, which was, she insisted, "structurally unsound" and at a point of deterioration that could make restoration prohibitively expensive. At the meeting were the twenty-five members of the newly appointed Summit House Task Force, a group of local residents, historians, and other interested individuals whom Commissioner Woody had asked to consider alternatives for the Summit House. Three of Woody's proposed alternatives involved the demolition of the building and its replacement with an observation platform or some other (more easily maintained) structure; one would entail restoration of the hotel and proposing a new function for it. In any case, Woody made it clear that the "real commitment" of her agency was to the "preservation and conservation of the Holyoke Range" and that no part of the $2.4 million that had been appropriated for land acquisitions could be used for restoring the Summit House.

But if public sentiment over various park proposals had been divided over the years, the old hotel had a way of bringing people together. Commissioner Woody discovered near unanimity among the 150 people present in favor of restoring the Summit House, as well as considerable anger that the state had let it deteriorate for so long. By the end of the month, Henri Forget, chairman of the Summit House Task Force, made it clear at a public meeting in Hadley that the task force members — and most of the public they had met with — strongly favored restoration.

From the beginning the Summit House Task

Force sought to find funding sources and creative suggestions for reuse of the building; demolition was never considered a desirable alternative.[48] One of the most successful efforts to build support for the Summit House at this time came from Gwendolyn Clancey, one of the task force members, who produced a film about the hotel's history. In the fall of 1976 the film was shown all over the region, usually picking up coverage by local newspapers when it was.[49] At a series of public meetings, the task force also solicited suggestions for new uses for the building and ways to fund its restoration. The grassroots campaign had an effect. That fall the state hired Maximillian Ferro, an architectural consultant, to study in detail the structural and economic feasibility of restoring the Summit House. Ferro's report, issued in January 1977, recommended restoring the existing structure to its historic use as a small hotel and restaurant. Guests would park at the Half-way House and proceed to the Summit House by horse-drawn carriage or sleigh.[50]

Public support for some kind of restoration was strong and relatively unified; but the Department of Environmental Management still remained ambivalent about the entire idea of having a hotel and restaurant in what agency officials increasingly characterized as an "overused" and ecologically sensitive area. By the end of the year, Bob Yaro, the Department of Environmental Management's chief planner, criticized Ferro's proposal because he considered such a business inconsistent with "the needs of the park as a recreation area and the frail ecology at the mountaintop."[51] With natural resource managers at the Department of Environmental Conservation openly ambivalent about the desirability of keeping the Summit House at all, the situation once again threatened to end in stalemate and inaction.

And then, remarkably, the state legislature surprised everyone, including the Summit House Task Force, and appropriated $600,000 for fiscal year 1979 to restore the Summit House and cover the cost of a new "visitor center" for the expanded Skinner State Park. The news was enough to re-activate the Holyoke Range Advisory Committee (the citizen group originally created in response to the federal recreation plans of the late 1960s), which had been inactive for years.[52] The architectural firm Alderman & MacNeish of West Springfield was selected in 1980 to design the new visitor center and the Summit House restoration. The goal of the plans for the hotel, according to Mark Sirulnik, the project architect, was to restore the hotel to its "former splendor," circa 1890, and even to rebuild a covered tramway up the hillside from the Half-way House. As engineering and architectural studies proceeded, the state was also acquiring land and easements along the Mt. Holyoke Range. When actual construction on the Summit House began in 1982, 2,500 acres of additional protected land had been obtained.[53] The preservation of both the mountain landscape and the mountain house proceeded together, the fate of each apparently linked to the other.

In 1981, the Holyoke Range Advisory Committee formed a nonprofit organization, eventually renamed the Friends of the Mt. Holyoke Range. This institutional stability for citizen participation and advocacy was a byproduct of the long preservation struggle.[54] Extensive restoration of the Summit House proceeded over the next six summers, as John Sadlow of the Department of Environmental Management supervised an in-house restoration crew that did most of the work. Completed in 1988, the building serves essentially as a visitor center and house museum, still featuring the "grandest cultivated view in the world."[55] Other uses, including a restaurant, continue to occasionally be discussed, but they are unlikely ever to be economically feasible when needed sewer, water, and transportation improvements are considered.

The Summit House restoration, done in the context of expanded land preservation by the state, and the increasingly active and organized citizen involvement in the management of the park symbolize an optimistic conclusion to the long and difficult history of "preserving" Mt. Holyoke in the twentieth century. Of course threats to the natural and cultural heritage of Mt. Holyoke continue to occur. In 1999, for example, a subdivision was planned for the former B&M traprock quarry. This was the site, ironically, that had originally activated the South Hadley Conservation Society in 1960 and had initiated an era of ambitious federal and state plans intended to prevent precisely this type of development. But in 1999, after the long and difficult history of proposed preservation plans for Mt. Holyoke, something else happened: citizens created a new organization, "Save the Mountain," which formed a partnership with conservation groups, civic organizations, and state and local governments to stop the development (see figure 54). In 2000, as a result of the advocacy and fundraising of Save the Mountain, a donation from a private individual to the state was used to acquire most of the quarry site through eminent domain. The town government of Hadley gave its full approval.[56] The right partners had come together in a cooperative way to achieve the further preservation of the Mt. Holyoke Range, something no federal recreation plan ever managed to achieve.

The very presence of the restored Summit House today embodies this evolution in the meaning and process of preservation. Its significance has continuously been altered in response to changing ideals for the management of the Mt. Holyoke Range and, in a larger sense, the balance of "man and nature" in the region. An unlikely survivor of an earlier era of tourism, the Summit House persists, despite all the vicissitudes of its history, as an active symbol of the mutual engagement of the people and the landscape of the Connecticut River Valley.

NOTES

1. The Mount Holyoke "Summit House" has also been known in the past as Prospect House and the Mt. Holyoke Hotel. It is referred to consistently here as the Summit House for the sake of clarity.

2. See Martha J. Hoppin, "Arcadian Vales: The Connecticut Valley in Art," *Arcadian Vales: Views of the Connecticut River Valley*, ed. Martha Hoppin (Springfield: George Walter Vincent Smith Art Museum, 1982).

3. The publication of George Perkins Marsh's *Man and Nature* (1864, second edition 1874), the success of J. Sterling Morton's suggestion for Arbor Day celebrations in the 1870s, and the establishment of the American Forestry Association in 1875, among other events and publications, all indicated a growing awareness for the need of some kind of protection for the rapidly disappearing trees of North America. See Hans Huth, *Nature and the American: Three Centuries of Changing Attitudes*, 3rd ed. (Lincoln: University of Nebraska Press, 1990), pp. 168–77.

4. In the Connecticut River Valley and elsewhere trolley companies and railroads did often remain important sponsors of resort development in the early twentieth century (as was the case on Mt. Tom, where the Holyoke Street Railway financed the reconstruction of the Mt. Tom Mountain House in 1901). The trend toward automobile tourism, however, coincided with the decline of most of the mountain houses. The last Mt. Tom Summit House was demolished in 1938. The Eyrie House, built on Mt. Nonotuck in 1861, burned in 1901 and was not rebuilt. The mountain house on Mt. Sugarloaf (the first built in 1864) was destroyed by the 1930s. For a history of Connecticut River Valley mountain houses, see David Graci, *Mt. Holyoke: An Enduring Prospect* (Holyoke: Calem Publishing Co., 1985). For an account of the dozens of mountain houses built on northeast mountaintops beginning in the 1820s, see Laura and Guy Waterman, *Forest and Crag: A History of Hiking, Trail Blazing, and Adventure in the Northeast Mountains* (Boston: Appalachian Mountain Club, 1989).

5. Shary Page Berg, *The Civilian Conservation Corps: Shaping the Parks and Forests of Massachusetts*, *Government Report* (Commonwealth of Massachusetts, Department of Environmental Management, 1999), p. 5.

6. Gordon Abbott, Jr., *Saving Special Places: A Centennial History of the Trustees of Reservations, Pioneer of the Land Trust Movement* (Ipswich: The Ipswich Press, 1993), pp. 15–21.

7. Graci, *Mt. Holyoke*, pp. 61–64. Both reservations remained under county administration, however, with privately owned and operated summit houses.

8. "Christopher Clarke Gets Mt. Holyoke Preserved," *Daily Hampshire Gazette*, March 23, 1908, Historic Northampton, Research Library (hereafter HNRL).

9. Graci, *Mt. Holyoke*, pp. 70–74.

10. "Mt. Holyoke as a State Reservation," *Daily Hampshire Gazette*, February 18, 1915, HNRL.

11. "Reservation Plans for Mt. Holyoke," *Daily Hampshire Gazette*, February 1, 1916, HNRL.

12. "Railway to Top of Mt. Holyoke is Electrified," *Springfield Union*, June 15, 1926, HNRL; Graci, *Mt. Holyoke*, pp. 74–76.

13. See Berg, *The CCC: Shaping the Parks and Forests of Massachusetts*.

14. Newspaper reports are unclear on the exact origin of this proposal, but by 1934 the Department of Conservation was actively planning for state park expansions with the National Park Service officials administering the CCC state park program. The Coolidge Memorial Park, however, seems to have been local in inspiration. "Memorial Plan Arouses Interest in Northampton," *Springfield Republican*, November 7, 1934, HNRL.

15. In 1936 Congress passed the Park, Parkway, and Recreational Study Act, which empowered the National Park Service to actively collaborate with state park departments (which it had been doing on a more limited basis since 1933) in planning state park systems and developing them with CCC labor. The result, in Massachusetts, was the *Park, Parkway, and Recreational-Area Study* (government report, Massachusetts State Planning Board in Cooperation with the Department of the Interior, National Park Service, 1941). This was the first truly statewide study of recreation needs and land uses in Massachusetts.

16. "Debate Buying Mt. Holyoke," *Daily Hampshire Gazette*, December 12,1936, HNRL.

17. "Would Have State Buy Mt. Holyoke Range," *Springfield Union*, January 15, 1937, HNRL.

18. Dean was also reported (after the fact, in the *Springfield Republican*) to have said that western Massachusetts had enough recreational lands for its population, while the denser population in the east was underserved. His reluctance to acquire and manage the Summit House, however, is the reason frequently mentioned in newspaper reports in 1937. "Public Hearing on Mt. Holyoke Plan Wednesday," *Springfield Union*, February 20, 1937, HNRL; "Large Group Asks for Purchase of Mt. Holyoke," *Springfield Union*, April 23, 1937, HNRL; "Dean Report on Taking of Mt. Holyoke," *Daily Hampshire Gazette*, December 6. 1937, HNRL.

19. "Mt. Holyoke Summit House Must Be Torn Down for Most Part," *Daily Hampshire Gazette*, September 29, 1938, HNRL; "Mountain Given to State by J.A. Skinner," *Springfield Republican*, June 20, 1940, HNRL.

20. "Mt. Holyoke Now Expected to Have a New Summit House," *Daily Hampshire Gazette*, September 7, 1940, HNRL; "Tablet Unveiled at Mt. Holyoke," *Daily Hampshire Gazette*, September 16, 1940, HNRL; "Old Summit House Not to be Razed," *Daily Hampshire Gazette*, September 16, 1940, HNRL; "State Accepts Skinner's Gift of Mt. Holyoke," *Springfield Union*, June 20, 1940, HNRL; Graci, *Mt. Holyoke*, pp. 80–81.

21. Graci, *Mt. Holyoke*, p. 81.

22. "Debate Buying Mt. Holyoke," *Daily Hampshire Gazette*, December 12, 1936, HNRL; "Century Old Prospect House Visited by 12,540 So Far This Year," *Daily Hampshire Gazette*, October 16, 1953, HNRL; "Record Number of Visitors View Valley," *Daily Hampshire Gazette*, December 1, 1954, HNRL.

23. A.K. Sloper to Roger Johnson, letter dated May 21, 1947, HNRL.

24. Roger Johnson to A.K. Sloper, letter dated May 31, 1947, HNRL; Roger Johnson to A.K. Sloper, letter dated June 12, 1947, HNRL.

25. "Johnson Denies Mt. Holyoke Railway Sliding Down Slope," *Springfield Union*, June 13, 1947, HNRL; "Battle Is Going On to Save Mt. Holyoke Cable Railway," *Springfield Union*, June 19, 1947, HNRL; "$20,000 Sought to Repair Railway on Mt. Holyoke," *Springfield Daily News*, January 10, 1949, HNRL; "Historic Mt. Holyoke Tramway Will Probably be Torn Down," undated clipping [1953?], Mount Holyoke College Archives and Special Collections; "State Bureau Burns Ruined Cable Line," *Holyoke Transcript-Telegram*, February 18, 195[4?], HNRL; Graci, *Mt. Holyoke*, p. 84.

26. "Once Famous Mt. Holyoke Summit House Now a

Shambles," *Springfield Daily News*, August 13, 1958, HNRL.

27. "Bill is Filed for Improving Skinner State Park," *Daily Hampshire Gazette*, September 7, 1956, HNRL; "Historic Prospect House Again Making Headlines," *Daily Hampshire Gazette*, March 13, 1957, HNRL; "Hadley Park Bill Signed by Furcolo," *Daily Hampshire Gazette*, August 16, 1957, HNRL.

28. Although the architects' model apparently was not preserved, photographs of it were published by the newspapers. See, for example, "Historical Nature Preserved in Famous Architects' Plans," *Daily Hampshire Gazette*, August 20, 1958, HNRL.

29. "$50,000 for Summit House Was Used to Make a Model," *Springfield Daily News*, August 15, 1958, HNRL; "Summit House Funds — Coming Or Not?" *Springfield Daily News*, August 20, 1958, HNRL.

30. The Town of Hadley passed an ordinance in 1956 preventing this land use in the future, but the B&M's operations were not affected.

31. The trail was surveyed by Professor Walter M. Banfield in the late 1950s. See "Mt. Holyoke Range Historical Timeline" maintained by Robb Strycharz for the Friends of Mt. Holyoke Range at *http://members. tripod.com*. The timeline is an excellent source for local history, and includes many historical documents, maps, and press clippings.

32. "Mt. Holyoke Summit House," *Springfield Republican*, August 21, 1960, HNRL.

33. Charles H.W. Foster to Robert E. Barrett, letter dated May 25, 1961, Papers of Roger Johnson.

34. The South Hadley Conservation Society, the Massachusetts Department of Natural Resources, and the U.S. Department of the Interior, National Park Service, "The Case of The Holyoke Range . . . and a Proposal," brochure, 1962, pp. 20–21.

35. "Mt. Holyoke Range Proposal Given Impetus by Brochure," *Daily Hampshire Gazette*, February 28, 1962, HNRL.

36. "Hadley Selectmen Have a Point," *Daily Hampshire Gazette*, March 9, 1962, HNRL; "Other Side of the Mountain," *Springfield Union*, March 15, 1962, HNRL; "Homes, Farms Not Needed in Plans for Park," *Springfield Union*, March 15, 1962, HNRL.

37. Edwin M. Fitch, John F. Shanklin, *The Bureau of Outdoor Recreation* (New York: Praeger Publishers,

1970), pp. 79–80, 89.

38. Barry Mackintosh, *National Parks: Shaping the System* (Washington, DC: GPO, 1991), pp. 72–75.

39. Department of the Interior, Bureau of Outdoor Recreation, *New England Heritage: The Connecticut River National Recreation Area Study* (Washington, DC: GPO, 1968); Gregory G. Curtis, "Connecticut Historic Riverway: A Case Study of Acceptance and Rejection of a National Recreation Area" (PhD diss., University of Connecticut, 1974), pp. 9, 19, 34–47.

40. Curtis, "Connecticut Historic Riverway," pp. 48–63, 70–74, 105–39.

41. Robert A. Shanley, "Attitudes and Interactions of Citizens Advisory Groups and Governmental Officials in the Water Resources Planning Process," unpublished report, University of Massachusetts, 1976, The Jones Library Inc. Special Collections, pp. 67–72; Curtis, "Connecticut Historic Riverway," pp. 78–85.

42. "The Mt. Holyoke Unit of the Proposed Connecticut Historic Riverway: A Report of the Massachusetts Citizens Advisory Committee, John W. Olver, Chairman," brochure, 1971, The Jones Library, Inc. Special Collections.

43. Curtis, "Connecticut Historic Riverway," p. 139.

44. *Massachusetts Department of Natural Resources, A Plan for the Protection of the Holyoke Range*, government report, 1973.

45. "Holyoke Range Park Is Praised in Amherst, Criticized in Hadley," *Amherst Record*, June 10, 1973, Special Collections, The Jones Library, Inc.

46. Curtis, "Connecticut Historic Riverway," pp. 139–45.

47. "Halfway House at Skinner State Park," *Springfield Union*, February 6, 1967, HNRL; "Summit House Still Draws Visitors," *Holyoke Transcript-Telegram*, August 9, 1966, HNRL; "Park Shows Valley's Nature — and Man's," *Springfield Union*, July 29, 1969, HNRL.

48. Mac Gress also served as chairman of the task force. "Foundations Weak, But Support for Summit House Strong," *Amherst Record Weekend*, October 4–5, 1975, HNRL; "Summit House Fans Seek Quick Action," *Daily Hampshire Gazette*, October 1, 1975, HNRL; "Restoration Sought for Summit House," *Daily Hampshire Gazette*, October 24, 1975, HNRL; Graci, *Mt. Holyoke*, pp. 89–90.

49. For example, "Movie Aims at Saving Hadley Summit House," *Greenfield Recorder*, October 23, 1976, HNRL.

50. Maximillian L. Ferro, "Historic and Economic

Assessment, Summit House," unpublished report, Department of Environmental Management, 1977, HNRL.

51. "Summit House: Debate Over Its Future Continues," *Daily Hampshire Gazette*, December 10, 1977, HNRL.

52. "Holyoke Range Committee Is Back," *Daily Hampshire Gazette*, September 18, 1978, HNRL; Graci, *Mt. Holyoke*, p. 91. John W. Olver probably was the moving force behind the appropriation.

53. Graci, *Mt. Holyoke*, pp. 92–93.

54. "Group Is Forming to Assist Holyoke Range Development," *Daily Hampshire Gazette*, August 24, 1981, HNRL.

55. The total cost of the restoration was about one million dollars. This figure was kept down by the Department of Environmental Management through the use of in-house restoration crews. "Summit House Renovations," *Daily Hampshire Gazette*, September 22, 1988, HNRL.

56. See Save the Mountain's comprehensive documentation of this entire issue at *http://frugalfun.com/ savemtholyoke.html*.

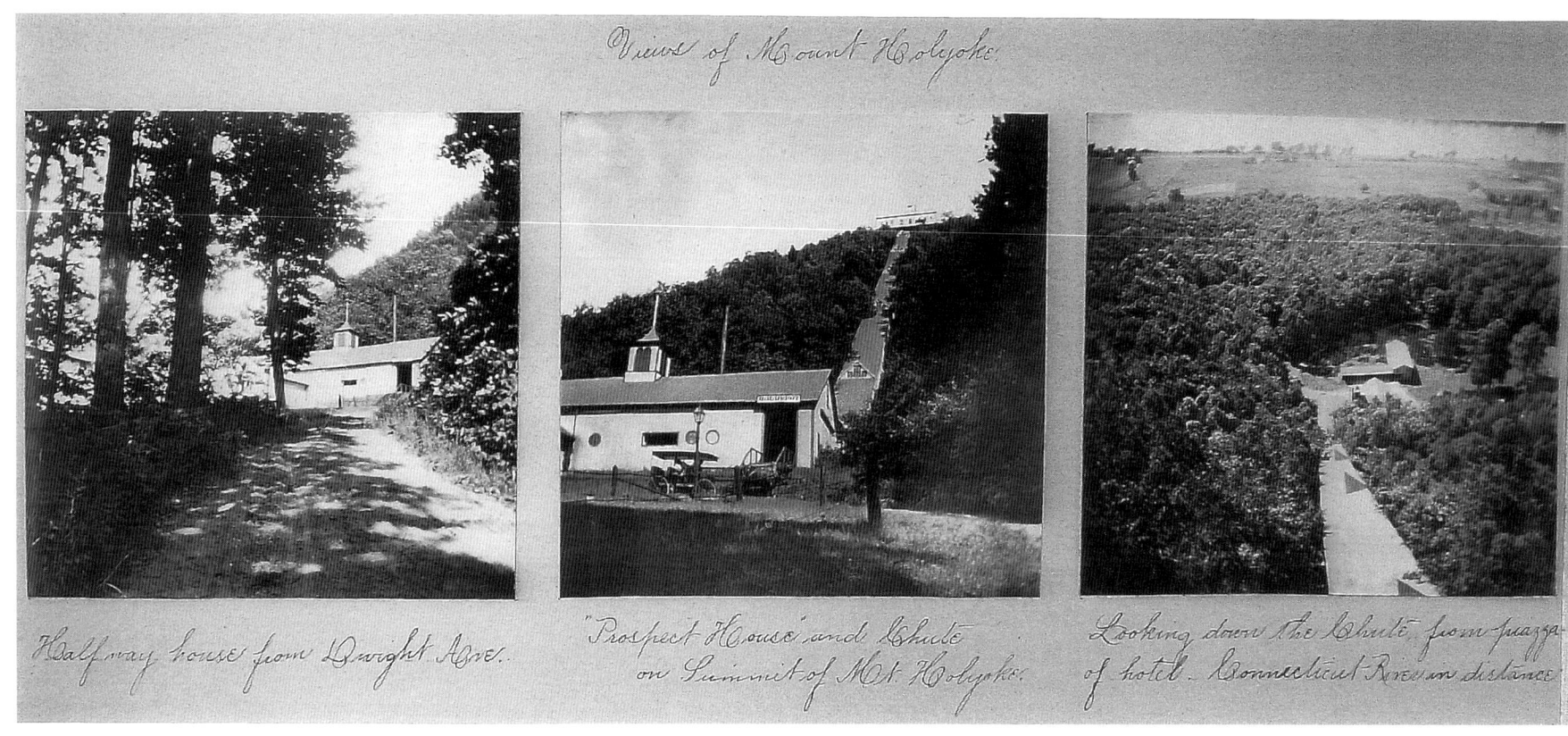

Views of Mount Holyoke.

Halfway house from Dwight Ave.

"Prospect House" and Chute on Summit of Mt. Holyoke.

Looking down the Chute, from piazza of hotel. Connecticut River in distance.

FIGURE 59. *Views of Mount Holyoke,* 1902–05, three mounted photographs from album. Mount Holyoke College Archives and Special Collections

Exhibition Checklist

Paintings and Drawings

Artist unknown
The Oxbow of the Connecticut River, ca. 1850
Oil on canvas, 16⁵⁄₁₆ x 21¹⁄₂ in.
Mead Art Museum, Amherst College, Amherst,
Massachusetts, Gift of Professor Charles H.
Morgan (1948.54)
(see figure 24)

Martha Armstrong (b. 1940)
Oxbow from the Summit House, 1993
Oil on canvas, 18 x 26 in.
Collection of the artist
(see figure 37)

Lewis Bryden (b. 1944)
Mid-Summer in the Valley, 2001
Oil on canvas, 24 x 36 in.
Courtesy R. Michelson Galleries, Northampton
(see figure 44)

Thomas Chambers (1808–after 1866)
View from Mount Holyoke, ca. 1845
Oil on canvas, 22¹⁄₂ x 30¹⁄₈ in.
Fruitlands Museums, Harvard, Massachusetts
(see figure 26)

Edmund C. Coates (1816–1871)
The Connecticut River from Mount Holyoke, 1855
Oil on canvas, 33³⁄₄ x 48 in.
Mead Art Museum, Amherst College, Amherst,
Massachusetts, Purchase (1955.674)
(see figure 28)

Thomas Cole (1801–1848)
*View from Mount Holyoke, Northampton, Massa-
chusetts, after a Thunderstorm (The Oxbow)*, 1836
Oil on canvas, 51¹⁄₂ x 76 in.
The Metropolitan Museum of Art, Gift of Mrs.
Russell Sage, 1908 (08.228)
(see figure 8)

Edward Corbett (1919–1971)
Mt. Holyoke, 1962
Oil on canvas, 50 x 39¹⁄₂ in.
Whitney Museum of American Art, New York,
Purchase with funds from the Friends of the
Whitney Museum of American Art (62.54)
(see figure 47)

Richard Crozier (b. 1944)
Kindred Spirits, 1987
Oil on canvas, 48 x 140 in.
Collection Citigroup
(see figure 35)

Victor de Grailly, (1804–1889)
The Valley of the Connecticut from Mount Holyoke,
ca. 1845
Oil on canvas, 17¹⁄₄ x 23¹⁄₂ in.
Private collection of an alumna
(see figure 27)

Thomas Charles Farrer (1839–1891)
Mount Holyoke, 1865
Oil on canvas, 16¹⁄₄ x 24¹⁄₄ in.
Vance Jordan Fine Art, New York
(see figure 18)

David Gloman (b. 1958)
Hockanum Road, 1996
Oil on canvas, 37 x 56 in.
Collection of the artist
(see figure 48)

Elizabeth Goodridge (1798–1882)
*View of Mount Holyoke, Massachusetts, and the
Connecticut River*
Watercolor on paper, 12 x 15 in.
Mount Holyoke College Art Museum, Purchase
with the Elizabeth Peirce Allyn Art Acquisition
Fund and Art Acquisition Fund
(see figure 17)

David John Gue (1836–1917)
View of Mount Holyoke, 1890
Oil on canvas, 48¹/₈ x 62³/₄ in.
Mount Holyoke College Art Museum,
Gift of John Dwight, 1903
(see figure 16)

David John Gue (1836–1917)
View from Mount Holyoke, 1903
Oil on canvas, 26 x 48 in.
Mount Holyoke College Art Museum,
Gift of John Dwight, 1903
(see figure 15)

Stephen Hannock (b. 1951)
The Oxbow, After Church, After Cole, Flooded,
1979–1994 (Flooded River for the Matriarchs,
E. and A. Mongan), 1994
Polished oil on canvas, 54 x 81 in.
Smith College Museum of Art, Northampton,
Massachusetts, Gift of Irene Mennen Hunter
(class of 1939), 1995
(see figure 32)

Elbridge Kingsley (1842–1918)
Springtime — Meadow and Mt. Holyoke, 1899
Oil on canvas, 31 x 43 in.
Forbes Library, Northampton, Massachusetts
(see figure 14)

Alfred Leslie (b. 1927)
Holyoke Range, near Oxbow, Easthampton,
Massachusetts, 1983
Watercolor on paper, 44¹/₂ x 45 in.
Collection of the artist
(see figure 53)

Alfred Leslie (b. 1927)
View from Mt. Holyoke, of the Oxbow, Oct 17–71,
1971
Pencil on paper, 28¹/₂ x 47 in.
Collection of the artist

Mark Meunier (b. 1949)
Valley View, 1995
Egg tempera on canvas, 30 x 40 in.
Collection of Joseph and Emily Partyka
(see figure 45)

Elizabeth Meyersohn (b. 1959)
Flooded Fields, 2001
Oil on linen, 36 x 78 in.
Private collection
(see figure 49)

David Moriarty (b. 1957)
New World: Red, 1996
Acrylic on prepared paper, 28 x 32 in.
Holyoke Community College, Holyoke,
Massachusetts
(see figure 41)

Cathy Osman (b. 1953)
Oxbow Revisited, 1993
Oil on canvas, 50 x 60 in.
Collection of the artist
(see figure 36)

Scott Prior (b. 1949)
View from Mt. Holyoke, 1996
Oil on board, 11¹/₄ x 15 in.
Collection of David K. Scott
(see figure 46)

Alan Robinson (b. 1950)
The Oxbow, 2001
Watercolor and gouache on topographical map,
26 x 34 in.
Courtesy R. Michelson Galleries, Northampton,
Massachusetts
(see figure 19)

James Winn (b. 1949)
The Connecticut River Near Northampton, 1987
Acrylic on paper, 24 x 72 in.
Collection of Andersen-Boston
(see figure 42)

John Douglas Woodward (1848–1924)
Mt. Holyoke, Mass. From Hockanum Ferry,
Aug. 28, 1872, 1872
Graphite and white gouache on paper,
9¹⁵/₁₆ x 7 in.
Courtesy of the Episcopal Diocese of Virginia,
Shrine Mont

John Douglas Woodward (1848–1924)
Oxbow, Conn. River from Mt. Holyoke,
Aug. 31, 1872, 1872
Graphite and white gouache on paper,
9¹⁵/₁₆ x 7 in.
Courtesy of the Episcopal Diocese of Virginia,
Shrine Mont

Prints and Photographs

Unknown photographers
Croquet Ground on Mt. Holyoke, ca. 1900
Platinum print photograph, 4 ⁵/₈ x 7 ⁵/₈ in.
(1981.48.10)
Hall on Mt. Holyoke decorated for the silver wedding
of Mr. and Mrs. F. E. Bliss, September 28, 1895
Albumen print photograph, 4⁷/₈ x 8 in.
(1981.78.23)
Interior of Prospect House, Mt. Holyoke, ca. 1870s
Stereoscopic photograph, 3¹/₂ x 7 in.
(1956.548)
Mount Holyoke College Senior Mountain Day,
ca.1890
Albumen print photograph, 4³/₄ x 7³/₄ in.
(1983.37.5)
North View from Veranda, late 1890s
Platinum print photograph, 4¹/₂ x 7³/₄ in.
(1981.48.16)

The Prospect House, Mt. Holyoke, late 1890s
Platinum print photograph, 4 1/2 x 7 in.
(1981.48.7)*
Tennis Court, Mt. Holyoke, ca. 1900
Platinum print photograph, 4 1/2 x 7 1/2 in.
(1981.48.11)
Thatched Roof Summer House, ca. 1900
Platinum print photograph, 4 1/2 x 7 1/2 in.
(1981.48.12)
Western View from Veranda. The Oxbow in the Conn. River, ca. 1900
Platinum print photograph, 4 1/2 x 7 3/4 in.
(1981.48.15)
Wordsworth Outlook, ca. 1900
Platinum print photograph, 4 1/2 x 7 1/2 in.
(1981.48.13)
Historic Northampton, Northampton, Massachusetts
*(See figure 7)

Unknown photographers
Mt. Holyoke, ca. 1860–70s
Albumen print photograph, 4 1/4 x 7 1/2 in.
Mt. Holyoke, ca. 1860–70s
Albumen print photograph, 4 1/4 x 7 1/2 in.
The Jones Library, Inc., Amherst, Massachusetts

Unknown artist
Mount Holyoke, from Amherst College, Massachusetts, from *Ballou's Pictorial Drawing-Room Companion*, 1855
Wood engraving, 7 x 10 1/2 in.
The Jones Library, Inc., Amherst, Massachusetts

Unknown photographers
Freshman Mountain Day, 1898
Gelatin silver print photograph, 3 1/2 x 4 3/4 in.*
Freshman Mountain Day, 1911
Gelatin silver print photograph, 2 3/4 x 3 3/4 in.
Group [of Mount Holyoke students] at Summit House, ca. 1910
Gelatin silver print photograph, 2 1/4 x 4 in.

Mountain Day, October 9, 1893
Gelatin silver print photograph, 4 x 5 in.
Mountain Day, ca.1903
Gelatin silver print photograph, 2 7/8 x 3 1/4 in.
Mountain Day, ca. 1930–31
Gelatin silver print photograph, 6 1/2 x 4 3/4 in.
Mountain Day, 1940
Gelatin silver print photograph, 6 3/4 x 4 3/4 in.
Mountain Day Seniors, 1912*
Gelatin silver print photograph, 3 3/4 x 4 3/8 in.
Senior Mountain Day, 1912
Gelatin silver print photograph, 4 1/8 x 2 3/8 in.
Senior Mountain Day, ca. 1914
Gelatin silver print photograph, 2 3/4 x 4 1/2 in.
View from Mount Holyoke [Mountain Day], 1940s
Gelatin silver print photograph, 7 x 5 in.*
Mount Holyoke College Archives and Special Collections, Student Traditions, Mountain Day
*(See figures 60, 3, 4)

On Summit of Mount Holyoke, 1902–05
Photograph album page with six gelatin silver print photographs, 3 3/8 x 3 3/8 in. each

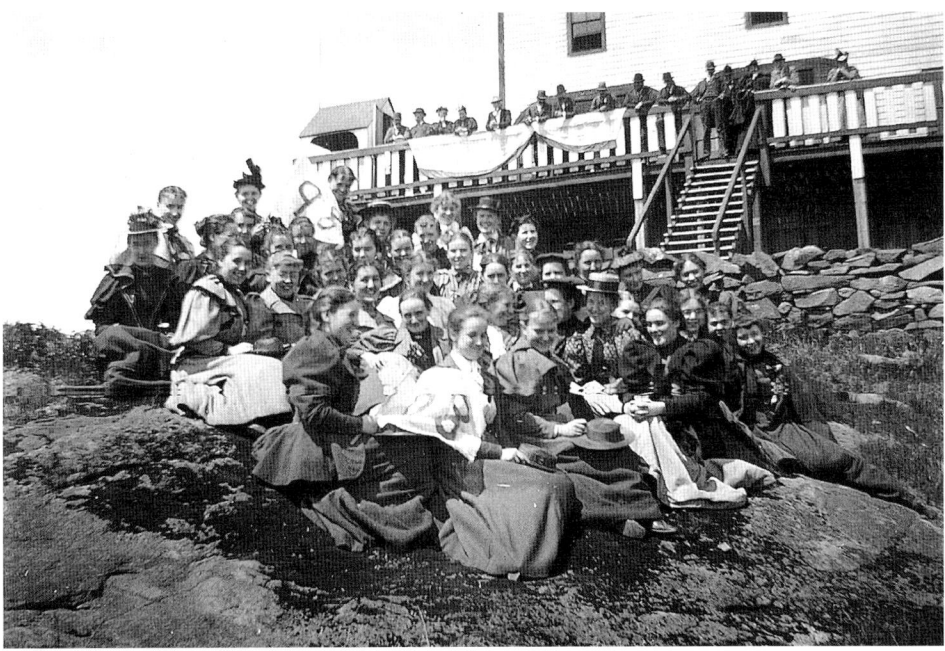

FIGURE 60. *Freshman Mountain Day*, 1898, gelatin silver print photograph. Mount Holyoke College Archives and Special Collections

Views of Mount Holyoke, 1902–05
Photograph album page with six gelatin silver print photographs, 3 3/8 x 3 3/8 in. each
Mount Holyoke College Archives and Special Collections, South Hadley Collection

Robert Aller (b. 1947)
Mt. Holyoke, 2001
Gelatin silver print photograph, 15 x 20 in.
Collection of the artist
(See figure 39)

Robert Aller (b. 1947)
Birch Tree, Mt. Holyoke, 2002
Half-way House, Mt. Holyoke, 2002
Rocks, Mt. Holyoke, 2002
Rocks, Mt. Holyoke, 2002
Digital print photographs, 4 x 5 1/4 in. each
Collection of the artist

William Henry Bartlett (1809–1865)
Valley of the Connecticut (from Mount Holyoke),
ca. 1838
Steel engraving, 4$^{7}/_{8}$ x 7$^{1}/_{8}$ in. (plate)
Published in Nathaniel P. Willis, *American Scenery*
(London: George Virtue, 1840)
Collection of Jill A. Hodnicki
(See figure 23)

William Henry Bartlett (1809–1865)
View from Mount Holyoke, ca. 1838
Steel engraving, 4$^{3}/_{4}$ x 7$^{7}/_{8}$ in.
Published in Nathaniel P. Willis, *American Scenery*
(London: George Virtue, 1840)
Collection of Jill A. Hodnicki
(See figure 22)

David Gloman (b. 1958)
Oxbow, 1993
Ething, 7 x 14$^{1}/_{4}$ in. (plate)
Collection of Samuel C. and Anne Nishimura
Morse

Orra White Hitchcock (1796–1863)
A View in Hadley, 1833
Handcolored lithograph, 5$^{3}/_{8}$ x 8$^{5}/_{8}$ in.
Published in Edward Hitchcock, *Report on the
Geology, Mineralogy, Botany and Zoology of
Massachusetts* (Amherst: Press of J.S. and
C. Adams, 1833)
Collection of Jill A. Hodnicki

Orra White Hitchcock (1796–1863)
West View from Holyoke, 1833
Handcolored lithograph, 5$^{5}/_{8}$ x 8$^{5}/_{8}$ in.
Published in Edward Hitchcock, *Report on the
Geology, Mineralogy, Botany and Zoology of
Massachusetts* (Amherst: Press of J.S. and
C. Adams, 1833)
Collection of Jill A. Hodnicki

Houghton and Knowlton
Prospecting on Mt. Holyoke, ca. 1860s–70s
Stereoscopic photograph, 3$^{1}/_{2}$ x 7 in.
Historic Northampton, Northampton,
Massachusetts (1956.574)
(See figure 10)

Clifton Johnson (1865–1940)
*Hockanum: The Winding Connecticut viewed from
Mt. Holyoke,* ca. 1909
Toned gelatin silver print photograph,
4$^{1}/_{2}$ x 6$^{3}/_{4}$ in.
The Jones Library, Inc., Amherst, Massachusetts
(See figure 12)

Elbridge Kingsley (1842–1918)
Sketching Car at Mt. Holyoke, ca. 1890
Toned gelatin silver print photograph,
4$^{3}/_{8}$ x 7$^{7}/_{8}$ in.
Mount Holyoke College Art Museum,
Gift of John Dwight, 1901

Elbridge Kingsley (1842–1918)
Untitled [View from Mt. Holyoke], ca. 1890
Toned gelatin silver print photograph,
4$^{1}/_{2}$ x 7$^{1}/_{2}$ in.
Mount Holyoke College Art Museum,
Gift of John Dwight, 1901

Elbridge Kingsley (1842–1918)
In the Shadow of Mt. Holyoke
Wood engraving on tissue, 5 x 7$^{3}/_{8}$ in.
Mount Holyoke College Art Museum, Gift of John
Dwight, 1901

L[ewis] H. Kingsley (1853–after 1910)
[Half-way Barn] At foot of Mt. Holyoke Railway
(No. 5 from series "Views of Mt. Holyoke and
Vicinity"), ca. 1880s
Albumen print photograph, 4$^{3}/_{4}$ x 7$^{1}/_{2}$ in.
Historic Northampton, Northampton,
Massachusetts (1981.78.7)
(See figure 11)

Knowlton Brothers
Interior View of Mt. Holyoke Railway (No. 101 from
series "Connecticut Valley Views"), ca. 1870s
Stereoscopic photograph, 3$^{1}/_{2}$ x 7 in. (1956.558.1)
Prospect House, Mt. Holyoke, from the foot of Railway
(No. 76 from series "Connecticut Valley Views"),
ca.1870s*
Stereoscopic photograph, 3$^{1}/_{2}$ x 7 in. (1956.530)
Prospect House, Mt. Holyoke from South (No. 75 from
series "Connecticut Valley Views"),
ca. 1860s–70s
Stereoscopic photograph, 3$^{1}/_{2}$ x 7 in. (1956.536)
Historic Northampton, Northampton,
Massachusetts
*(See figure 6)

E.J. Lazelle (active from the 1870s)
Mount Holyoke Boat (No. 64 from series "Springfield
and Vicinity in Stereoscope"),
late 1870s
Stereoscopic photograph, 3$^{1}/_{2}$ x 7 in.
Historic Northampton, Northampton,
Massachusetts (1956.566)

Jerome Liebling (b. 1927)
Summit House, Mt. Holyoke, 1996
Type C color photograph, 11 x 14 in.
Collection of the artist
(See figure 51)

John Marcy (b. 1952)
Houseboat on the Connecticut River, 1985
Platinum/palladium print photograph, 13$^{1}/_{2}$ x 17 in.
Collection of the artist
(See figure 52)

Henry G. Peabody (1855–1951)
*Down Connecticut River from Mt. Holyoke, South
Hadley, Mass.,* ca. 1900
Gelatin silver print photographs (four panoramic
prints), 9 x 6$^{7}/_{8}$ in. each
Society for the Preservation of New England
Antiquities, Boston, Massachusetts

T. Addison Richards (1820–1900)
Top of Mount Holyoke, 1856
Wood engraving
Reproduced in *Harper's New Monthly Magazine*,
vol. 13 (August, 1856)
The Mount Holyoke College Library
(See figure 29)

Stephen Petegorsky (b. 1954)
The Meadows from Rt. 91, 1989
Gelatin silver print photograph, 16 x 2 in.
Collection of the artist
(See figure 50)

David Ryan (b. 1951)
Connecticut River, Holyoke Range, 1998
Digital print photograph, 11 x 16 in.
Collection of the artist

Illustrated Books and Magazines

Theodore Dwight (1796–1866)
The Northern Traveller, 2nd ed.
New York: A.T. Goodrich, 1826
Amherst College Archives and Special Collections

Basil Hall (1788–1844)
*Forty Etchings, from Sketches Made with the Camera
Lucida, in North America, in 1827 and 1828*
Edinburgh: Cadell & Co., 1829
Mount Holyoke College Archives and Special
Collections

Edward Hitchcock (1793–1864)
Final Report on the Geology of Massachusetts, vol. 1
Northampton: J.H. Butler, 1841
Mount Holyoke College Archives and Special
Collections

Edward Hitchcock (1793–1864)
The Religion of Geology and its Connected Sciences
Boston: Phillips, Sampson, and Company, 1852
Collection of Diane and Dale Schläppi

Edward Hitchcock (1793–1864)
*Sketch of the Scenery of Massachusetts with Plates
from the Geological Report of Professor Hitchcock*
Northampton, Mass.: J.H. Butler, 1842
Mortimer Rare Book Room, Smith College

Clifton Johnson (1865–1940)
Mount Holyoke and Vicinity Illustrated
Northampton: Gazette Printing Company, 1887
Mount Holyoke Archives and Special Collections

John Douglas Woodward (1848–1924)
William Cullen Bryant, editor, 1794–1878
*Picturesque America ; or, The Land we live in. A
delineation by pen and pencil of the mountains, rivers,
lakes, forests, water-falls, shores, canons, valleys, cities,
and other picturesque features of our country.*, vol. 2
New York: D. Appleton and Company, 1874
Mount Holyoke College Archives and Special
Collections

Miscellany

Broadside, *Prospect House, Mount Holyoke*, ca. 1895
5$^1/_2$ x 7$^1/_2$ in.
The Jones Library, Inc., Amherst, Massachusetts

Claude Glass used at Prospect House Hotel,
ca. 1855
Glass in wood frame, 8$^1/_2$ x 10 x 1 in.,
Historic Northampton, Northampton,
Massachusetts (1861.161.1)

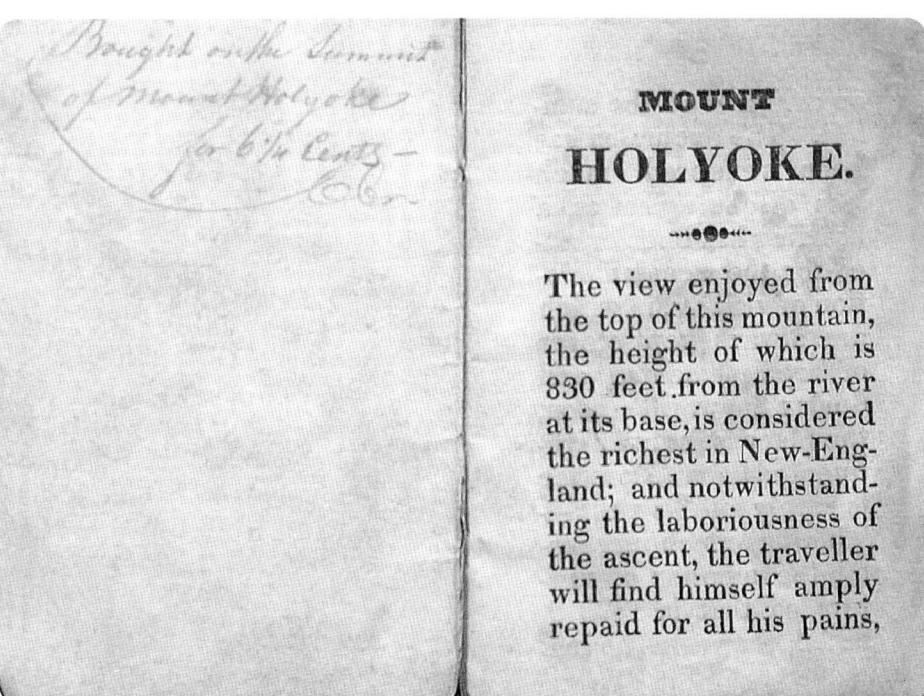

FIGURE 61.
Mount
Holyoke,
guidebook, ca.
1825. Private
collection

FIGURE 62.
Mount
Holyoke
Company
Stock
Certificate,
1908. Mount
Holyoke
College
Archives and
Special
Collections

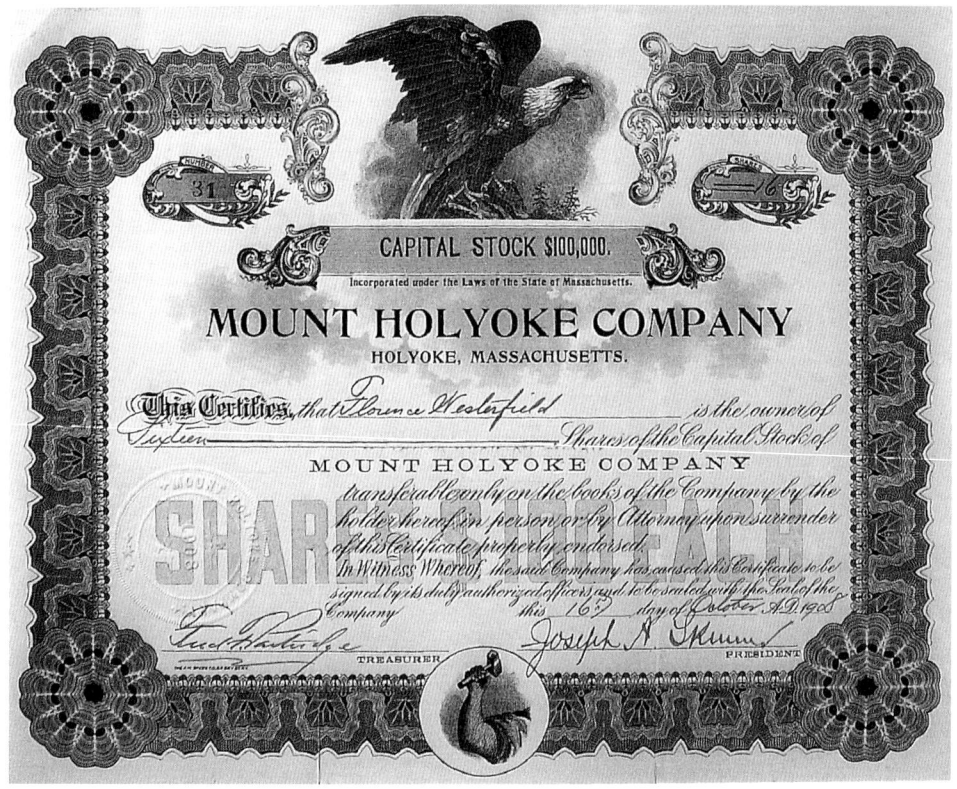

Newspaper from Prospect House, *Mount Holyoke Pathfinder*, 1870
Mount Holyoke College Archives and Special Collections, South Hadley Collection

Offset reproduction of *Valley View*, a painting by Mark Meunier, 1995
21½ x 28½ in.
Collection of WGBY Gallery, Springfield, Massachusetts

Plan of the Town of Northampton, 1831
Lithograph, 27¾ x 20½ in.
Pendleton's Lithography, Boston
Historic Northampton, Northampton, Massachusetts (72.668)
(See figure 62)

Prospect House Souvenir Book, *Golden Thoughts from Great Authors*, ca. 1890s
Register Books from Mount Holyoke, 1823 and 1864
Register book, *Automobile Arrivals on the Summit of Mount Holyoke*, 1908–1914
Historic Northampton, Northampton, Massachusetts (01.1287; A.Md.18.303; A.Md.18.327; A.Md.18)

Prospect House Souvenir Tea Cup and Saucer, ca. 1890s
cup: 2½ x 3 in., saucer: 4½ in. diam.
Historic Northampton, Northampton, Massachusetts (1972.671.a and b)

Scrapbook of clippings and photographs assembled by Roger Johnson, 1930s–1980s
Collection of Charles M. and Dorothy A. Johnson, Wilbraham, Massachusetts

Selection of ephemeral materials from *Save the Mountain* campaign (sign, bumper sticker, decal), 2001
Collection of Save the Mountain

The Class Book of Nineteen Hundred and Twelve
9½ x 6¾ in.
Mount Holyoke College, Class of 1912
Mount Holyoke College and Special Collections

Detroit Publishing Company, *Connecticut River from Mount Holyoke Hotel*, ca. 1903
Panoramic postcard, 3½ x 16½ in.
The Florence History Project, Florence, Massachusetts
(See figure 55)

Envelope from Mount Holyoke, 1927
3¾ x 6⅜ in.
Brochure, *The Oxbow As Seen from Mount Holyoke*, 1888
6 x 3¾ in.
Mount Holyoke College Archives and Special Collections, South Hadley Collection

Guidebook, *Mount Holyoke*, ca. 1825
Author and publisher unknown
Private collection
(See figure 61)

Letterhead, Mount Holyoke, 1890s
6½ x 9 in.
The Jones Library, Inc., Amherst, Massachusetts
Letters, selection of "Mountain Mail" sent to Helen Sweet, Class of 1907
Mount Holyoke Archives and Special Collections, Alumnae Biographical Files

Mount Holyoke Company Stock Certificate, 1908
Engraving, 8¼ x 10⅜ in.
Mount Holyoke Archives and Special Collections, South Hadley Collection.
(See figure 62)

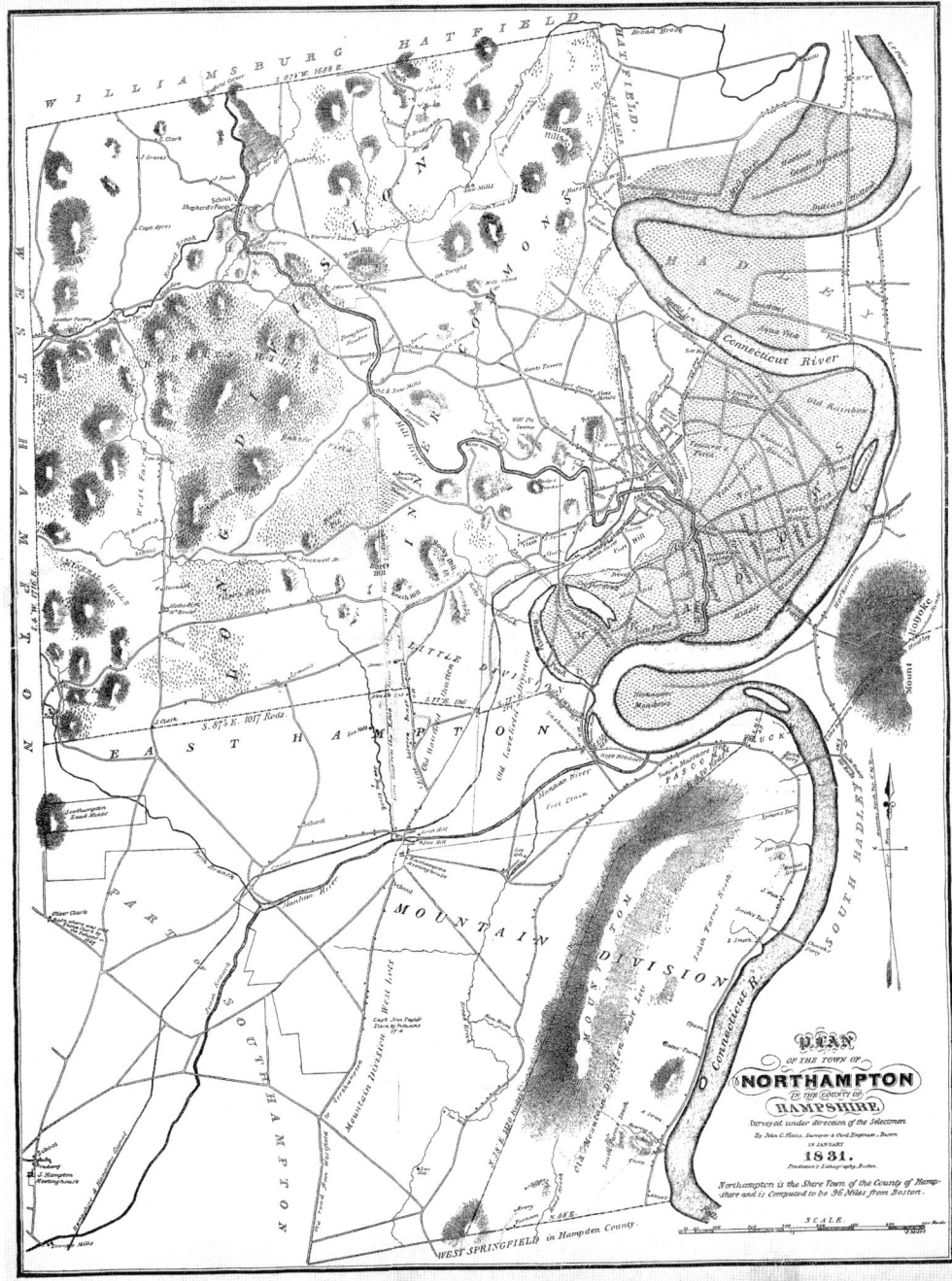

FIGURE 63. *Plan of the Town of Northampton*, 1831,
lithograph. Historic Northampton, Northampton,
Massachusetts

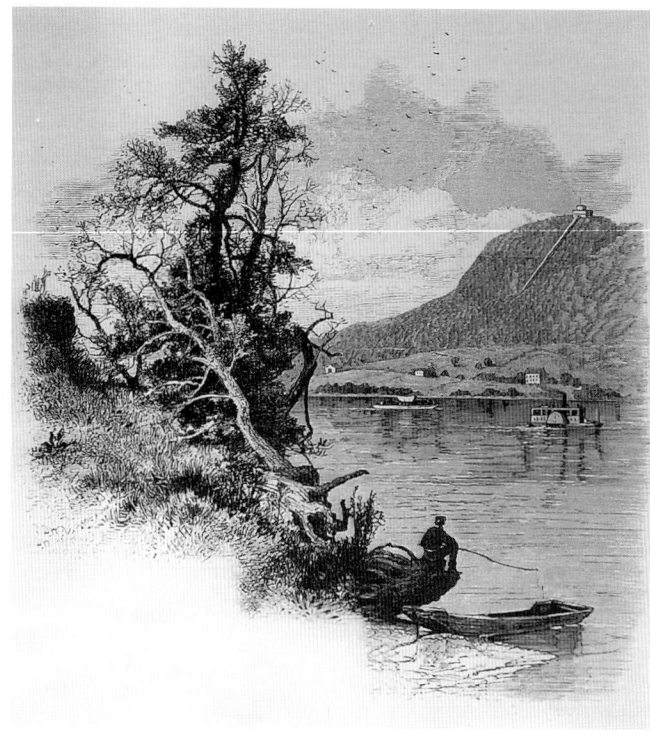

Figure 64. J. Douglas Woodward, *Mount Holyoke*, in *Picturesque America*, vol. 2, 1874. Mount Holyoke College Archives and Special Collections